Take my leaves America,
    take them South and take them North,
Make welcome for them everywhere,
    for they are your own offspring,
Surround them East and West,
    for they would surround you ....

Land of the pastoral plains, the grass-fields of the world!
    land of those sweet-air'd interminable plateaus!...

Land of the ocean shores! land of sierras and peaks!...

See, on the one side the Western Sea
        and on the other the Eastern Sea,
        how they advance and retreat upon my poems
        as upon their own shores,

See, pastures and forests in my poems --
        see, animals wild and tame ...

See, lounging through the shops and fields
        of the States, me well-belov'd,
        close-held by day and night,
Hear the loud echoes of my songs there--
        read the hints come at last.

                    Walt Whitman
            from "Starting from Paumanok"
                in Leaves of Grass

Our Threatened

By Ron Fisher   Photographed by James P. Blair
Prepared by the Special Publications Division, National Geographic Society, Washington, D. C.

CHINCOTEAGUE NATIONAL WILDLIFE REFUGE, VIRGINIA

INHERITANCE
Natural Treasures of the United States

CARIBOU IN DENALI NATIONAL PARK AND PRESERVE, ALASKA

OUR THREATENED INHERITANCE:
NATURAL TREASURES OF THE UNITED STATES

By RON FISHER   *Photographed by* JAMES P. BLAIR

Published by the National Geographic Society
GILBERT M. GROSVENOR, *President*
MELVIN M. PAYNE, *Chairman of the Board*
OWEN R. ANDERSON, *Executive Vice President*
ROBERT L. BREEDEN, *Vice President,*
    Publications and Educational Media

Prepared by the Special Publications Division
DONALD J. CRUMP, *Editor*
PHILIP B. SILCOTT, *Associate Editor*
WILLIAM L. ALLEN, WILLIAM R. GRAY, *Senior Editors*
MARY ANN HARRELL, *Consulting Editor*

Staff for this book
MARGERY G. DUNN, *Managing Editor*
JOHN G. AGNONE, *Picture Editor*
JODY BOLT, *Art Director*
PENELOPE DIAMANTI DE WIDT,
    Senior Researcher and Assistant to the Editor
K. M. KOSTYAL, *Assistant to the Editor*
RUTH L. CONNOR, PATRICIA F. FRAKES, BONNIE S. LAWRENCE,
    Researchers; MARILYN WILBUR CLEMENT, JOHNNA F. JONES,
    Assistant Researchers
TONI EUGENE, *Contributing Writer*
PENELOPE DIAMANTI DE WIDT, K. M. KOSTYAL, JANE R. McCAULEY,
    H. ROBERT MORRISON, JENNIFER C. URQUHART,
    SUZANNE VENINO, *Picture Legend Writers*
PAMELA A. BLACK, ELIZABETH A. BRAZEROL, *Editorial Assistants*
CAROL ROCHELEAU CURTIS, *Illustrations Assistant*
PAMELA J. CASTALDI, JENNIFER WOODS, *Assistant Designers*
ELENI CONSTANTOPOULOS, *Calligrapher*

JOHN D. GARST, JR., PETER J. BALCH, JOHN G. LEOCHA,
    SEAN O'NEILL, with the assistance of the Computer Map Lab,
    Cartographic Division, *Map Research and Production*

Engraving, Printing, and Product Manufacture
ROBERT W. MESSER, *Manager*
GEORGE V. WHITE, *Production Manager*
GREGORY STORER, *Production Project Manager*
MARK R. DUNLEVY, DAVID V. SHOWERS, GEORGE J. ZELLER, JR.,
    Assistant Production Managers; MARY A. BENNETT,
    Production Assistant; JULIA F. WARNER, *Production Staff Assistant*

NANCY F. BERRY, MARY FRANCES BRENNAN, DIANNE T. CRAVEN,
    SUSAN CROSMAN, LORI E. DAVIE, MARY ELIZABETH DAVIS,
    JANET A. DUSTIN, ROSAMUND GARNER, VICTORIA D. GARRETT,
    NANCY J. HARVEY, SANDRA K. HUHN, JOAN HURST,
    ARTEMIS S. LAMPATHAKIS, KATHERINE R. LEITCH,
    MARY EVELYN McKINNEY, CLEO E. PETROFF,
    SHERYL A. PROHOVICH, KATHLEEN T. SHEA, NANCY E. SIMSON,
    VIRGINIA A. WILLIAMS, *Staff Assistants*

JOLENE M. BLOZIS, MICHAEL G. YOUNG, *Indexers*

HARDCOVER: BALD EAGLE BY GEORGE FOUNDS
FROM A PHOTOGRAPH BY WILLIAM L. ALLEN.
ENDPAPERS: ART BY GEORGE FOUNDS
FROM A PHOTOGRAPH OF BIG BLUESTEM AND HEATH ASTERS BY JAMES P. BLAIR.

Contents

CHANNEL ISLANDS NATIONAL PARK, CALIFORNIA

Sheer red walls enclosed us as we drifted lazily beneath the hot desert sun. Occasionally, our wooden dories plunged through boulder-strewn rapids, engulfing us in frigid, muddy waters. Of the many trips I've taken throughout the world, one of the most memorable—and educational—was that 18-day rafting vacation down the Colorado River through the Grand Canyon.

The reality was brought home to me that more than half the people in the West depend on Colorado water, which powers distant cities and irrigates fields as far as California. The population grows, but the water volume does not. Pressures intensify as outfitters vie with farmers, cattlemen, utilities, and mining companies for a share of the river. On the Colorado—as in the entire nation—we must come to grips with increasing demands on our natural resources. Some 14,000 people run the Colorado each year, while more than two million visitors view the splendors from above in Grand Canyon National Park. Their avid appreciation threatens the very wonders they cherish. Crowds menace the delicate ecology of the canyon; pollution obscures the view from rim to rim—18 miles across the widest part—100 days out of every 365.

The canyon and the river have changed radically since 1869, when Maj. John Wesley Powell, a one-armed Civil War veteran, first mastered the Colorado. He and his party of nine battled the uncharted rapids in four wooden boats. Four men abandoned the expedition, and supplies dwindled in the 98 days it took to course the thousand miles. But Powell accomplished his aim: "to add a mite to the great sum of human knowledge."

In 1888 Powell and 32 other men with a zest for knowledge and a concern for the environment founded the National Geographic Society. A 1916 issue of its monthly journal devoted entirely to our national parks helped bring about the creation of the agency that administers them—the National Park Service. That same year the Society contributed funds to preserve California's giant sequoia trees—the first national organization to do so. More recently, Geographic support helped in almost doubling the size of Redwood National Park. Each year the Society's research grants enable individuals to study subjects as varied as the impact of wild horses on the ecology of Nevada's Great Basin and the plight of the gravely endangered black-footed ferret in Wyoming.

The Editor of NATIONAL GEOGRAPHIC in 1916 called our country "the treasure-house of nature's scenic jewels." Since then, as pressures on our national parks, refuges, forests, and other federal holdings have increased, the Society has presented up-to-date coverage of those jewels and the growing threats to them. Reflecting a century of concern, *Our Threatened Inheritance* depicts the federal lands and their varied uses, explains how we have cared for them, and describes the problems we must solve to preserve our natural heritage.

The public lands belong to all Americans, and their conservation must begin with us. For 50 years I have sailed Chesapeake Bay and have seen it deteriorate through pollution, overuse, and neglect. Since the 1960s, when a group of dedicated citizens established the Chesapeake Bay Foundation, interest in returning the area to health has grown to include state and federal governments. Now that its plight is recognized, the bay has a chance to be rejuvenated.

As American citizens, we have the privilege of sharing the natural treasures of our nation. We also have the responsibility of preserving and nurturing that inheritance and bequeathing it, intact, to future generations.

GILBERT M. GROSVENOR
President, National Geographic Society

TUFA FORMATION AT MONO LAKE, CALIFORNIA

Introduction

More than that of most nations, the history of the United States has been a story of a people's interaction with the natural environment. The story began as an effort to carve out farms in the forests, to create villages in the wilderness, but in the long run the main script for our epic of pioneering was written by the spaciousness of the country and the sheer abundance of its resources.

At the individual level, this abundance translated into a chance for ordinary immigrants to achieve something unthinkable in the Old World—the outright ownership of land for the taking and the working of it. Thomas Jefferson recognized the transforming importance of free soil when he called small landholders "the chosen people of God," and stated that the independence of yeoman farmers was the taproot of the American political system.

Once these Jeffersonian concepts were intertwined with the idea that the nation's resources were, in effect, unlimited, they influenced everyone's thinking about America's future. They became a beacon to the landless folk of western Europe; they developed a mystique that lured newcomers westward as long as a frontier of free land remained; and they permeated our politics and dictated our 19th-century land policies. Land was a commodity to be sold cheap or given away, and administrations were judged by the celerity with which they got rid of the lands owned by the federal government.

The vigor of this disposal policy can be measured by the circumstance that nearly all of the 19th-century land laws were designed to hasten the transfer of public lands into private hands—and its success can be reckoned in the realization that by the time of our Centennial in 1876 almost the only large areas east of the Mississippi River remaining in national ownership were military posts and isolated tracts of "worthless" swamplands and forestlands.

Doubts about the wisdom of the disposal policy began to surface after the Civil War, when huge General Land Office giveaways created scandals, and the public realized that immense herds of buffalo on the Great Plains were being wiped out and timber barons were destroying some of the nation's finest forestlands from Maine to California. Unbridled disposal had invited unbridled individualism and greed. The first effective calls for reform came from scientists such as John Wesley Powell and Gifford Pinchot; from nature lovers, such as John Muir, who wanted scenic masterpieces preserved; from hunter-conservationists, such as young Teddy Roosevelt, who were outraged by the wholesale slaughter of wildlife. Change came slowly, but the enactment in 1872 of the bill establishing Yellowstone National Park and the passage in 1891 of a "sleeper amendment" enabling Presidents to designate existing federal lands as forest "reserves" set the stage for far-reaching reforms during the presidency of Theodore Roosevelt.

Books have been written about how the nation's disposal policy was gradually reversed and replaced by laws and plans designed to conserve—and manage—a national estate of resources for the benefit of future generations. The creation of this national heritage, however, has not been accomplished without controversy. Even now, some western states complain that too much land is "retained" in national ownership, just as some landowners in eastern states have objected vehemently when their lands were reacquired by the federal government and placed in national parks, forests, seashores, and wildlife refuges.

The four categories of national lands that form the subject of this book are the final result of a century-long process of rethinking our relationship to the resources of our country. Their status has been determined by Presidents and Congress through decisions that much of our prime forestland, including millions of acres repurchased east of the Mississippi, should be kept and managed according to scientific principles in a system of national forests; that the country's scenic wonders and historical treasures should be preserved in perpetuity in a system of national parks; that habitats necessary for the survival of wild species should be maintained throughout the country in a system of national wildlife refuges; that all "leftover" federally owned areas not encompassed by the other three systems—the Bureau of Land Management holdings—will be retained to ensure that their resources are available to serve national needs.

This is a felicitous book, for it not only affirms that these decisions were correct, but also hews to the thesis that our country must make a permanent commitment to sensitive stewardship if it is to discharge its duty to future generations. With this volume, the National Geographic Society gives new vitality to Theodore Roosevelt's axiom that a nation is obligated to manage its resources for the greatest good of the greatest number over the long run.

A central theme of this work is that piecemeal conservation will always fall short: Ecology tells us that no park or forest or wildlife sanctuary can be "saved" unless the ecosystem of which it is a part is fully protected. We are warned that superb national parks such as Florida's Everglades and Montana's Glacier will not survive as we know them unless intrusions that threaten their water and quietude are brought under control.

It is not surprising that many of the threats depicted in this book were unknown to conservationists a few decades ago. Insidious contaminants such as acid rain, toxic chemicals, and radiation are invisible, and it often takes intensive investigations by scientists to measure their impacts and prescribe programs to curb or slow their inroads. Similarly, many of our national treasures will be impaired unless we control short-sighted development that will despoil them. We must disabuse ourselves once and for all of the idea that where our national estate is concerned we can have our cake and eat it, too. Neither laws nor boundary lines can protect these assets if we are unwilling to identify grave threats and spend whatever is necessary to conserve areas that are imperiled.

Each generation must form its own action agenda, for the work of environmental enhancement is never done. Just as fresh leadership emerged in the 1960s and '70s to establish a wilderness policy, to create new systems to save some of our remaining seashores and wild rivers, and to devise plans to protect endangered species from extinction, so today's concerned conservationists must evolve plans that will secure the resources needed tomorrow.

In this connection, one of the most inspiriting things about *Our Threatened Inheritance* is that it throws a spotlight on the BLM lands, long the orphans of our national estate. These neglected areas include rich mineral, range, forest, and recreational resources, and it is a hopeful sign that the stakes involved in the controversies over these assets are underscored here.

I am convinced that visible trends in the next half century will inculcate an ethic of national thrift—which will deepen our appreciation of our rich land legacy. As the petroleum age winds down and we are forced to use science to expand our renewable resources, we will realize what Aldo Leopold meant when he urged us to "see land as a community to which we belong. . . ."

To paraphrase Robert Frost in "The Gift Outright": The land will really be ours when we care enough about the land.

STEWART L. UDALL
Secretary of the Interior, 1961-69

*P*atterned by moraines, 22-mile-long Russell Glacier winds down from the University Range in Wrangell-St. Elias National Park and Preserve. Perhaps Alaska's most rugged wilderness, it testifies to the awesome power of ice, which still shapes much of its terrain. The 12-million-acre park—the nation's largest—holds dense forests, alpine meadows, untamed rivers, and the continent's greatest concentration of glaciers and of peaks higher than 14,000 feet. In Alaska, said naturalist John Muir, "one learns that the world, though made, is yet being made; that this is still the morning of creation. . . ."

PRECEDING PAGES: Fountains of molten lava explode 250 feet into the air above Hawaii's Kilauea volcano. While nature alters landscapes, mankind has the choice of preserving them— or destroying them.

Life-giving water flows through a wilderness of saw grass and
palmettos in Everglades National Park, sustaining a
subtropical ecosystem that once covered much of southern Florida.

This Land...

*T*erri Martin sat at her kitchen table, coffee cup cradled in her hands, remembering her childhood in California, and the day she invented guerrilla warfare. She was seven years old. "It's funny. I want to go back to being a child and playing in the orchards around my house. The orchards were my frontier, a wonderful place to play. There were rabbits and deer there, and the kind of imaginary adventures kids have.

"I can still remember the shock of one day finding wooden stakes driven into the ground, with little orange ribbons tied to them. I knew without being told what it meant. It meant that they were going to come in and cut the trees down and clear the land and build more houses. Even at that age I remember thinking: 'They can't do this. They can't take away the orchards. Where will the rabbits go? Where will the deer go? Where will I play?' So I pulled up all the stakes and threw them over a fence.

"I guess I knew it wouldn't really stop them, but I thought it would give me some more time."

In a way, Terri is still buying time by pulling up stakes and throwing them over fences. She works for the National Parks & Conservation Association, an organization based in Washington, D. C., that for more than 60 years has operated as a watchdog for the national parks. When I met Terri, her major project was trying to stop the U. S. Department of Energy from building a nuclear waste repository—a dump, Terri calls it—less than a mile from Canyonlands National Park. Her living room in Moab, Utah, was piled so full of reports, studies, correspondence, maps, proposals, counterproposals, court records, and memorabilia of the struggle that her front door literally would not open.

Terri is one of thousands of Americans caught up in a battle that is being waged in boardrooms and courthouses all across the country. It is a battle to answer one of the hardest of questions: How do we make the best and wisest use of our remaining federal lands?

An American historian once proposed that our entire history could be considered as one continuous real estate transaction. In many ways it's true. When Europeans first splashed ashore here, they found a continent of unimaginable richness, inhabited by scattered tribes of Indians who were unable to stop them from calling it their own. Since those earliest days we have been busy claiming, settling, and disposing of this enormous Eden.

Seven of the original Thirteen Colonies had claims to western lands between the Appalachian Mountains and the Mississippi River. With the ratification of the Articles of Confederation, which created a national government, the landed states yielded all their western holdings to the new government. Congress had already determined that the government would own those lands—lands that would be "disposed of for the common benefit of the United States, and be settled and formed into distinct republican states. . . ."

The new country set about gathering to itself much of the broad continent stretching from sea to sea. By treaty and purchase, by conquest and cession, territory was added. The Louisiana Purchase, acquired from France in 1803, nearly doubled the nation's size; in 1819 Florida was ceded by Spain; in 1845 the Republic of Texas was annexed; in 1846 the Pacific Northwest was acquired by the Oregon compromise with Great Britain, which earlier had relinquished claims to a smaller area along the Canadian border. After its defeat by the United States in 1848, Mexico ceded the land now comprising the southwestern states and California; the Gadsden Purchase in 1853 filled out the southern portion of Arizona and extended east into New Mexico, giving the contiguous

United States its final shape. When the territories of Alaska and Hawaii became states in 1959, they pushed the nation's area to its present 2.3 billion acres.

In the 1780s the fledgling Congress approved three landmark pieces of legislation, including the Constitution itself. These set in motion forces and policies that remain influential today as Americans debate how best to manage the federal lands.

The Land Ordinance of 1785 established the familiar survey grid of townships, each with an area of 36 square miles, each containing mile-square sections of 640 acres. One section from each township was to be given to the new states for the support of public schools. If you look today at a land-use map of the country—especially the West—you'll see the little mile-square sections, usually blue, marching across the continent.

The Northwest Ordinance of 1787 put each new state on equal footing with the older states and specified that each new state formally renounce any claim to lands in the public domain—the federal lands. Texas was the exception; it retained its own public holdings when it entered the Union.

Finally, in 1789, the new Constitution, which replaced the ineffective Articles of Confederation, gave Congress the authority to regulate and dispose of all federal lands.

The disposal began at once, for the Founding Fathers never thought the government should hold on to the lands indefinitely. Early policy was simply to survey the public domain and auction it off at a dollar an acre.

Millions of acres were sold at bargain prices under various settlement acts, and in 1812 the General Land Office was set up as a unit of the Treasury Department to handle the booming business. The Homestead Act, which the South had opposed for years, fearing the establishment of more free states, was finally passed in 1862 and signed by President Lincoln. The act gave any settler the right to claim a 160-acre parcel if he would agree to improve it and establish residence there for five years. About 287 million acres were claimed under this system. The intent of the act—and it was a noble one—was to urge settlers westward, to populate the fertile plains. Appropriately, the person officially recognized as being the first to file was named Daniel Freeman; his application for a tract in Gage County, Nebraska, is dated January 1, 1863.

The railroads were another prod to westward movement, and Congress cooperated with the companies that were building them in a scheme beneficial to both. Congress granted to the railroads the rights-of-way and the lands along them. As the tracks were laid, the lands increased in value, and the railroads could sell them to finance construction and operations. Congress kept title to alternate sections, which also increased in value as the railroads progressed. The extent of the giveaway to the railroads was enormous—nearly 100 million acres—and the alternate-section scheme created the devilish checkerboard pattern of land ownership that persists in large areas of the West today.

In addition to the lands homesteaded or given to the railroads, about 328 million acres were granted to the states, and another 61 million to veterans as bonuses. Included in the state grants were 30,000 acres for each representative and senator in Congress; the proceeds from the sale of those lands were to be used in support of agricultural and mechanical colleges.

Lured by the land and the dream of owning a piece of the continent, the emigrants poured westward in irresistible waves. Many became the victims—and a few the perpetrators—of the massive land frauds that robbed the nation of millions and millions of acres of prime land during the Gilded Age, from 1865 to the turn of the century. If there were opportunities for the yeoman farmer and his family, so too were there opportunities for shysters and hucksters.

Some of the forestland in Oregon and California, for instance, fell into private hands as timber companies hired sailors from the waterfronts to file claims in the forests, then bought the claims back from them. Mining companies in the West acquired priceless mineral rights for practically nothing, and ranchers, by securing the sources of water on the western range, ended up effectively controlling thousands of acres of choice grazing land.

Town jobbing—the practice by speculators of picking and promoting sites for new settlements—was rampant along western rivers and some of the Great Lakes, particularly in the 1830s. "Hundreds of tracts were laid off in town lots where the original forests were still standing," reported a resident of Indiana. ". . . On the Maumee River, from its mouth on Lake Erie, there was for miles a succession of towns; some of them . . . were realities, but most of them existed upon paper only." Bribery and influence-peddling became commonplace during the scramble for railroad loans and rights-of-way, especially during the administration of President Ulysses S. Grant.

Skulduggery regarding federal lands continued in the 20th century. Teapot Dome was a scandal that fascinated the nation in the 1920s. It involved a Secretary of the Interior, Albert B. Fall, secretly leasing strategic naval oil reserves to private interests. He was convicted of accepting a bribe of $100,000 in a "little black bag."

A colorful Westerner, William Andrews Clark, enriched himself by buying up mining claims in Montana and Arizona, and a dozen members of the Montana legislature were bribed to elect him to the U. S. Senate. He died in 1925 worth some 200 million dollars, then one of the largest fortunes in the world. He had opposed early steps to conserve the forests for future generations, saying, "Those who succeed us can well take care of themselves."

By 1976 the government had disposed of more than a billion acres of public land. Today 730 million acres—about a third of the nation—remain under federal management.

*A*ssorted departments and agencies have been given responsibility for this management. The largest of the land guardians is the Department of the Interior, which was signed into existence by President James K. Polk on March 3, 1849, the last night of his term. Thomas Ewing, the first Secretary of the Interior, requested a staff of 10 and a budget of $14,200 to run the department. Today Interior employs some 72,800 people and has a budget of 6.6 billion dollars. The department oversees more than half a billion acres, nearly 70 percent of the federal lands, through a number of agencies.

Most familiar of these is the National Park Service, with responsibility for 11 percent of the federal lands, most of it extraordinarily beautiful. The service was established in 1916 and now administers areas in every state—not only parks, but also national monuments, seashores, lakeshores, scenic rivers and trails, recreation areas, and battlefields and other historic sites.

The U. S. Fish and Wildlife Service takes care of the more than 400 national wildlife refuges. The refuge system got its start in 1903, when President Theodore Roosevelt designated a sanctuary for brown pelicans off the east coast of Florida. The service assumed its present form with the passage of the Fish and Wildlife Act in 1956 and is now entrusted with 12 percent of the federal lands.

The Interior agency in charge of the most land is the Bureau of Land Management—the BLM—which looks after 47 percent of the federal domain. The BLM, long the whipping boy of ranchers and miners in the West, was established in 1946 when the old General Land Office, which had overseen the homesteading programs, and the Grazing Service, which since 1934 had attempted to manage the vast western rangelands, were combined.

For many years the BLM was the poor country mouse of federal agencies, hopelessly underfunded and understaffed. It performed a largely custodial role, with no clear management goals and no administrative machinery for correcting the overgrazing that was seriously damaging the western range. Often the BLM could field only one representative to oversee thousands of acres of rangeland. Some ranchers reckoned they knew that land better than anyone and felt it belonged to them; they ran more cattle on the range than it could support.

The Bureau of Reclamation, originally called the Reclamation Service, was organized when Congress finally realized the Homestead Act would not work in arid regions of the West. It was all very well to offer a homesteader 160 acres of land, but if that land had no water on it, it was worthless for farming. Visionaries genuinely believed for a time that "rain follows the plow," and predicted that once farmers began tilling the dry western soil, the desert would bloom. No such thing happened, of course, and thousands of homesteaders saw their dreams blow away with the dust on western winds. To improve the situation, Congress passed the Reclamation Act of 1902, which provided that "all moneys received from the sale and disposal of public lands" in 16 western states would be used to build and maintain irrigation works such as dams and canals in those states. The bureau oversees about one percent of the federal holdings.

Another department with a major role in managing federal lands is Agriculture, whose Forest Service controls 190 million acres of national forests and grasslands in 44 states—25 percent of the public domain. The forest reserves were managed originally by Interior, but in 1905 Teddy Roosevelt, distrusting that scandal-ridden department, moved them to Agriculture and named Gifford Pinchot Chief Forester.

The Departments of Defense and Energy, and NASA and other agencies also administer federal lands, many of them off limits to the public or requiring special visitor permits. And Interior's Bureau of Indian Affairs acts as trustee for Indian-owned properties amounting to more than 52 million acres.

All these agencies are responsible for managing the federal lands, but Congress has the final say in *how* those lands are managed. Over the years Congress has enacted various pieces of legislation that are essential to understanding today's conflicts.

The 1872 Mining Law, a legislative dinosaur that still lumbers across the front pages of newspapers, said that "all valuable mineral deposits in lands belonging to the United States . . . are hereby declared to be free and open to exploration and purchase. . . ." It was clearly intended to give a boost to the lonely prospector with his mule and shovel, but today multinational corporations with platoons of lobbyists and lawyers invoke the law to mine lands for hard-rock minerals such as gold, silver, copper, and uranium. Though heavily amended over the years, the law remains on the books.

The 1920 Mineral Leasing Act removed coal, oil, natural gas, and a few other minerals from the "free and open" category. The federal government retains ownership of lands where these minerals occur, and the Secretary of the Interior may allow exploration and development, impose conditions, and collect fees—which go into the U. S. Treasury.

The Taylor Grazing Act of 1934 organized western rangelands into districts and authorized the Interior Secretary to charge ranchers modest fees for grazing privileges they had previously enjoyed without cost on public lands.

"The fees are almost always much lower than those on other lands," one conservationist, a Westerner, told me, "and they are often criticized as being subsidies to grazers."

The Multiple-Use Sustained-Yield Act of 1960 required that all federal lands under the Forest Service be classified and used for "outdoor recreation, range, timber, watershed and wildlife and fish purposes." The Classification and Multiple Use Act of 1964 required that the same be done with BLM lands. Much of the controversy surrounding federal lands arises from disagreements about which purposes should take precedence.

Also appearing in today's headlines is the Wilderness Act of 1964, intended "to secure for the American people of present and future generations the benefits of an enduring resource of wilderness."

"A wilderness," says the act, "in contrast with those areas where man and his own works dominate the landscape, is hereby recognized as an area where the earth and its community of life are untrammeled by man, where man himself is a visitor who does not remain." The Interior Department and the Forest Service were instructed to examine their holdings, inventory locations that met the definition of wilderness, and recommend them to the President, who in turn recommends them to Congress for inclusion in the National Wilderness Preservation System. By 1984, 80 million acres of forest, park, refuge, and BLM lands had been set aside as wilderness; another 24 million were under study.

The Wilderness Act is the legislative cannon shot that most antagonizes developers. Miners, loggers, energy companies—many insist it is a mistake to "lock up" valuable resources that the country needs. Conservationists answer that our need for wilderness is just as great as our need for other resources, and that there are plenty of resources outside the wilderness areas that remain unexplored and undeveloped.

In 1969 Congress passed the National Environmental Policy Act (NEPA), which has been called "one of the most far-reaching measures for protecting this country's land, air and water that has ever been enacted." Its Section 102 requires federal agencies to assess any action they are planning that might significantly affect the environment and to produce an environmental impact statement (EIS) on it. The EIS must state the purpose of the action and analyze its environmental consequences as well as the consequences of reasonable alternatives. The draft EIS is made public for comments by officials and citizens and review by the Council on Environmental Quality. Citizens can challenge the adequacy of the statement and bring suit to halt or postpone the action.

People at first assumed it would be a fairly simple matter to prepare an EIS, but it didn't turn out that way. As environmentalists challenged the statements and the courts rigorously upheld the law, the statements became more and more exhaustive. Now a statement on proposed coal leasing in a BLM district, say, or on a change of management for a forest area can easily run to hundreds of pages of detailed research, alternative proposals, and public comment. It sometimes seems that half the federal employees in the country are involved at one time or another in preparing environmental impact statements.

Pieces of land-management legislation continued to pour out of Congress in the 1970s. One of them, with the tongue-twisting title of "Forest and Rangeland Renewable Resources Planning Act of 1974," directs the Forest Service to assess its renewable resources—water, fish, wildlife, outdoor recreation, and wilderness as well as timber and range—and to develop programs for its activities. This law was amended by the National Forest Management Act of 1976 to provide for new timber management policies and a planning process that requires full public participation.

After decades without a legal mandate, the BLM finally received its own organic act in 1976—the Federal Land Policy and Management Act (FLPMA), pronounced "flipma" by those who deal with it. The act specifically states that BLM lands are to remain in federal hands, unless the "disposal of a particular parcel will serve the national interest." It charges the BLM with managing those lands and the resources on them so as not to cause "permanent impairment of the productivity of the land and the quality of the environment. . . ." At the same time, the agency must recognize "the Nation's need for domestic sources of minerals, food, timber, and fiber." The BLM is trying to strike a balance between those two sometimes contradictory charges—protection and use. The act also prevents some of the worst abuses that occurred under the 1872 Mining Law.

Many of these laws, especially those of the past 20 years, reflect changing public attitudes toward the federal lands and the ways they are managed. "People have come to recognize the value and vulnerability and increasing scarcity of the country's natural resources," Terri Martin pointed out, "and they want a say in how those resources are used."

*T*oday the federal lands are coveted as never before by interests as diverse as birders and beryllium miners, rock climbers and motorcyclists. Cattlemen want grazing for their herds; energy developers want to mine the enormous reserves of coal, oil, and natural gas; hard-rock miners want to extract gold, silver, copper, and uranium; loggers look with longing at thousands of acres of timber; vacationers in greater and greater numbers each year seek undisturbed solitude for their camping and rafting; hunters want to hunt; hikers want to hike; archaeologists and paleontologists want their discoveries protected from damage; off-road vehicle enthusiasts deplore fences and gates and want to ride in dusty thunder across the desert. And the wildlife! The deer and the grizzlies, the prairie falcons and the prairie dogs—can they survive all this?

So many want so much.

Certain activities threaten to degrade or destroy the remaining federal lands, according to many who are intimately involved in their management. Surface mining would leave some areas so churned and scarred that they couldn't be restored. Increased cutting in some forests exposes mountainsides to erosion. Wildlife suffers if too many cattle are allowed to graze on prairie refuges. Coal-fired power plants breathe veils of haze that threaten to obscure some of the Southwest's most magnificent scenery. Overuse of parks invariably means more vandalism and littering.

Standing watch in the trenches, meanwhile, are the environmental organizations. Some of them have been around a long time; others emerged from the environmental movement of the 1960s and '70s. Their very names can set some people's teeth on edge and chins to quivering. The Sierra Club, The Wilderness Society, Friends of the Earth, Defenders of Wildlife, Earth First!, the National Parks & Conservation Association. They have become very sophisticated during the last couple of decades in the ways they do business. No longer relying solely on public forums and appeals to federal agencies, the environmentalists have discovered "the law," and they don't hesitate to use it. The machinery for combat is now in place. The laws exist, the courts exist, the data exist, and when environmentalists get wind of something they perceive as a threat—

mining, logging, road building, whatever—their response is often simple and straightforward: See you in court.

Lately they have seen much they don't like. Administrations come and go, each with its own policies for managing the federal lands. Some policies worry those interested in developing more of our natural resources. Other policies worry conservationists, especially today. President Ronald Reagan has asked various agencies to determine if certain federal lands could produce more revenue. Increased coal mining, increased oil and gas leasing, increased grazing, increased timber sales—all have been urged by the President as sources of revenue for the Treasury. Conservationists say the federal lands are being forced to play a role that was never intended for them. Should oil wells be drilled on a wildlife refuge? they ask. Is strip-mining compatible with wilderness?

To get a good look at the battlefield, I recently spent ten months touring the country, from southern Florida to northern Montana, from Hawaii to Virginia, visiting national parks and forests, wildlife refuges and BLM lands that for one reason or another have become subjects of controversy.

I found much that was disturbing. On the beach at Chincoteague National Wildlife Refuge in Virginia, tern chicks become trapped in ruts made by off-road vehicles. Around the Snake River Birds of Prey Area in Idaho, irrigated farmland has replaced some of the native rangeland where golden eagles, prairie falcons, and other raptors hunt. Geothermal development near Yellowstone National Park could take the steam out of Old Faithful, just 13 miles away.

I visited unfamiliar BLM lands, exquisite areas where massive coal draglines waited at the boundaries for clearance to move in. I saw the troubles that can result when people with the best of intentions begin tampering with the natural flow of water: Swamps die, lakes flood, waterfowl crowd onto dwindling wetlands. Off the coast of Texas I watched an oil-laden barge pass within 50 yards of a pair of feeding whooping cranes, one of the most seriously endangered species on earth—and one of the most beautiful. I saw the damage that exotic plants and animals can do when they are introduced into areas that have no natural mechanisms for resisting them. I visited, with armies of summer tourists, national parks in danger of being loved to death.

"We just underwent some reorganization here," a wildlife biologist told me in heavily used Great Smoky Mountains National Park, "and one of the divisions—the Ranger Division—was renamed 'Resource Management and Visitor Protection.' I think it should be the other way around: 'Resource Protection and Visitor Management.'"

Much was disheartening, but much else exhilarating. I visited places that were genuinely breathtaking, some familiar, some all but unknown. I awoke in the Nevada desert one night to stars and the howls of coyotes. In Arizona I saw a roadrunner actually running across a road, something I had suspected never really happened. In Hawaii I saw a hang glider descend from the rim of Haleakala Crater *toward* a layer of clouds. With other tourists I gaped at Yosemite's famous granite features, Half Dome and El Capitan. I visited deserted parcels of BLM land that in any country less blessed with scenic wonders would be national parks. I leaned into prairie winds in North Dakota and stood hushed beneath California's redwoods. Despite generations of exploitation, development, mistakes, and the backfiring of good intentions, this remains a beautiful country.

Everywhere I went, too, I talked with people whose lives are wrapped up in the federal lands. The men and women of the Park Service and the Forest Service, passionate with concern for their parks and forests, dropped everything to show me around and point out the problems they face. BLM employees, unaccustomed to the glare of the spotlight after decades of obscurity, fell over backward to open their files and their territories to me. The Fish and Wildlife people—a folksy bunch—sometimes reminded me of the critters in their care. A biologist darted shy glances my way like one of the herons he studies.

Many of these people, some with tears in their eyes, would talk deep into the night of the battle to ward off corporations bent on development, or of policies originating in Washington that they had to implement, even though the result might be further degradation of the land. They lamented budget cutbacks that forced them to stand by and watch their resources deteriorate.

"Who am I responsible to—the people above me, or the public?" a wildlife refuge manager asked. "What they tell me is, 'If you can't support your superiors, you ought to quit.' But I'm not working for *those* people. I'm working for the public. And quitting isn't going to help anything. I should be allowed to express publicly my disagreement with policies, to say 'The government position is *this,* and my position is *that.*' But they don't see it that way."

Environmentalists, too, described their frustrations and fears, the constant compromising, the hostility and anger they encounter. I asked Terri Martin if she ever became discouraged, and she said, "I feel sometimes as if I'm plugged into an environmental bureaucracy that is the mate of the federal bureaucracy, as if we're doing nothing but churning out reams of paper and keeping a finger in the dike. The real message is much more fundamental. It's a set of values, a perspective.

"I know the value of the paperwork, but it seems . . . I get a little bit tired of being a fighter all the time, of forever being on the defensive. And there are always 16 more issues to address than there is time to address them."

If everyone agreed on what constitutes threats, it would be easy to eliminate them. But perhaps it's well to remember through all of this that one person's threat may be another's livelihood, and a conservationist may also be an out-of-work logger with a house that needs to be lighted, heated, and cooled. "Our own backyard is usually someone else's front yard," said Terri, "and in the long run *all* our livelihoods depend on wise stewardship of the land."

Nearly every threat I encountered has its roots in economics. The business of America is business, perhaps, but business unrestrained will destroy our natural heritage. In wildness is the preservation of the world, perhaps, but wholesale preservation can lead to a shortage of resources that the country needs. The attempt to balance these two powerful forces, to find the middle ground, produces the conflicts and threats I set out to chronicle. And in resolving them we dare not make too many mistakes.

In the 1940s and early '50s there was a move by western stockmen to get hold of BLM and Forest Service grazing lands. Various bills were introduced in Congress, the most far-reaching of which would have virtually eliminated the public domain in the West. The scheme didn't succeed, of course, and now it is highly unlikely that anything of the kind ever will. But what journalist and historian Bernard DeVoto wrote during that battle is worth keeping in mind as we survey the federal lands today.

In an article published in 1953, DeVoto said: ". . . the public lands are the only responsibility of the government besides atomic energy about which Congress could make an irretrievable mistake, one that could not be corrected later on. For if the public lands are once relinquished, or even if any fundamental change is made in the present system, they will be gone for good."

*C*urtain of mangrove leaves shelters a little blue heron in J. N. "Ding" Darling National Wildlife Refuge, a major rookery on Florida's Gulf Coast. At Cape Romain Refuge in South Carolina (below), tidal creeks braid nutrient-rich marshland. In 1903 President Theodore Roosevelt set aside three-acre Pelican Island in Florida as the country's first wildlife preserve. The system now embraces 89 million acres in more than 400 refuges from Maine to American Samoa, from Alaska to Puerto Rico. Many early sanctuaries were created to protect wetlands along flyways of migratory waterfowl. In today's world of dwindling wild lands, refuges also provide retreats for human visitors.

FOLLOWING PAGES: Alone in morning mist, a sika deer comes to nibble marsh grass in Black Duck Pond at Virginia's Chincoteague National Wildlife Refuge. Autumn brings thousands of geese, ducks, and other waterfowl here, to overwinter or to rest and feed before continuing the journey south.

Snugly chinked against autumn's chill, an oak-log house built around 1830 stands restored in Cades Cove, Tennessee, part of Great Smoky Mountains National Park. Several such homesteads here recall the region's pioneer past. The half-million-acre park also encompasses one of the largest wild areas in the East, including an extensive virgin hardwood forest. Designated a park in 1934, later than many western preserves, these rolling mountains straddling the North Carolina-Tennessee border rank, in the words of an early park supporter, "second to the West in rugged grandeur," but "first in beauty of woods, in thrilling fairyland glens, and in the warmth of Mother Nature's welcome."

*S*houlder-deep in summer pasture, a month-old bison calf nurses at Fort Niobrara National Wildlife Refuge in Nebraska. Of the millions of bison that once roamed the prairies, perhaps 55,000 survive, many in parks and refuges. Below, four young black-tailed prairie dogs cluster around their burrow entrance. Often destroyed as pests on private rangeland, the rodents thrive in their town at Fort Niobrara. For visibility—and safety—they burrow where bison, pronghorns, and other animals have cropped the grass. Before the coming of the plow, dozens of grass species and abundant wild flowers blanketed much of the nation's heartland. Today virgin prairie exists only in a few scattered pockets.

FOLLOWING PAGES: *Granite peaks of the Teton Range glow at sunset in Wyoming's Grand Teton National Park. Donations of land and money by private citizens helped create this and other federal preserves.*

fternoon storm builds over wild flowers and sagebrush at the Snake River Birds of Prey Area in Idaho. Scarlet paintbrush (below, left) and penstemon brighten the rangeland. Birds of Prey draws one of the world's largest concentrations of nesting raptors—such as eagles, hawks, and owls. By 1980 the Bureau of Land Management had expanded a protected area along the Snake River from 27,000 to 483,000 acres of public land to include more of the birds' hunting ground. Formed in 1946, the BLM oversees 342 million acres—more than any other agency. After the wholesale disposal of the public domain in the 19th century, these "lands nobody wanted" remained in federal hands. Today pressures to develop BLM holdings in the West threaten many wildlife habitats.

*F*rothing waters of Yosemite Falls (opposite) plunge 2,425 feet, in three long steps, to the valley floor near the Merced River. Farther upstream at Nevada Falls (left), the Merced hurtles 594 feet down a granite cliff below Liberty Cap. The concept of setting aside government-owned land for public use originated in 1864, when Yosemite Valley became California's first state park; it reverted to federal control in 1890. Eighteen years earlier, Congress had established Yellowstone as the first national park. The system has grown to 335 parks and other preserves totaling some 80 million acres—and representing, in the words of an English observer, "America's unique contribution to the democratic idea."

FOLLOWING PAGES: Breaking through rain clouds, the setting sun gilds part of the Black Rock Desert below Trego mountain. These alkali flats in Nevada and other deserted tracts of BLM land possess a special kind of beauty, stark and untamed.

intry dawn illumines massive buttes and mesas of the Grand Canyon. Carved by the Colorado River, at far left, the vast chasm exposes rocks nearly two billion years old. Grand Canyon National Park in northern Arizona protects what naturalist Joseph Wood Krutch called "the most revealing single page of earth's history anywhere open on the face of the globe."

FOLLOWING PAGES: Centuries-old giants, redwoods pierce the morning fog in northern California. Redwood National Park preserves remnant groves of old-growth trees, which once flourished on two million acres in the moist coastal fog belt.

*C*ompanions in September, three Dall rams graze flowering mountain avens in Alaska's Denali National Park and Preserve. The rams band together until the mating season in late fall, when they clash horns over the ewes. On a misty summer morning, ewes and their lambs (above) scamper up a steep slope. With more than 250 million acres of federal land, most of it remote and unspoiled, Alaska is the nation's last frontier, rivaling in wealth and grandeur the West of a century ago.

FOLLOWING PAGES: Sunset casts an ethereal veil over peaks of the Alaska Range, looming beyond the Susitna River in Denali.

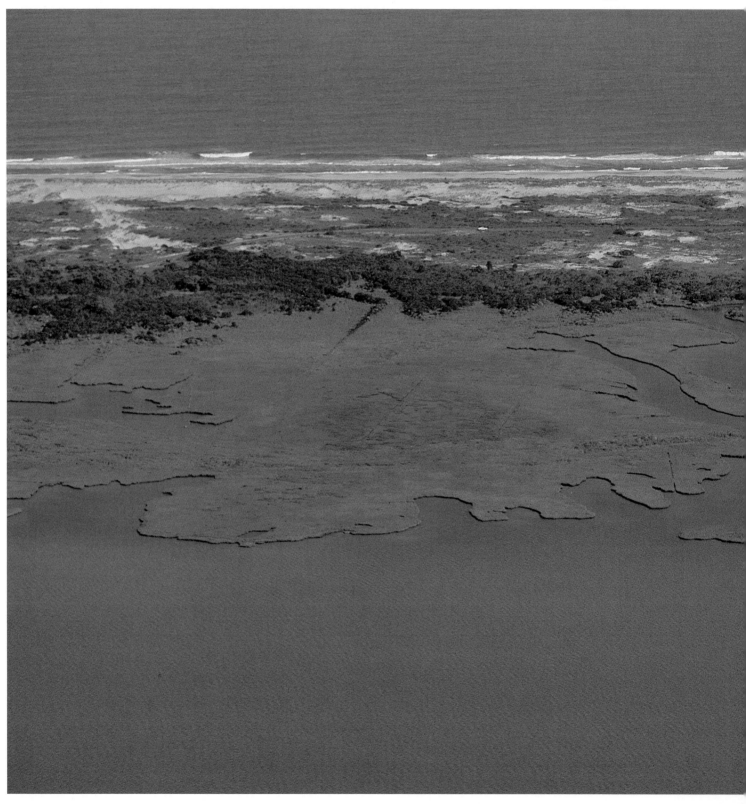

Pounded by surf on the east, edged by salt marsh on the west, Maryland's Assateague Island National Seashore endures as a rare unspoiled strand along the Atlantic coast.

Land of

the Eastern Sea

*O*f the many tales about the ponies of Assateague, one strikes me as especially poignant. In the New World as in the Old, the Spaniards used ponies to work in their mines, to labor alongside slaves extracting gold and silver. So that they wouldn't panic while being lowered into the mines, the ponies were blinded. They toiled in a darkness that was indistinguishable from the darkness of their short, unhappy lives.

Around 1820, so the story goes, a hundred ponies were put aboard a ship in what is now Panama. The mines there were being shut down because of rebellion among the Indians, and the ponies were sailing home to work in the mines of Spain. The ship broke up in a storm off the coast of Maryland. With the sea crashing over them, the blind ponies somehow found their way out of the stricken ship and swam instinctively with the surf toward shore. Their landfall was what we know as Assateague Island.

Though some ponies may have reached Assateague this way, the first ones probably belonged to English colonists who moved them off the mainland in the 1600s. Today their bright-eyed descendants stand among the trees like shy Indians, watching with considerable interest the goings-on around them.

Assateague is a narrow, 37-mile-long blade of sand and marsh, divided about two-thirds of the way down by the Maryland-Virginia state line. North of the line is Assateague Island National Seashore, with small Assateague State Park near its center. South of the line is Chincoteague National Wildlife Refuge. A confusion of authorities—the Maryland state government, the Park Service, and the Fish and Wildlife Service—shares the management of the island.

Opposite its northern tip sprawls Ocean City, Maryland, a resort town where the boardwalk on hot summer days reeks of suntan lotion and pizza. Opposite the southern end is Chincoteague, Virginia. Lying as it does on the edge of Megalopolis, Assateague receives many visitors—more than a million a year on the wildlife refuge alone. The goings-on that intrigue the ponies include swimming, biking, hiking, birding, boating, surf fishing, a yearly oyster festival, and the launching of rockets from the nearby NASA installation on Wallops Island. And every July there is the famous roundup of the ponies themselves.

Many local surf fishermen use off-road vehicles (ORVs) to get to the beach, and that worries refuge biologist Irvin Ailes. He and assistant refuge manager Bob Wilson drove me to the southern tip of the island, where it curves toward the mainland. In the loose sand just back from the surf, our four-wheel-drive vehicle rocked and pitched like a small boat on a rough sea. A few fishermen stood knee-deep in the surf, casting for flounder. Vehicle ruts several inches deep crisscrossed the sand, and here and there least terns were nesting.

"You can see the problem," said Irvin. "The terns nest in the open areas. Their nesting season is approximately May 1 to August 1, which coincides with our period of heaviest use, so the terns have to share the beach with a lot of visitors—many of them fishermen in ORVs. It takes about three weeks for the eggs to hatch and another three weeks before the chicks can fly, so for about six weeks the eggs and young are very vulnerable."

We saw several tern chicks—little black-and-gray fuzz balls with matchstick legs—running in comic haste as if on a mission of desperate importance.

"When the chicks move out of the nest, they get in the ORV ruts and use them like highways. But if they get in a rut several inches deep, they sometimes can't get out. The ORVers tend to use the same ruts over and over, so we lose a lot of chicks that way. When something startles them, they squat down and freeze. That's the wrong thing to do if an ORV is bearing down on you."

Virgin forests and marshes teeming with wildlife greeted the first European settlers of America's eastern lands, but in time overhunting and overcutting depleted nature's largess. Today this once formidable wilderness has become a vanishing treasure, confined to a sprinkling of what one conservationist called "islands in fact and islands drawn on land." Amid the urban sprawl extending from Maine to Florida, these federally held "islands"—most designated national wildlife refuges or national seashores—provide habitat for birds migrating along the Atlantic flyway and for dwindling numbers of larger animals. One of the East's few national parks, Everglades preserves the most extensive subtropical wilderness north of Mexico.

Near Toms Cove at the southern end of the island we came to a section of beach that had been set apart by a single-strand fence. Signs dangling from it said, "Caution: Shorebird Nesting Area."

"Inside this 8-acre exclosure," said Irvin, "are 7 piping plover nests, 2 oystercatcher nests, about 30 common tern nests, and 220 least tern nests." ORV ruts ran along the edges of the exclosure but not through it. "The ORV people are good about not driving into the exclosures, though we get a few people—mostly beach strollers—walking through. Curiosity gets the best of them."

Jerry Liechty, president of the Assateague Mobile Sportfishermen Association, thinks policies are too strict. As head of a 1,500-member ORV club, he resents the restrictions imposed on ORV users in recent years.

"We're limited to only about 15 miles of beach now, with just a few access points to the bay side. Sometimes you want to go there for clamming or crabbing. And they've restricted us to 190 vehicles a day—about 12 vehicles per mile of beach, which is practically no use at all."

Jerry, who has lived just a few miles from the beach for 40 years, likes to hop in his four-wheel-drive Scout on weekends and go surf fishing for blues and sea trout. "I guess you could say Assateague Island is my backyard sandbox. It's a real pleasure to be out there, whether you catch any fish or not."

Jerry raised an issue that troubles many people: In the management of federal lands, who should carry more weight—local residents or national conservationist organizations? "We have so many people from the Midwest and even the West Coast trying to tell us how to run Assateague Island," he said. "That doesn't seem fair to me. We don't try to tell them how to run Yellowstone National Park. We're all conservationists here, too, because we love Assateague and want to protect it. To us, it's home."

The problem of ORVs on Assateague may eventually solve itself. Every year the island becomes a little narrower as winter storms wash sand away from the beach and onto the bay side. And jetties at Ocean City are aggravating the situation as they trap or divert southward-moving sand that once replenished the Assateague beach.

"Our policy on this is up in the air right now," Bob Wilson told me. "We have to decide whether we want to spend the money to keep building up the dunes on the seaward side, or let the area go. It's just a matter of time before the sea cuts through the island."

"From a biological point of view, that would be the best thing that could happen," said Irvin. "It would separate the people and the terns. But politically that's probably not feasible."

Probably not, but it points up a question that confronts many wildlife refuges today: Are they intended for wildlife—or for people?

In the beginning, certainly, for wildlife. The first refuges were established to save various species from the threat of extinction, largely from commercial hunting. They were "inviolate sanctuaries" where hunters, fishermen, and sometimes even tourists were denied access. President Theodore Roosevelt, an early advocate of refuges, established 55 of them but failed to put in place the management machinery that would protect them. Understaffed, neglected by Congress, the refuges made out as best they could until the Depression years. By then they encompassed more than four million acres.

President Franklin D. Roosevelt appointed conservationist and political cartoonist J. N. "Ding" Darling of Iowa to head the Biological Survey, which included the refuges among its responsibilities. Darling in turn named biologist J. Clark Salyer II to oversee the refuges. Salyer was tireless, visiting refuges from one end of the country to the other. He found that the birds were increasing in number and overcrowding their refuges—largely because new laws successfully prohibited egg collecting and market hunting and limited the seasons and bag limits of hunters. He and Darling began acquiring lands for new refuges, and they put the Civilian Conservation Corps—the CCC—to work on them. Between 1935 and 1939 they doubled the size of the refuge system.

One device Darling employed to raise revenue was the duck stamp. Every waterfowl hunter had to buy one, and most of the revenue was used for acquiring wetlands. In 1949 Congress authorized the doubling of the price of a duck stamp—from one dollar to two—on condition that parts of refuges be opened to hunters. That ended the inviolate nature of the refuges, and now not only hunting but also grazing and oil and gas drilling are allowed on some of them.

Today the Fish and Wildlife Service, successor to the Biological Survey, manages more than 400 refuges, at least one in every state except West Virginia; they range from 19 million acres to less than an acre, for a total of more than 89 million acres. They provide cover and food for at least 600 species of birds, 220 kinds of mammals, and hundreds of reptile, amphibian, and fish species. Some refuges are so remote as to be almost invisible; others are visited by armies of birders, fishermen, hunters, and picnickers.

The refuges are under assault today. In the summer of 1983, the Fish and Wildlife Service published the results of a survey of refuge managers citing a broad range of external threats. Many named poaching, erosion, decrease in water flow, and land development; some cited grazing, oil and gas extraction, timber harvesting, acid rain, agricultural and toxic chemicals, air and water pollution, and urban encroachment. Most of them mentioned the internal problems of vandalism, littering, and wildlife disturbance.

Disagreement about the function of refuges exists even within the Department of the Interior. Shortly before the survey results came out, the head of Fish and Wildlife issued a controversial memorandum to the regional directors urging them to expand the economic and public uses of their domains. Singled out for possible increases were such activities as timber harvesting, grazing, and farming. "The increases," said the memo, "must be compatible with refuge objectives." Even so, many critics saw the memo as encouraging those activities *inside* the refuges that managers perceived as *external* threats.

Many refuges on the East Coast were established as breeding grounds and feeding areas for waterfowl. Moosehorn Refuge in the easternmost part of Maine has abundant waterfowl, but it was established chiefly to study and protect the American woodcock.

Of the many bird species on the refuge—some 200 in all—the woodcock is the charmer. A small, round, brown bird, it disappears almost completely in dead leaves and undergrowth. Its mating antics are something to behold. In April and May, early in the morning and late in the afternoon, the male woodcock finds himself a clearing in the forest and strolls around it, chuckling to himself. Suddenly he leaps into the air, spiraling higher and higher, reaching maybe 300 feet. There he pauses, sings a short, melodious song, then plummets like a stone toward the ground. A few minutes later he repeats the show. The female evidently finds it irresistible.

Moosehorn is divided into two units, the wooded, upland habitat where the woodcocks frolic, and another tract on Cobscook Bay, where waterfowl flock. At the mouth of the bay is the town of Eastport. An oil company proposed building a refinery there, only 20 miles from the refuge.

"Everybody agreed it wasn't a matter of *if* there would be an oil spill, but *when*," assistant manager Tom Goettel told me. "Cobscook Bay has 24-foot tides. If there were an oil spill at the mouth of the bay, the tidal bore would wash it right up against the refuge."

Public opinion, initially in favor of the project, gradually swung the other way. In late 1983, after more than a decade of hearings and court battles, plans for the refinery were canceled.

If one of the Moosehorn woodcocks were to look for a place along the Atlantic flyway to spend the winter, he might consider Cape Romain National Wildlife Refuge on the coast of South Carolina. Along a 20-mile stretch of uninhabited shoreline, he'd find sea islands, salt marshes, coastal waterways, and sandy beaches. He'd find a perfect resting place—Bulls Island—covered with live oaks, magnolias, pines, and palmettos. Tundra swans would arrive later in the winter, to rest and feed along with coots, gallinules, and other water birds. The noisy duck contingent would be there—black ducks, pintails, mallards, gadwalls, blue- and green-winged teal, scaups, buffleheads, shovelers, and the like. The enormous family of waterfowl would turn the refuge into a quacking chaos of feathers and webbed feet.

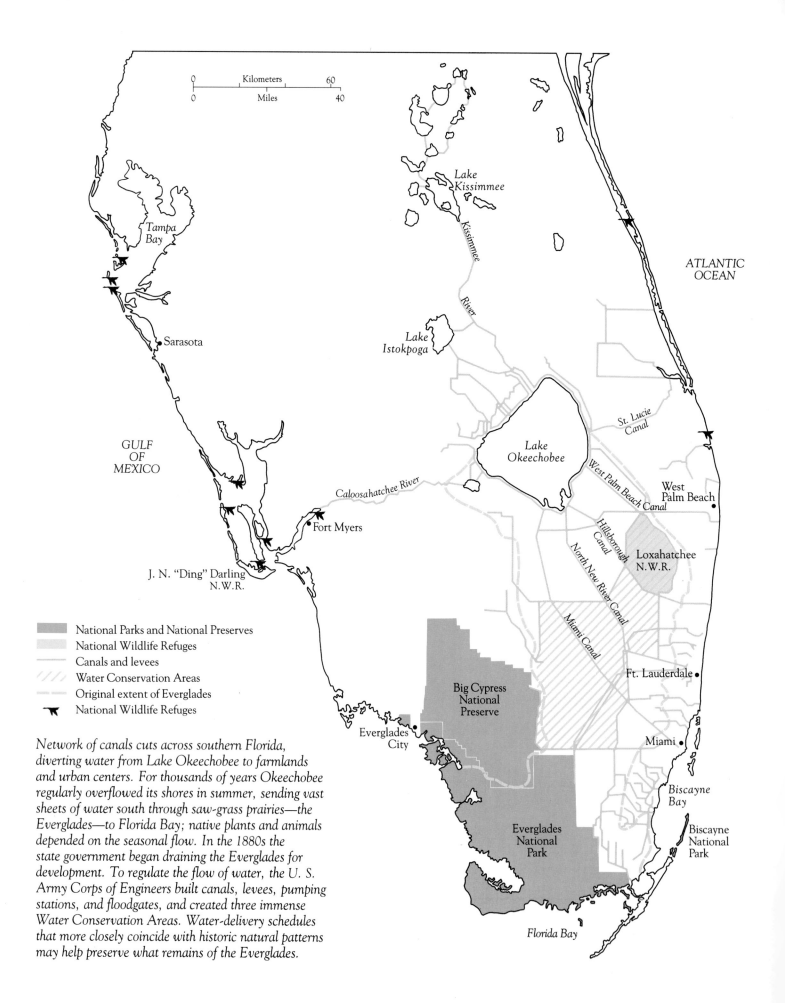

Kilometers 0 — 60
Miles 0 — 40

Lake Kissimmee

Kissimmee River

Tampa Bay

ATLANTIC OCEAN

Sarasota

Lake Istokpoga

GULF OF MEXICO

Lake Okeechobee

St. Lucie Canal

Caloosahatchee River

West Palm Beach Canal

West Palm Beach

Fort Myers

Hillsborough Canal

North New River Canal

Loxahatchee N.W.R.

J. N. "Ding" Darling N.W.R.

Miami Canal

Ft. Lauderdale

National Parks and National Preserves
National Wildlife Refuges
Canals and levees
Water Conservation Areas
Original extent of Everglades
National Wildlife Refuges

Big Cypress National Preserve

Miami

Everglades City

Biscayne Bay

Everglades National Park

Biscayne National Park

Network of canals cuts across southern Florida, diverting water from Lake Okeechobee to farmlands and urban centers. For thousands of years Okeechobee regularly overflowed its shores in summer, sending vast sheets of water south through saw-grass prairies—the Everglades—to Florida Bay; native plants and animals depended on the seasonal flow. In the 1880s the state government began draining the Everglades for development. To regulate the flow of water, the U. S. Army Corps of Engineers built canals, levees, pumping stations, and floodgates, and created three immense Water Conservation Areas. Water-delivery schedules that more closely coincide with historic natural patterns may help preserve what remains of the Everglades.

Florida Bay

Our woodcock would fly through some of the cleanest, freshest air in the United States. If he flew high enough, however, he might see a disturbing sight on the horizon—the hazy skyline of Charleston, just 20 miles to the southwest. And if he came back to Cape Romain every year during his brief life, he might notice that Charleston was creeping ever closer.

To orient myself to Cape Romain, I mimicked the birds and went for a flight in a small plane around the edges of the refuge. The Atlantic Intracoastal Waterway, a busy thoroughfare for pleasure craft, runs along the western boundary. Once we were across it the land below became a flat, marshy maze where tiny muddy streams ran into larger muddy streams, which ran into tidal creeks. Beyond the refuge shrimp boats bobbed in the ocean, spars extended like the feelers of crustaceans. Thin, pale spits of sand became long, deserted beaches. At the northeast corner an abandoned lighthouse stood like an exclamation point. Scallops of sand changed color as they disappeared into blue depths. In coves and bays, whorls of mud, shaped and patterned by tides, baked in the sun. It was lovely and remote, and deserted by all except the birds.

When I visited refuge headquarters, little barn swallows with blue backs and orange stomachs were darting back and forth beneath the pier where they nested. Manager George Garris, a folksy and forthright nine-year veteran of Cape Romain, plans to finish his career here, "unless they want to give me a refuge in New Mexico; the humidity here hurts my sinuses." I told him I had read that Cape Romain was one of the country's outstanding refuges.

"It depends on who you're talking to," he said. "Birders come from all over the world to Bulls Island. Roger Tory Peterson comes every few years. And Gerald Durrell, the British wildlife writer, said that this was one of the places he *had* to see.

"Our population of brown pelicans—an endangered species—is on the rise. It got down to between six and seven hundred nests here in the early '70s. DDT was getting into the water and from there into fish the pelicans were eating. It made their eggshells so thin they couldn't produce young. They'd lay this blob of . . . of *stuff*. Now DDT has been banned, and the pelicans have built back up in the eight years I've been here to about three thousand nests. We also have probably the country's largest population of the threatened loggerhead turtle outside Florida. And we have the nicest natural marsh you'll ever find."

About 29,000 acres of the refuge are designated a wilderness area, and amendments to the Clean Air Act in 1977 brought every wilderness area larger than 5,000 acres under the umbrella of Class I air standards. That means pollutants reaching the refuge must be so benign as to have no adverse effect on the most sensitive plant or animal there. In 1981, Alumax, a firm operating an aluminum smelter 35 miles from the refuge, wanted to expand its plant by 50 percent. It applied for a variance to emit slightly more sulfur dioxide than standards at Cape Romain would allow. The Interior Department approved the variance, and the state government issued the permit.

No one seems much worried by Alumax, a responsible company, but many fear a precedent has been set that will allow other industries to develop in the same area. It's an ideal spot for industry, according to Jim Decker, director of the Charleston Development Board. "There's vacant land up there, a railroad, fresh water, and saltwater estuaries where companies could discharge saline effluents. But the problem is, companies looking for a place to build know that Alumax spent a quarter of a million dollars over the course of a year just getting their permit to expand. That naturally makes them leery of the area."

Richard Watkins of the South Carolina chapter of the Sierra Club told me, "Any major new or expanded source of pollutants that might affect Cape

Romain's air quality will have to go through the same process as Alumax, and the development board is anything but happy with the restraints. They'd like to have Cape Romain downgraded to Class II air standards, or else get a blanket exemption for industry in the Cape Romain area."

And how are things going at Alumax, meanwhile?

"We still haven't expanded the plant," the technical director, Bob Dickie, told me. "As soon as we got the permit, the country went into a recession. I'd say there's a fifty-fifty chance we'll expand before our permit expires in 1985. Alumax has done a good job of building in the right pollution-control techniques. It's company policy to be a good neighbor, so we're willing to go one step beyond what the law says a plant must do."

Betty Spence, executive director of the South Carolina Wildlife Federation, said, "It's potentially a classic case of confrontation between industrial development and maintenance of air quality. We need to find out if emissions under Class II standards would harm the biological integrity of Cape Romain. If they would, then no change from Class I should be contemplated. If they wouldn't, then redesignation would remove one obstacle to Charleston's development and at the same time provide continuing protection for the refuge."

Prompted by public concern, South Carolina's Department of Health and Environmental Control has begun continuous monitoring of air quality at Cape Romain.

Suppose our migrating woodcock tired of the bustle at Cape Romain, or found the winter nights a little nippy there. He might consider moving farther south to the lower end of the Atlantic flyway, where Loxahatchee Refuge offers 145,000 acres of lush Everglades habitat in southeastern Florida.

Loxahatchee has a double-barreled designation. It is both a national wildlife refuge and a flood-control and water-storage area for the state. It's one of three large areas engineered with dikes and canals that capture water flowing southwestward across the lower third of Florida and dole it out to farms and cities along the east coast. And so the wildlife refuge must compete with civilization for water—a precious commodity in Florida.

The refuge faces an assortment of problems. The survey of managers in 1983 listed 35 threats to Loxahatchee—among them urban encroachment, increased public use, airboat traffic, exotic vegetation, pesticide runoff from surrounding agricultural areas, and erratic fluctuations in the water level.

From the air you can see most of the refuge—and many of the problems. Loxahatchee is rimmed by a dike and a canal, making it a true island of everglades in a sea of development and agriculture. Checkerboard fields of radishes, lettuce, strawberries, and sugarcane edge the refuge. A new town under construction crowds one corner. The southeastern quarter of the refuge is open to airboats, and their trails show clearly throughout the marsh, like the strands of a spiderweb. At the northern end, canals from central Florida converge on a giant pumping station, capable of flooding the refuge with more than 600,000 gallons of water a minute—much of it fertilizer-rich runoff from farmlands. Crop dusters emit puffs of pesticides as they skim back and forth above the lettuce fields.

Refuge manager Burkett Neely became relaxed and expansive when we left his office and went for a drive and a stroll along one of the levees.

"The Loxahatchee is probably the best preserved northern Everglades habitat that's left," he said, "but it's a leased piece of property, leased from the state of Florida. Federal money was used to construct it, so there are three agencies involved in managing it: the Army Corps of Engineers, the South Florida Water Management District, and us. When you're trying to satisfy three different needs you always wind up with conflicts and compromises. We've negotiated a water schedule that gives us a range of water that neither floods us out nor dries us up completely. It's usually worked out very well."

We walked down to the edge of a dike. Burkett fished around in the shallows and came up with a couple of snail shells, translucent brown whorls of fragile beauty.

"This area is one of two that we own outright, so we can manage it the way we want. Two years ago we drained it completely, worked it really good with fire and disk, set the cattails back, then reflooded it to the right level to get the most desirable vegetation. We had a tremendous response from these apple snails—about the only food the snail kite will eat. It's one of our rarest birds. Only 437 of them have been counted this year in all of Florida. We had three of them out here last year, feeding on the snails.

"I've read some of the early histories of settlement along the coast—in Delray Beach and West Palm Beach—and people used to talk about going 'out west.' Well, they weren't talking about Texas or Arizona. They meant right here. Now we're averaging between 350,000 and 400,000 visitors a year. Nearly 6,000 people went through our new visitors' center in March, before we even announced it was open.

"The problem in Florida is more and more people and more and more development. They're developing out of existence the very things that made people want to come here in the first place. They've cleared all the easy stuff; now they're down to the hard stuff—the wetlands. I don't know where it will end. They're up to the refuge boundary, and I can't say they'll stop there."

I asked about the airboat trails I had seen from the plane. "Airboating is allowed only in the southeastern 30,000 acres of the refuge. It's very tightly controlled. There's just one entrance and one exit for airboats, and a special-use permit is required. The things do alter the habitat, certainly. They create paths through the vegetation, which permit the water hyacinth to spread."

Earlier Burkett had said to me, "Everglades National Park was established not for its scenery but for its ecology, and it's probably going to be one of the first parks to die."

As I drove south toward the park, I understood his concern. In this part of Florida, development has run amok. Cropland alternates with subdivisions as civilization—heralded by little orange ribbons—creeps westward from the coast. I contemplated the past of southern Florida and began to recognize the awful price the state is paying today for yesterday's mistakes.

The trouble began in the middle of the last century, when the government agreed to cede to Florida the 2.8 million acres of land called the Everglades if the state would agree that "the proceeds of such lands shall be applied to the purpose of reclaiming said lands by means of levees and drains." This seemed such a good idea that Congress went further and passed the Swamp and Overflow Lands Act of 1850. Florida and other states with swampland were quick to take advantage of it. Florida alone obtained more than 20 million acres.

To speed the draining and development, the state turned to the railroads, the only organizations with the financial resources to undertake such massive projects. By 1900 the state had given the railroads more land than it possessed. But as railroads failed, and many did, they lost their grants, saving the state from considerable embarrassment. Still, Florida gave the railroads some nine million acres—about one-fourth of all its land.

Between 1907 and 1926 Florida built a series of six drainage canals from Lake Okeechobee to the state's east and west coasts; four of the canals cut directly across the path of the natural flow of the Everglades. Southern Florida was developing with a vengeance. In 1911, Everglades land was being sold by 50 real estate agencies in Chicago alone.

Since those days, hundreds of miles of canals have been built in the Everglades to capture, control, and distribute every drop of rain that falls there. Every road and highway in southern Florida crosses canals as straight and sterile as surgical incisions. Fishermen with bamboo poles line many of them, with sunfish and bream flopping in the grass at their feet. Billboards hawk "pesticide enhancer," crop-dusting services, and "U-pic" tomatoes.

My first night in Everglades National Park, the night before Easter, I went for an after-dinner stroll and was overtaken by an eerie storm. Dark clouds rolled in, and silent lightning began to flash like artillery, first to the north, then overhead, then all around me. It blazed without letup. White birds soaring against the dark sky were lighted as if by strobes. The wind rose as the temperature dropped. Across the road, hundreds of frogs came suddenly to life, croaking a rackety chorus of alarm. A lightning bug hurtled past, out of control, blinking what looked like an insectile SOS. For half an hour the silent storm raged, then thunder rumbled and muttered and finally crashed overhead. Palm trees swayed, and the fierce lightning continued. Then, as the wind died, the sky opened and an all-night rain began to fall.

A downpour was the last thing park superintendent Jack Morehead wanted. In the perpetual struggle to maintain water in the right places, at the right times, and in the right amounts, an unusually dry or wet year can have serious consequences, and 1983 was unusually wet.

A tall, rangy man, Jack was eager to help me understand the park's complex problems. "We've only got about half our usual number of birds this year because of the high water," he said when we talked in his large, sunlit office at headquarters. "You might think high water would attract more wading and swimming birds, but actually the opposite happens: High water lets the fish the birds prey on disperse, and the birds follow them out of the park."

Over the years, development, drainage, and the resulting loss of habitat have had a devastating effect on bird populations in the park. For example, there are perhaps about 90 percent fewer white ibises here now than in the 1930s. It's hard to imagine what the place must have been like then, because even today birds are everywhere—sandhill cranes, pelicans, snowy egrets, herons, limpkins—more than 300 species in all.

I went for a stroll around Ecopond one afternoon and saw hundreds of birds, including a bald eagle soaring high overhead. Toothy alligators dozed in the sun on muddy banks. Diving for fish, least terns hurled themselves into the lake like rocks. A little egret stood swaying in the tall shore grass, mimicking the motion of the windblown vegetation. With a rapierlike lunge, it plucked a small frog out of the shallows. A feeding coot, dipping its head to scour the bottom, misjudged and went too far, turning a complete somersault, pedaling its feet in the air. As evening approached, two roseate spoonbills settled in a tree across the lake, looking like pink nighties hung out to dry.

Another evening I took a boat ride from Florida Bay up a man-made canal to Coot Bay—and saw nary a coot.

"The canal was built to give boaters easier access to the interior of the park," explained Dr. William Robertson, park biologist. "But it also let in sea water. The brackish water killed the vegetation the coots eat. Once you could see 20,000 coots on Coot Bay; now there are none. They've moved elsewhere."

The Park Service recently closed the canal—"plugged it," in their words—and gradually the water is becoming fresh again, and the vegetation the coots need is coming back.

The plight of wildlife in the Everglades can be illustrated by one endangered species—the wood stork. It's a tall wading bird, mostly white, with a face like a buzzard's and a long, downward-curving bill. In the 1930s there may have been as many as 10,000 storks in the park. In 1983 there were fewer than 1,500 in all of southern Florida.

I drove out to the Everglades Research Center to visit Dr. James Kushlan, a research biologist who seems too young to have devoted a dozen years to the study of wading birds in the park. In his work-cluttered office he filled me in on the "very complicated system" that governs the lives of the wood storks.

"Since the levees were built north of the park, our population of wood storks has dropped from more than 2,000 to about 600. Because it's a very large bird, it needs a lot of food, and if you're going to raise a big chick, you need a lot of time to do it. If you're a little bird, a wren, say, you go through your nesting season in about 25 days. A wood stork takes about four months. And it needs special kinds of food presented to it in special ways during those four months.

"It's what we call a 'tactile feeder.' It feeds by sticking its bill into the water and waiting for something to bump into it. It shuffles along with one wing raised, stirring up the water, sort of herding the fish into its open mandibles.

"Think of the conditions that would be best for the feeding wood stork: big fish and lots of them. In the park, the size and density of the fish depend on the water conditions. The wood stork can't stand in one pond and feed for four months. So the number and kinds of wading birds in any given place change over the course of a year."

In the dry season, during late winter and spring, water in the Everglades recedes to its lowest point—often into alligator holes. Fish congregate there, and the wood storks gather to feed on them. For wood storks to survive, there has to be a dry season, and it has to last for four or five months. Anything that disrupts this drying pattern will interfere with the nesting of the storks. If the water level rises even as little as an inch and a half, the fish will disperse, the wood storks' feeding method won't work, and they will abandon their nests.

"We've had successful wood stork breeding seasons here just twice in the last 20 years," Dr. Kushlan said. "The real problem now is that we rarely have a dry season. Back in the '60s there was a period of drought, aggravated by the new levees, which impounded water that should have flowed into the park. There were fires, alligators dying, no fish. A schedule was devised guaranteeing a minimum flow each month so the Everglades wouldn't dry up. But now the opposite is happening. The park isn't drying enough. It's the only place to dump potential floodwater. This causes unpredictable peaks and valleys of water— pulses of water—in the park. Nature's way was gradual.

"We need to restore patterns of water delivery to the park that will in turn restore historic biological conditions."

A few days before I met with Jack Morehead, he had forwarded to the South Florida Water Management District a statement by his research director, Gary Hendrix, outlining seven steps that needed to be taken at once "to save Everglades National Park." It ended: "We do not think the wildlife, fisheries, and natural functioning of Everglades National Park can be safely protected for another year under the current water management practices." The district board had called a special meeting to respond to the statement.

The meeting was held in a small auditorium at the district headquarters in West Palm Beach. The board sat in high-backed leather chairs behind a bench, facing an audience of some 200 people. Television cameras hummed, and photographers crouched and clicked. Jack Morehead sat with the board, looking slightly ill at ease, like a fish in a favored wood stork pond.

The board's secretary, Jack Maloy, opened the session with a short account of the congressional action that had dictated Florida's water policies, and reminded the audience that the system now being criticized, in a time of high water, was built in response to drought. A board member spoke in a slow Florida drawl of the longtime cooperation between state and federal agencies. A biologist with maps and a pointer showed us the canals and levees causing the trouble. I realized with a jolt that they were talking about actually removing some of the offending structures—in effect, dismantling mistakes of the past.

Representatives of various points of view rose to speak. The National Audubon Society, the Florida Audubon Society, the Friends of the Everglades, the Dade County Farm Bureau, the Florida Game and Fresh Water Fish Commission, the Martin County Conservation Alliance, the Dade County Water and Sewer Authority—all took their brief turns at the podium.

Then, subdued and thoughtful, the board voted. Unanimously, they adopted an emergency order that seemed to surprise even them: to fill in canals, to remove levees, to discharge some excess water into drier areas, to devise a new delivery schedule.

The mood in the room afterward was buoyant. Board members and environmentalists alike seemed pleased with what they had done. They had come together, recognized a problem, reasoned it out, agreed on a solution, and acted.

So Everglades National Park was saved. Or was it?

A few weeks later I talked with Jack again. "As you know, the board approved the seven steps we asked for, but the whole deal has fallen apart. The Corps of Engineers, even though they were represented at the meeting, stopped us cold. Subsequently, some agricultural interests and landowners have threatened suit against both the water management district and the Corps if those seven steps are implemented."

At issue is the fact that the Corps is legally mandated to provide flood protection. So if there is a decision to change existing water control structures, the Corps has to determine if any private property will be affected. And if there is any possibility that homes would be flooded or crops damaged, the Corps is constrained from doing anything without congressional authority.

"The governor has announced his support and introduced a Save-Our-Everglades initiative," Jack continued. "We've still got the support of the water management board and most of the public, and our congressional delegation in Washington is continuing to press for legislation and authorization of funds to protect the Everglades. But even that wouldn't guarantee action.

"After that meeting with the board, we were so elated. It seemed that finally, after years of talking, we were actually on the way to solving some of the park's problems. It really took the wind out of our sails to get stopped. We keep having to come back here to the park, sit down, catch our breath, rethink what needs to be done, and start all over again."

Seaside goldenrod emblazons dunes behind a solitary sweep of beach at Chincoteague National Wildlife Refuge on the Virginia portion of Assateague Island. Waves of reedy brown dune grass act as natural barriers to erosion, holding the sand in place. The refuge restricts one ten-mile stretch of wild beach to foot access only, but in some other areas local surf fishermen drive their off-road vehicles—ORVs—onto the sand. The deep tracks cause further erosion—and affect the refuge's population of least terns. Tern chicks, such as one awaiting a meal under its parent's wing (below), often toddle into ORV ruts, where drivers inadvertently run them down. New restrictions imposed by the refuge severely limit ORV use on beaches favored by the terns as nesting grounds.

MICHAEL L. SMITH

64

*A*bundant marsh grass makes a feast for Chincoteague's wild ponies, whose roundup each July draws thousands of spectators. The refuge's 9,460 acres of forest, marsh, and beach support a rich mix of wildlife, including some 260 species of birds. A young black-crowned night heron (opposite) fishes in a marsh. Attracted by the promise of wilderness still intact, some of Chincoteague's million visitors a year seek out such secluded spots as Janey's Creek (below).

FOLLOWING PAGES: In the golden haze of dawn, a mallard visits a Chincoteague marsh. Here, as on many other federal refuges, hunting regulations ensure the safety of waterfowl.

*S*tark sentinels against a winter sky, loblolly pines guard the edge of a high marsh in Maryland's Blackwater National Wildlife Refuge. The lofty trees provide prime nesting spots for bald eagles. During the fall waterfowl migration along the Atlantic flyway, thousands of ducks, geese, and swans flock to Blackwater and nearby Chincoteague, where a snow goose (below, left) plunges its bill into mud to feed on plant roots. Canada geese (below, right) peck for food, and a great blue heron nearly five feet tall (bottom) wades on stiltlike legs in a Blackwater marsh. Reversion of refuge marshland to open water, caused in part by a rise in sea level, has reduced the habitat of wading birds and waterfowl. Dredge-and-fill operations now under way should save and augment Blackwater's existing marshes.

N.G.S. PHOTOGRAPHER BATES LITTLEHALES (ABOVE, BELOW, AND OPPOSITE)   NATHAN BENN

70

ardinal flowers bloom above eddying waters in one of many streams draining the wetlands of Moosehorn National Wildlife Refuge. In a refuge upland, delicate red maple leaves against a lichen-patterned rock (below) mark the coming of fall to Maine's North Woods. Established in 1937 to protect the American woodcock, Moosehorn continues research on the mottled brown birds, banding them (right) to monitor their movements. Their numbers have decreased in northern Maine, where much former farmland has grown to forest now too old for woodcocks and other animals that need young stands. Refuge officials hope to halt the decline by educating local landowners in habitat management.

PRECEDING PAGES: Brooding waters of a Moosehorn marsh face an insidious peril—acid precipitation, both rain and snow, caused by the burning of fossil fuels. Falling on lakes and wetlands throughout the northern United States and parts of Canada, the deadly pollution destroys fish and aquatic plants on which birds and other wildlife feed.

*S*ummer sunrise unveils salt marshes and tidal creeks of Cape Romain National Wildlife Refuge near

Charleston, South Carolina. Fish and crustaceans hatch in this warm, shallow estuary, where streams and tides deposit nutrients, and dense aquatic vegetation provides protection from larger fish and hungry wading birds. Draining and filling have destroyed similar coastal wetlands, but so far industrial and urban expansion has spared pristine Cape Romain. An American oystercatcher (above) surveys its prey. The shorebird wields its bill like a knife to pry open mussels, oysters, and clams.

FOLLOWING PAGES: American alligator, one of about 500 at Cape Romain, glides toward a clump of marsh grass on Bulls Island. The reptiles remain a threatened species along the South Carolina coast.

*C*abbage palmettos spread spiky
fronds in the maritime forest on Bulls
Island. With its thick vegetation
and shifting channels, the island reputedly
served as a pirates' hideaway in the early
1700s. Today it attracts avid bird
watchers from around the world.
Turnstones and sanderlings throng
the beaches; cormorants and horned grebes
fish offshore; and black ducks, wigeons,
and mallards congregate on freshwater
ponds. Hikers in the live oak forest
may glimpse white-tailed deer, wild turkeys,
and glossy black fox squirrels.
The few reptiles on the refuge include
nonpoisonous rat snakes such as
the 16-inch specimen below. In a tannin-
stained pond (bottom), decaying plants
fuel a fragile food chain.

*L*ush tree islands dot the waters of Loxahatchee National Wildlife Refuge in Florida. The islands form wherever slight elevations in the soil offer toeholds to red bay, wax myrtle, and dahoon holly. Herons and egrets roost in the branches, deer browse in the undergrowth, and robins feast on the berries in winter. For canoeists (opposite, upper), the trees relieve a relentlessly flat landscape of water and saw grass. Good fishing and wildlife watching along the 57 miles of levees and canals surrounding Loxahatchee also lure visitors from nearby cities, and now hunters and airboaters seek wider access to the 145,636-acre refuge. Fields of winter vegetables and sugarcane crowd Loxahatchee's borders (opposite, lower); polluted runoff flows in, and unseasonal fluctuations in water levels, engineered to satisfy farmers and city dwellers, disrupt natural rhythms in this remnant of the northern Everglades.

*G*raceful neck extended, a great egret stalks its prey in the marshy shallows of Florida's J. N. "Ding" Darling Refuge. Memorial to a pioneering conservationist, this sanctuary on Sanibel Island also shelters solitary green-backed herons (above, right) and other wading birds. Cardinal wild pine (top), an air plant, survives on sunlight, moisture, and airborne particles.

alancing on a
mangrove branch, an
anhinga stretches its two-foot
wings to dry. When hunting,
this fish-eater swims
submerged to the neck,
spearing prey with its sharp
bill. Here in subtropical
Everglades National Park,
tangled mangrove forests
reach out to sea; inland,
hardwood-covered
hammocks punctuate
seemingly endless saw-grass
prairies. Dolphins play in
tidal rivers; panthers prowl
the cypress swamps;
manatees graze in shallow
bays; and deer splash
through marshes to feed in
pine woods. Raccoons,
otters, opossums, and
bobcats also frequent the
1,400,533-acre park. But
the profusion of birds at this
crossroads of migration is the
main attraction for the
nearly one million visitors
a year.

*S*ocial and solitary—and often showy—birds representing some 300 species find haven in Everglades National Park. White ibises (above) perch on mangrove roots in a marsh, where they probe the mud for crayfish. Nearly extinct as a breeding species in Florida 45 years ago, roseate spoonbills like the one at far right number more than a thousand nesting pairs today. Once slaughtered for its plumes, the snowy egret (opposite) now thrives under a hunting ban.

FOLLOWING PAGES: Silhouetted at sunset, red mangroves appear to rise from the sea on arching prop roots. Their seeds sprout in salt water and float until the roots take hold.

Carpeted with autumn leaves, a woodland trail leads
backpackers past birches and rhododendrons in the North Carolina
section of Great Smoky Mountains National Park.

Land of

Pastures and Forests

*G*o carefully and observantly into another place and time," the Park Service booklet says, in a tone unusually lyrical for a government publication. The place it has in mind is Cades Cove, deep in Great Smoky Mountains National Park; the time is the 19th century.

The first permanent white settler, John Oliver, arrived in Cades Cove around 1820. Seven generations later a descendant of his, Judy Johns, became a park ranger assigned to Cades Cove. We went for a drive around the 11-mile loop road that winds through the cove, and she told me what it was like to grow up in a national park.

"The first house I lived in was up here on the right," she said, pointing to a grassy knoll. "There was an old CCC camp over there. The barracks were still standing, so we had real houses to play in.

"My brothers and sisters and I thought the tourists had been brought in for our amusement. This creek—Tater Branch—we'd try to charge the tourists to cross it. Most times they wouldn't pay. They wouldn't even stop. Mom had a garden near the road, and when she wasn't looking, we'd sell strawberries to the tourists. Watermelon, too. When we saw a ranger coming, we'd hide the sign and wave to him as he went by. We got sick once on a cigar a tourist threw away. We were awful. If I caught my daughter doing anything like that. . . .

"Our drawl is typical east Tennessee, and they liked to hear us talk. They'd do just about anything we wanted if we would just talk to them a little. And I liked to talk, so. . . .

"Over there"—across a broad meadow, tucked among trees—"is the home of the only person still living here. He's my double second cousin, Kermit." Double second cousin? "More or less. My grandfather and his mother were brother and sister, and his wife's mother and my grandmother were sisters.

"All of us kids worked for Dad leading horse rides for tourists. We figured up once that we'd each ridden somewhere near 20,000 miles taking horseback tours. My ten-year-old daughter is here today, riding. She'd leave me in a minute for one of those horses."

In the late 1920s, park commissions in Tennessee and North Carolina began acquiring land to turn the area into a national park. People were given a choice: Sell to the commission and move out, or sell and then lease the land back. It was a disruption of their lives that many had trouble accepting.

"I'm on a fence," said Judy. "I understand why it became a park. It's beautiful and needed to be protected. But I sympathized with my grandfather. It bothered him tremendously to sell his farm. But time heals. It bothered my father only a little bit, it *barely* bothers me, and my daughter couldn't care less."

At several places along the road in Cades Cove and around a couple of the old cabins, the ground had been churned and chopped as if someone had been at work with a garden tiller. Wild boars had paid a visit during the night.

In 1912 European wild boars were imported to a private hunting preserve on Hooper Bald in North Carolina. In 1920 about a hundred escaped and, despite heavy hunting, began to spread. By the late 1940s they had reached the park, and in 1976 the Park Service estimated they occupied three-fourths of it. Today they are everywhere.

The females and the young travel in family groups, rooting as they go. They compete with bears and other mammals for mast—acorns, hickory nuts, beechnuts, and other tree fruits. They feed on tubers of wild yams, pitch pine roots, and plant bulbs. They also eat small animals such as salamanders, snakes, and rodents. They have greatly reduced some wild flower species—spring

Younger and less extensive than their western counterparts, national forests east of the Mississippi River range from the hardwoods of Wisconsin's Chequamegon and Pennsylvania's Allegheny to the pines and cypresses of Osceola in Florida. Beginning in the 1800s, virtually all forests in the region were cut over at least once. After the turn of the century, the federal government began acquiring and reforesting land for watershed protection and timber management, and for wildlife refuges such as Hatchie and Lower Hatchie in western Tennessee. Established in the 1930s, Great Smoky Mountains National Park encompasses more than half a million acres in Tennessee and North Carolina.

beauty, yellow adder's-tongue, wake-robin. They damage tree roots and seedlings. They uproot the grass on the Smokies' famous grassy balds. They destroy the nests and eggs of ground-nesting birds. They can turn a small trout stream into a bulldozed quagmire. They create ugly patches of destruction that the tourists complain of. They may even be spreading diseases.

In short, it's hard to find anything good to say about the wild boars in the Smokies—but how do you get rid of them?

"Talk with Kim Delozier," Judy advised me. "Kim 'the Wall' Delozier, I call him. Whenever the staff gets together for basketball, I make sure Kim is on my team. He's a big, husky wildlife handler from Tennessee working on the boar problem in the park."

I found Kim at park headquarters near Gatlinburg, Tennessee. He has a number of traps set at various points around the park—simple wood-and-wire cages with sliding doors and triggers that, when tripped, trap the unsuspecting pigs. A hole in the top lets innocent raccoons escape. Kim makes his rounds every day, checking traps, rebaiting them, turning captured pigs over to the Tennessee Wildlife Resources Agency, which takes them to a game management area south of the park. Over the 1983 Memorial Day weekend just before my visit, he had caught 12.

"Our objective is to reduce the number of hogs in the park," he told me, "and our justification is that they do a lot of damage and they're exotics. They don't belong here."

I rode with Kim in his Park Service jeep to check his traps. Summer was coming to the Smokies, and the air had a moist, heavy feel.

"We've managed to reduce the number of hogs in certain areas of the park," Kim told me, "but I don't think we'll ever eradicate them. Not with the methods we're using. They breed too prolifically and have adapted too well to this area. It's good habitat for hogs—plenty of food most years, few natural enemies, fairly mild climate, isolation."

I visited three traps with Kim that morning. At one, the door was down but the trap was empty. A raccoon had been in it. At the next, the door was still up but all the bait was gone.

"We had one here, but someone has let him go," Kim said as he took a shovel and bucket of corn and laid a trail of grain to the trap door. "Some of the local people oppose what we're trying to do. They want us to leave the hogs alone so they'll spill out of the park and can be hunted. A lot of times I'll find someone has cut the cord that holds the trigger up." At the third trap, the door was still up and all the corn had been eaten. "The darn pigs are getting smarter," Kim said. "We catch the little dumb ones first."

"How do you get them out of the trap when you *do* catch them?" I asked. "Don't they put up a fight?"

"You get hold of the end that doesn't bite."

Since 1978, Kim has helped remove some 1,700 hogs, most of them by trapping. "We do shoot them. It's no secret. They're nocturnal, so we hunt primarily at night." Kim's catch has improved each year—405 in 1982 and 520 in 1983. But the pigs keep breeding, and they are nearly impossible to count. Estimates of the number in the park at any given time range upward to 2,000.

Back at park headquarters, wildlife biologist Bill Cook told me, "If we had four more Kim Deloziers, we'd be in fairly good shape."

The boar problem is a regional one, he stressed. "The movement of the boars throughout the southern Appalachians is what we should be concerned about. There is constant traffic of hogs into and out of the park.

"A while back, we didn't talk about reduction of pigs here; we talked about eradication. Now we're more realistic."

Stu Coleman, chief of the park's Division of Resource Management, explained the change in policy. "A few years ago, the Park Service said, 'Look, every park has its exotic species, and there's no way to get rid of them all. But each park must study its exotics and determine if they really are harmful to the native ecology, and if they are, then spend the money and manpower to control them.' We have more than 280 species of exotic plants here, but we intensively campaign against just four: kudzu, mimosa, Canadian thistle, and multiflora rose. Same with animals. We campaign against only the wild boar and the rainbow trout, which was introduced into the park early in this century. A 1963 report on wildlife management in the parks probably said it best: There is no way you're going to be able to restore an ecosystem that is 'primitive American,' but you should try to recreate a 'reasonable illusion' of what primitive America looked like. That has become Park Service policy all over the country."

In western Tennessee, a reasonable illusion is about all that's left of the once extensive bottomland hardwood forest. All but one of the slow-moving swamp streams that used to wind through the rolling countryside have been channelized, their banks made arrow-straight. Alongside them, lush stands of oak, maple, elm, ash, and hickory have given way to fields of soybeans.

The lone exception is the Hatchie, which rises in Mississippi, wanders across Tennessee, then joins the Mississippi River. Near its junction with the Mississippi, two small national wildlife refuges—the Hatchie and the Lower Hatchie—hug its banks. They were established to provide protection and food for overwintering and migrating waterfowl within the Mississippi flyway.

"The Hatchie is the last major stream in west Tennessee that hasn't been significantly altered by channelization and wetland drainage," said refuge manager J. C. Bryant. Further, the Tennessee portion of the river—185 miles—has been classified as a Class I State Scenic Swamp River under the Tennessee Scenic Rivers Act of 1968, which means it won't be channelized.

But extensive channelization and clearing upstream of the refuges have caused serious problems. Tributary waters, freed from the former restraints of a broader, meandering streambed, rush into the Hatchie. The river, now laden with silt from newly cleared farmland, slows down and deposits its burden on the floodplain. Silt collects around the roots of trees and smothers them; oaks and hickories are particularly sensitive. Silt also fills wetland areas, alters drainage patterns in the forest, and degrades wildlife habitats.

As you might expect, all of the agencies and each of the landowners involved have different ideas about what should be done. Some farmers would like to see the Hatchie channelized. A straight, deep channel would drain the river bottom and hurry the water on its way to the Mississippi.

Chuck Cook, director of the Tennessee Nature Conservancy, said: "The bottomlands of the Hatchie are so productive that everybody is after them. You can grow 30 to 35 bushels of soybeans an acre down there."

Not when I visited. It was late summer, and water was everywhere. It spilled through breaks in dikes and out of channels, flowed over fields, pushed chocolate-colored fingers up valleys, and threatened towns. It oozed across farmland and roadways, and eddied in sinister whorls beneath highway bridges. With assistant refuge manager Glenn Stanley, a soft-spoken Southerner, I went for a short motorboat ride on the flooded Hatchie. The muddy water, disregarding the channel entirely, flowed in a broad, shallow sheet across the land and through the dark forest on either side of us.

"If you like a river for its bends, you'll love the Hatchie," said Glenn. One minute the sun was full in my face; the next, on the back of my neck. Occasionally we'd shut off the engine and drift. Bird songs were constant, and the birds themselves flitted among bushes and trees. Indigo buntings, cardinals, a red-winged blackbird with a beakful of nest, a red-bellied woodpecker and a red-shouldered hawk, a brood of wood ducks, a yellow-billed cuckoo, and two big barred owls—we saw all these in just a couple of hours.

Earlier, over cheeseburgers at a little restaurant near refuge headquarters, I had talked with Glenn and J. C. Bryant about the clearing of bottomland, the accumulation of silt, the threat of channelization.

"It all comes down to stewardship, pure and simple," said J. C. "Many people here are very enthusiastic about the refuges and what we're trying to do, but these same people may own 2,000 acres of bottomland hardwood timber that they're clearing as fast as they can, right up to the river's edge. The government can't solve that problem. It's up to individual people.

"Also, there's a lot of tenant farming in west Tennessee, where a man farms land he doesn't own. I think that's been bad for land stewardship. We have lands that are losing 40 tons of topsoil an acre every year. There's a lot of sheet erosion, where you can lose two inches in one rainfall. If we'd just do what we know how to do, that is, farm this land properly, we'd be in pretty good shape."

"The very worst thing," said Glenn, "is to have two or three dry years. People see all that good land; bulldozers go to work and the soybeans go in; then the rainfall gets back to normal and the land is underwater. More erosion."

Paul Thomas, resource management specialist for the state's Department of Conservation, told me, "It's not entirely a matter of poor agricultural practices. The farmer is caught in the middle, trying to make a living. He feels that if he can clear a few more acres, get them into production, he'll make it."

The threats to the Hatchie refuges come from outside, but many threats to our public lands are internal ones—as I discovered when I visited some of our national forests.

The eastern forests are remnants of the vast sea of trees that once flowed from the East Coast to the Mississippi River. To early loggers and to settlers pushing westward, those trees seemed inexhaustible. One of the first men to realize they weren't was Gifford Pinchot. He was born in Connecticut in 1865; after graduating from Yale in 1889, he studied forestry for a time in Europe, then came home and took a job managing the forests on George W. Vanderbilt's North Carolina estate, Biltmore. There he began developing the new science known today as silviculture. It was new not just to Pinchot, but to everyone, for, as he wrote, ". . . I knew little more about the conditions necessary for reproducing the Yellow-poplar than a frog knows about football." Late in the century he was a member of a commission that created what were then called "forest reserves." He became head of the Division of Forestry in the Department of Agriculture, and when the forest reserves were transferred there from Interior in 1905, President Theodore Roosevelt named him Chief Forester.

Theirs was an era of what one observer called "wanton, barbarous, disgraceful vandalism" in the nation's forests, when loggers engaged in "cut-and-run," leaving hideous devastation in their wake. Pinchot, however, had little patience with "preservationists" who bewailed the cutting of a tree. When New York forbade logging in the Adirondacks, he wrote: "As for me, I have always regarded the sentimental horror of some good citizens at the idea of utilizing the timber . . . as unintelligent, misdirected, and shortsighted." But he warned of a "timber famine" unless the forests were managed wisely.

Half a century later, Congress passed the Multiple-Use Sustained-Yield Act of 1960, which states that "the national forests are established and shall be administered for outdoor recreation, range, timber, watershed, and wildlife and fish purposes"—in other words, for multiple use. But how do you decide which use or uses will predominate? Suppose cattle and wildlife are competing for forest grazing land. Which should get the grass? Or suppose rich deposits of phosphate lie beneath part of a national forest. Should they be mined?

That's the big question in Osceola National Forest, 157,200 acres of pine flatlands and cypress swamps in north-central Florida. Though there's no mistaking Osceola for one of the rugged national forests of the West, it's a beautiful place, one that residents of nearby Jacksonville like to visit. The Osceola Trail winds through the forest; the fishing, in slow-moving streams, is good, especially for bream and crappie; hunters stalk deer, squirrel, quail, and bear; and a recreation area offers boating, swimming, picnicking, and camping.

Osceola is also prime habitat for the red-cockaded woodpecker, an endangered species. It's a bird that doesn't help its situation much, being fussy about its housing. It usually will drill its nest hole in a living pine tree that has heartwood disease. This finickiness annoys foresters, whose first impulse on seeing a diseased tree is to cut it down. Osceola foresters carefully flag pines with nests in them so that loggers will leave them standing.

Beneath the western third of the forest lie perhaps 120 million tons of phosphate, a mineral used chiefly in fertilizers. In the 1960s the Forest Service issued prospecting permits to nine different mining, oil, and chemical companies, allowing them to begin exploratory drilling on more than 144,000 acres. The Osceola phosphate controversy has been raging ever since.

Phosphate has long been important to Florida's economy, contributing three billion dollars in 1983 alone. But even its proponents admit it's a messy industry. Giant draglines tear up the land, leaving it radically altered. Enormous amounts of fresh water are required, which worries people concerned about Florida's fragile and falling water table. Phosphate mining also creates aptly named slime ponds, unsightly bodies of water that stand for years.

All in all, it's no wonder that environmentalists went to war over Osceola. They soon had the state government on their side. Between 1969 and 1972, four companies applied for leases to strip-mine 52,000 acres in the area, and Florida officials countered with a suit to prevent the leases from being issued. The state delegation introduced legislation in Congress that would have closed Osceola to mining while requiring the government to compensate the companies.

"Nobody knows how much money would be involved in compensation," Paul Steinmetz, Forest Service information officer, told me. "It would depend on the price of phosphate and whether they were paid in ground value or processed value. And nobody knows how much phosphate is down there. Estimates vary, depending on who does the test drilling."

In 1983 President Reagan vetoed the bill that would have compensated the companies for the value of their claims; he said it would be too expensive. At the same time, the Interior Department rejected the lease applications on the grounds that the mined areas could not successfully be reclaimed.

Environmental groups are relieved; mining companies are suing; another bill is pending that would close Osceola to mining and designate part of it a wilderness area. The forest appears safe for now.

Osceola's district ranger, Dick Bonyata, has seen Forest Service policies change over the years. "When I first started working for the service back in 1957," he told me, "we were under fewer restrictions. We were doing things right from a silvicultural point of view, but from an environmental standpoint we were making mistakes. For instance, there were no limitations on clear-cutting. We could clear any size area we wanted. Then environmental laws passed by Congress made us look differently at how we managed the land. Now when we go out, we try to consider every resource."

Many of the changes Dick has seen came about because of an old controversy up north in West Virginia. When the economy boomed after World War II and returning veterans began moving their growing families into single-dwelling homes, the demand for lumber skyrocketed. With the Forest Service's blessing, timber companies expanded their logging operations.

Clear-cutting—removal in one cut of all trees in a given area—had become the foresters' favorite method of harvesting. It's the most economical; it allows them to manage even-age stands of trees; and they say it's good for animals such as deer because it creates open areas for them to browse in. But whatever else is said about it, clear-cutting is ugly.

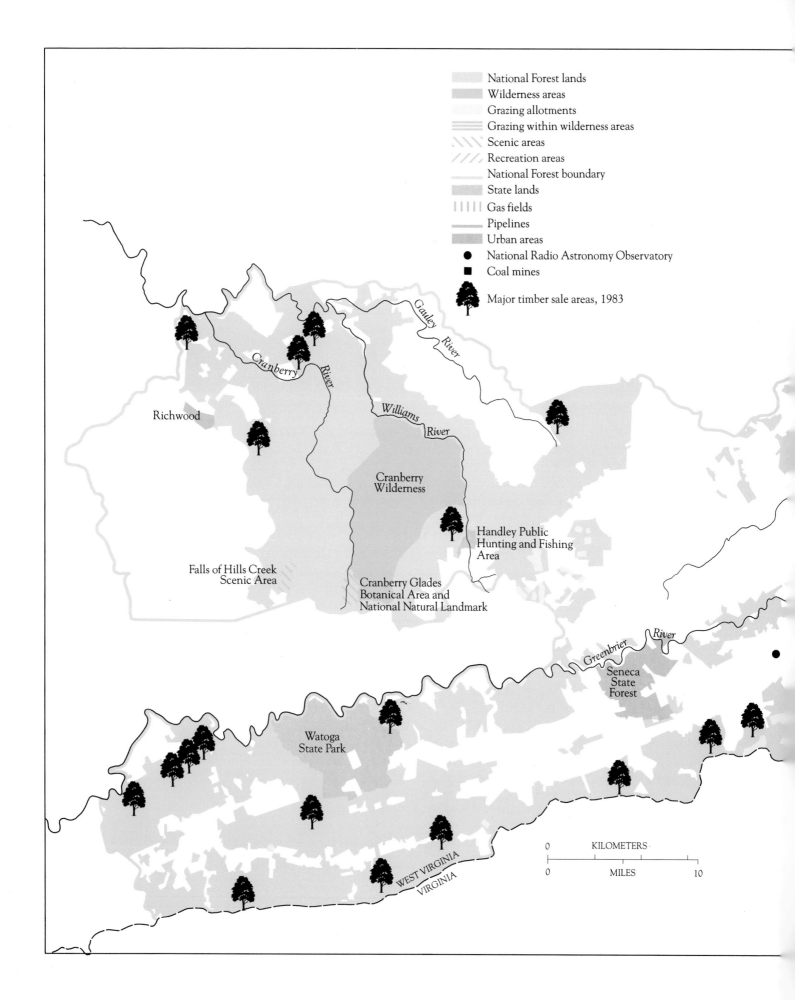

National Forest lands
Wilderness areas
Grazing allotments
Grazing within wilderness areas
Scenic areas
Recreation areas
National Forest boundary
State lands
Gas fields
Pipelines
Urban areas
● National Radio Astronomy Observatory
■ Coal mines
🌲 Major timber sale areas, 1983

Gauley River

Cranberry River

Williams River

Richwood

Cranberry
Wilderness

Handley Public
Hunting and Fishing
Area

Falls of Hills Creek
Scenic Area

Cranberry Glades
Botanical Area and
National Natural Landmark

Greenbrier River

Seneca
State
Forest

Watoga
State Park

WEST VIRGINIA
VIRGINIA

KILOMETERS
0   10
0   MILES   10

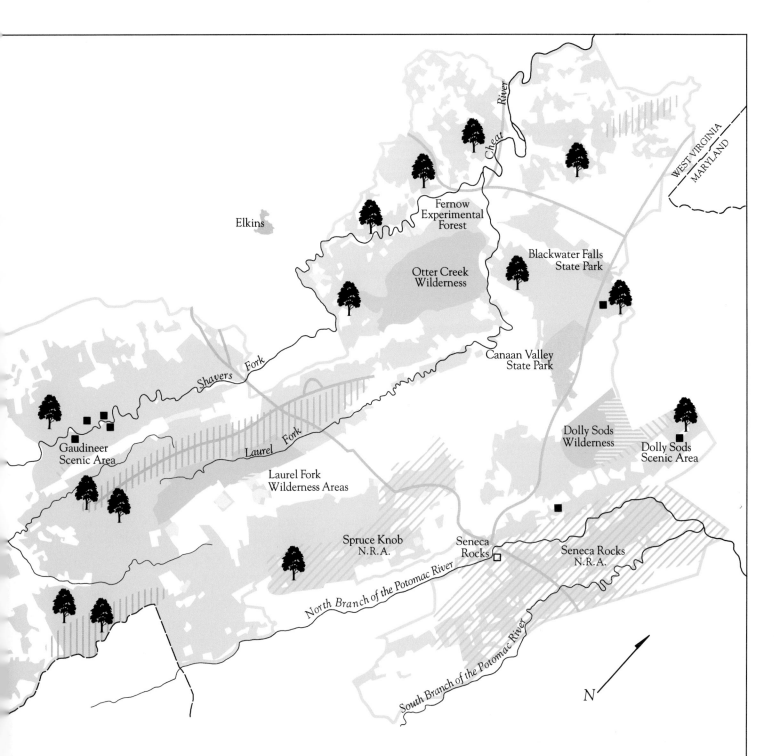

Elkins

Fernow
Experimental
Forest

Otter Creek
Wilderness

Blackwater Falls
State Park

Canaan Valley
State Park

Dolly Sods
Wilderness

Dolly Sods
Scenic Area

Shavers Fork

Laurel Fork

Gaudineer
Scenic Area

Laurel Fork
Wilderness Areas

Spruce Knob
N.R.A.

Seneca
Rocks

Seneca Rocks
N.R.A.

North Branch of the Potomac River

South Branch of the Potomac River

Cheat River

WEST VIRGINIA
MARYLAND

N

Resembling a crazy quilt, Monongahela National Forest spreads across more than 1.6 million acres in the Allegheny Mountains of West Virginia. Only about half the area consists of federal land; state forests and parks and thousands of privately owned parcels make up the remainder. In the Monongahela from October 1982 through September 1983, farmers grazed 1,833 cows and 274 sheep on more than 7,000 leased acres; wells in 2 major fields produced 10,268,000 cubic feet of gas a day, and another field stored gas pumped from the Southwest for winter withdrawal; 2 mines yielded 104,425 tons of low-sulfur bituminous coal; and loggers purchased more than 23 million board feet of lumber and nearly 1.5 million cubic feet of pulpwood from 13 major and 610 small timber sales. In addition, the Forest Service recorded more than a million "visitor days"—a visitor day meaning 12 hours of recreational use by one person or more.

The people of West Virginia, already up in arms over the ravages of strip-mining in their state, began seeing from their windows the mountainsides scraped bare of trees.

"Here is where the clear-cutting controversy perhaps grew most heated—and certainly received the most publicity," Gil Churchill, forest planner in West Virginia's Monongahela National Forest, told me. "And it could rightfully be called the Monongahela controversy.

"Around 1964 the Forest Service switched from a selective system of cutting—taking out individual trees and leaving the rest—to an even-age system—taking out all the trees. There wasn't much public involvement in that change of policy. In fact, there wasn't *any!* People here didn't like it one bit. They remembered the widespread clear-cutting here 50 years before and the awful fires and flooding that followed it, and they objected. The Forest Service, I'm afraid, wasn't very tactful in its response, which was something like 'Go peddle your papers; we know what we're doing.' That wasn't very smart. The controversy really got going in the late '60s."

Clear-cutting was one of the issues that led to the first Earth Day celebration in 1970, when hundreds of thousands of people in scores of cities across the country took time to look at their planet, to listen to speeches, to participate in discussions on the environment. The uproar over clear-cutting led directly to the National Forest Management Act of 1976, which requires extensive public involvement in Forest Service decisions. Regulations now limit clear-cuts to carefully designated areas and sizes—usually 100 acres or less.

Earth Day is still held every spring, but many people seem to have lost interest, and a new generation of college students, less committed to environmental issues, has come of age. I did find one young man, Jozef Antolin, who was trying to keep Earth Day alive. He was a student at Davis and Elkins College in Elkins, West Virginia.

I found him in a Forest Service cabin near the Dolly Sods Wilderness within the Monongahela. A biology major, he was spending a few weeks conducting a water-quality study of streams in the wilderness area. He and his new German shepherd puppy, Muki, accompanied me on a drive up the mountain.

Under the Wilderness Act of 1964, more than 25 million acres of national forest lands have been set aside in the National Wilderness Preservation System. Wilderness areas such as Dolly Sods must remain in a natural state.

"Dolly Sods is about 10,000 acres," Jozef said. "It was logged a long time ago and then burned. It burned right to the bare rock because it was an old spruce forest and there was a very thick layer of humus. Since then it's been going through all of its successional stages. There's a wide diversity of vegetation. You go from this deciduous forest we're in now to low upland types—laurel, blueberries, huckleberries."

We emerged from the forest onto the "sod"—a local word for pasture. "I've never been to Alaska," Jozef said, "but I've always thought it would look something like this." There *was* an Alaskan feel to it: big sky, rolling, rocky hills, and short, scrubby vegetation.

We left the car and strolled through a bog, pursued by a little yellow and green warbler that fluttered from branch to branch, warbling fluty cadenzas. Azaleas were just starting to bloom, and ferns grew along the trail.

Earlier in the year, Jozef had organized the college's Earth Day celebration. "A lot of people 'expressed interest' and showed up at meetings, but then wouldn't do anything to help. A man from the West Virginia Citizens Action Group spoke on hazardous wastes, and one professor spoke on population, another on alternative agricultural techniques. A band from Morgantown came down and played, and a fraternity planted some trees around campus. It wasn't as successful as we had hoped. Maybe 75 people showed up.

"The shame is, you have kids here from all over the country, but they've never heard of Dolly Sods. They wouldn't even know they were next door to the Monongahela unless they happened to drive by a sign. It's really hard to get them interested in the environment. They label you 'granola.' That's why I got a band for Earth Day—music's a big drawing card. *Granola!*"

*F*arther north, in Pennsylvania's Allegheny National Forest, two problems face supervisor John Butt and his staff. Drive through the forest and you're likely to notice evidence of both: an odor, in many places, of crude oil; and a browse line on the trees at the height of a deer's farthest reach. Allegheny has too much of two things: deer on the surface and oil and gas beneath it.

The undergrowth in millions of acres of Pennsylvania forest has been severely affected by deer. In logged areas, the deer prevent reforestation by eating new sprouts and seedlings. The disappearance of wild flowers, the absence of songbirds and ground-dwelling wildlife, the growing shortage of valuable black cherry, ash, and hard maple seedlings—all are blamed on the deer.

"Seedlings that started naturally here in the '60s and '70s have failed at the rate of 50 percent because deer eat them," John Butt told me when I visited him at his office in Warren, a town on the Allegheny River. "We've found that the best way to handle the deer is to overwhelm them with food. If we can get a tremendous number of seedlings started, and open them up to the sun, the deer can't eat them all. Another technique, if it looks like the deer are getting the best of the situation, is to do some spring fertilizing. We can sometimes get three to four feet of growth in a year, and the deer can't keep up. The final resort is fencing—eight-foot, deer-proof fences—but that's awfully expensive.

"There's a secondary problem related to the deer. When they destroy the undergrowth, thick beds of fern take over, which seems to be about the only thing deer won't eat. When the ferns build up to a certain point, they give off a toxic chemical that prevents the germination of seedlings. The answer to *that* is herbicide, but then we're faced with a whole new environmental concern. One thing triggers another. The best solution would be for the state game commission to allow hunters to shoot enough deer to restore the natural balance."

Much of John's scientific data comes from the nearby Forestry Sciences Laboratory. Its research project leader, David Marquis, joined John and me for lunch at a little roadhouse on the edge of Warren.

"Deer are a problem, certainly," said David, "but oil and gas extraction is the biggest threat here, especially in the Tionesta Research Natural Area."

Because of a surveyor's error back in the '20s, one section of forest in northwestern Pennsylvania was never logged. The 4,000-acre stand is one of the few remaining examples of the virgin forest that once covered six million acres of the Allegheny Plateau. The federal government purchased it in 1936 and made half of it a scenic area and the other half a research natural area for studying the ecology of a climax hemlock-beech forest.

But when it bought the land, the government did not acquire the rights to subsurface minerals, and today oil companies can legally drill beneath 98 percent of the national forest, including the scenic and research areas. Some of the studies in the research area have been going on since the '30s, and I asked David what sort of impact drilling would have.

"No question at all," he said. "The area will be destroyed for most research purposes. Most of what we know about how trees grow in this part of the country comes from areas that have been disturbed, because all of our forests had been logged over by the turn of the century. A climax forest needs 200 to 500 years to become established, so we can't study that kind of steady-state ecology anywhere except in places like Tionesta."

Over apple pie and coffee, John told me, "There are more than 10,000 active oil and gas wells in Allegheny National Forest, and there are more than 400 new ones drilled each year. That's more activity than is found in all the intermountain national forests of the West combined."

John sent me off on a tour of the forest with Nils Johnson and Jim Schuler, the first the lands staff officer for oil and gas, the other a district ranger.

"We really have two national forests here," said Nils, "one on the surface and one underneath. It's like owning a blueberry pie when somebody else owns the blueberries."

We drove out to the Tionesta Research Natural Area along a checkerboard of logging and oil company roads, then strolled down a narrow lane. Tall beech and hemlock trees cast a blanket of quiet shade. In the road ahead of us, three fox kits looked up from their play, saw us, and slid into the shadows. Birds whistled and chirped. A few yards down the road we came to an oil well where a clump of machinery was quietly doing its job.

"A well site may clear only an acre or so," Nils told me, "but it's going to affect light intensity, animal populations, vegetation, and so forth for several hundred feet in every direction. So, if you put in a well every 500 feet. . . ."

And that's what they've done. "In about 10 percent of the forest, there's an oil well every 500 feet," said Jim.

Abandoned wells are supposed to be plugged, but many old ones haven't been, and in places oil and gas seep into underground water or creep to the surface. "Over at Chapman State Park there's gas in the groundwater," said Jim. "People can set fire to the water coming out of their faucets. Another area has gas coming up everywhere. You can light bubbles in the streams."

*I*n Wisconsin's two national forests, it's not so much what's coming out of the ground that worries the Forest Service, but what's falling out of the skies: acid rain, or, more properly, acid precipitation. I went to Nicolet and Chequamegon to find out how those forests were faring.

I asked Nicolet's supervisor what was the prettiest part of his domain. "I don't want to say it's *all* pretty," said Jim Berlin, "but it's all about the same."

Indeed it is. And pretty, too. The glaciers left northern Wisconsin smoothed and rounded, and hardwoods now clothe its gentle hills. Thousands of little lakes catch cloud reflections and bat them back. Hunters and fishermen troop through the woods.

"This area had been just about destroyed by the time it was made a national forest 50 years ago," Jim told me. "We've managed it for five decades now, and to me it's like a rose that's ready to flower. But it's threatening to overwhelm us if we can't cut more trees from it. We're selling about 75 million board feet a year from Nicolet. We should be selling about a hundred million."

As for acid rain, Jim is not sure. "In my book, the jury is still out. I've read a lot of conflicting reports, and there seem to be some pretty credible sources on both sides of this issue."

"This issue" is: What is acid rain, where does it come from, and what harm, if any, does it do?

Acid rain is created by chemical reactions between sulfur dioxide and nitrogen oxides and moisture or dry particles in the air. Coal-burning power plants, largely in the East, and smelters in the West produce most of the 25 million tons of sulfur dioxide emitted annually in the United States. Cars, trucks, and factories are responsible for most of the 21 million tons of nitrogen oxides.

The acidity of precipitation is measured on a pH (concentration of hydrogen ions) scale of 1 to 14. Seven is neutral and, since the scale is logarithmic, a pH of 4 is ten times more acidic than a pH of 5. "Normal" rainfall has a pH of 5.6. The lower the pH level of a lake, the less biological diversity you'll find in it.

"The lakes in the northern third of Chequamegon are especially sensitive to acid rain because of their low alkalinity," said forest hydrologist Bonnie Ilhardt. "Alkalinity is an index of a lake's buffering capacity, its ability to absorb and neutralize acids." She's concerned about what might happen to the poorly buffered lakes if acid rain keeps falling.

"Certain species of leeches and mollusks are the first to go," said Bob Martini, who studies acid rain for the Wisconsin Department of Natural Resources. "They drop out of the system at about pH 6. But fish and amphibians may not be affected till pH 4. So we can't wait for the fish to die off before we do something. By then the lake will be drastically altered.

"The impact of air pollution on human health was noticed some time ago in cities, so laws were passed requiring taller smokestacks. They keep the emissions out of the cities, certainly, but they lift them into high-level air masses that may drift halfway across the continent before they drop as acid deposition."

I asked Bob where Wisconsin's acid precipitation was coming from.

"We'd sure like to know. So far we can't trace it to a single source. Nationally, most of it is probably coming from a string of plants along the Ohio River, but that presents a political problem. Most representatives in Congress come from states that are emitters. So it's the dumpers versus the dumpees. That's why the most stringent air-quality bills originate in the Senate. Lots of representatives from Ohio, but only two senators."

Park Falls, Wisconsin—a town, one resident told me, with "no park and no falls"—is near Chequamegon, and I spent the Fourth of July weekend there, helping residents celebrate. The Knights of Columbus had a three-day fete planned, with fireworks, a parade, softball games, and Vic's Polka Band.

But, as often seems to happen when a little town tries to throw a party, it rained. And I confess to a new uneasiness as I felt the first sprinkles. Because rain isn't what it used to be. "The precipitation in Wisconsin stays right around pH 4.6 as a weighted annual mean," Bob Martini had told me. "That's about ten times as acid as normal rain." It drizzled on children in "E.T." T-shirts and on little boys scouring the grounds for aluminum cans. It rained on ballplayers and on the plywood stand where the Veterans of Foreign Wars were selling beer. "We've monitored rain here that had a pH of 3.5," said Bob. "That's about the same as orange juice." Rain emptied the bleachers, and a gust of wind turned an umbrella inside out. "Even if we decided today to cut back on sulfur dioxide emissions, it would be eight or ten years before the rain would change," said Bob. It rained on canoes strapped to the tops of cars at motels, and water ran in rivers across parking lots and down streets. "Virtually no species of fish found in Wisconsin could survive in the rainwater now falling on the lakes in our state," Congressman David R. Obey told his constituents in 1982. It rained on the just and the unjust, on towns and farms, on forests and lakes and streams. It rained in horizontal sheets through the night. It rained as if the world would end.

FOLLOWING PAGES: Waves of shadowed ridges roll toward sunset in Great Smoky Mountains National Park. Here the hand of man rests lightly, and visitors can sense some of the spaciousness and tranquillity of the forests that once covered most of eastern North America. Like other federal preserves, this one provides a haven for wildlife and for the human spirit. Planning for a national park here began in the 1920s, when extensive logging threatened the Smokies. Private contributions—including five million dollars from financier John D. Rockefeller, Jr.— augmented state and federal funds to buy the land.

$\mathcal{M}$aples and the reddening leaves of a dogwood frame a pioneer cabin in Cades Cove, a sheltered valley in Great Smoky Mountains National Park. White-tailed deer (below) bound across a nearby meadow. First settled in the early 1800s, Cades Cove by mid-century had developed into a community of 685 people in 132 households. They grew, gathered, hunted, or made nearly everything they needed, from corn to walnut-plank coffins. Self-sufficient but not isolated, the community kept in touch with its neighbors through newspapers, circuit-riding preachers, and regular mail service. Eventually, the lure of factory jobs and the creation of the park doomed subsistence farming here. Today a handful of log cabins, churches, and other structures—and a few open fields where cows still graze—preserve the flavor of a vanished way of life.

*B*urnished gold of maple leaves gleams above traffic snaking through Cades Cove.
About a quarter of the U. S. population lives within a day's drive of Great Smoky Mountains,
our most heavily visited national park; more than 8.5 million people came here in 1983.
Autumn's crush of visitors adds to the demanding work of park rangers. Below, Judy Johns
explains parking regulations at a picnic area; at bottom, she administers first aid to a cyclist.

*S*pring floodwaters of the Hatchie River swirl around swamp privet bushes and dead oaks at Hatchie Refuge in Tennessee. Channelized streams such as arrow-straight Muddy Creek (opposite, lower) carry silt eroded from farmland; deposited on tree roots, the silt smothers them. Assistant refuge manager Glenn Stanley measures the depth of a gully in a field upstream.

 antle of moss covers fallen timber in Florida's Osceola National Forest. The Forest Service controls the surface resources here, regulating timber harvest, water conservation, grazing, and recreational activities; but mineral rights fall under the jurisdiction of the Department of the Interior. In the 1960s companies permitted to prospect in this area found deposits of phosphate—a primary ingredient of fertilizers—under the swamps and pine stands. From 1969 to 1972, four companies applied for leases to strip-mine the deposits, arousing the protests of conservationists, state officials, and Florida's entire congressional delegation. Saying the companies could not properly restore the strip-mined land, Interior denied the applications in early 1983. For now, flowers such as wild azaleas (below) bloom where draglines might have excavated.

Morning mist hovers above sedges and marsh grasses at Alder Run Bog in Monongahela National Forest. Opposite, crimson huckleberry leaves glow near green mountain laurel; below them, a young eastern red spruce has taken hold amid sandstone boulders. Congress has designated certain parts of the forest as wilderness areas—among them the Cranberry Backcountry, where a company held coal-mining rights. For surrendering them, it will receive monetary credits it can use to purchase coal resources on other federal lands.

FOLLOWING PAGES: Worm fence zigzags about a 19th-century homestead in the rolling Monongahela. The Forest Service leases these and other pastures for grazing.

*S*pray of gold, a sugar maple branch emerges from the mist on a mountain ridge in the Monongahela. When the government set aside the forest in 1920, timbering and fires had devastated the land to such an extent that local people called it the "Monongahela Burn." Furor over clear-cutting here and in Montana's Bitterroot National Forest led in 1976 to new regulations that restrict the practice to areas of no more than 40 to 100 acres, depending on location and kind of timber. Below, leaves of yellow poplar, as well as birch, basswood, oak, and maple, nestle at the base of a hollow snag.

FOLLOWING PAGES: Setting sun spotlights Seneca Rocks, where climbers stand nearly a thousand feet above a valley floor in the Monongahela.

*C*linging to an alder branch, a trio of green-backed heron fledglings less than three weeks old surveys an unfamiliar world. A young cottontail (left), ears alert, crouches amid a feast of clover and timothy. At bottom, a red-spotted newt about four inches long scampers over a mossy hummock. Eastern forests shelter a variety of animals and plants, among them the saprophytic herb known as Indian pipe (below). Lacking chlorophyll necessary for photosynthesis, the herb obtains nourishment from living roots and decaying vegetation on the moist and shady forest floor.

HAL S. KORBER

SCOTT RIDGEWAY/VIEW FINDER

PAUL G. WIEGMAN

*T*orrent of drilling mud sprays into a pit sunk to contain it in Pennsylvania's Allegheny National Forest. After completing the well, workers will fill in the depression. At least 10,000 oil and gas wells already exist here, and drillers sink more than 400 new ones each year. Individuals and corporations—not the federal government—hold 98 percent of the mineral rights in the half-million-acre forest. Besides creating management problems, the drilling threatens one of the largest remaining virgin stands of hemlock and beech in the East. Managing national forests for multiple use means additional duties for federal employees. Above, district ranger Jim Schuler sniffs his fingers to detect leakage from a wellhead. At right, forest supervisor John Butt explains how sediment, brine, and oil residues from a nearby oil field have polluted Grunder Run, reducing its entire fish population and eliminating its native brook trout.

*R*arity in a glacier-smoothed land,
Morgan Falls tumbles down a course of black
granite in Wisconsin's Chequamegon National
Forest. Marsh marigolds (below) bloom in

swamps that cover about a quarter of
Chequamegon and nearby Nicolet National
Forest; lakes large and small lace the terrain.
Poorly buffered soils make these forests
especially vulnerable to acid rain. Forest Service
employees test the water of some lakes for
increased acidity three times a year; so far they
detect no significant change. At right,
hydrologist Bonnie Ilhardt prepares to draw a
sample from Chequamegon's Reynard Lake.

FOLLOWING PAGES: Lacy white foamflowers
contrast with the verdure of moss, lichen, and
leaf in Nicolet National Forest. On Wisconsin's
endangered species list, the flowers thrive in a
''no-cut zone'' established to protect them.

Home on the range: Under boundless Nebraska skies, a small herd of bison grazes native grasses on the rolling prairie at Fort Niobrara National Wildlife Refuge.

Land of

the Pastoral Plains

tand amid the big bluestem, just as the sun begins to nudge the tops of the shadowed sandhills, and listen to the warm prairie wind. Heat and light seem to seep out of the sandy ground, as if from fires smoldering far below. A bobwhite whistles its name. As twilight falls over Fort Niobrara, I find a vantage and watch and listen.

An enormous rack of antlers suddenly rises from the grass—and a big bull elk appears. Shadows creep across the prairie, and so does a flock of feeding Canada geese. An owl, its wings slowly pumping, scours the ground for mice. Two more elk, top-heavy with tremendous racks, canter through the grass, followed by one with short, stubby antlers like cigars.

Prairie dogs squeak, then race pell-mell to a burrow hole. Two stand back to back like bookends, wiggling their tails and whispering. Another holds a leaf in his little brown paws and nibbles it, like someone playing a harmonica.

Burrowing owls stand about, occasionally lunging at grasshoppers. Their scowling look and the way they fold their wings remind me of stern schoolteachers, their hands behind their backs. One owl stands beside its burrow. Another glides in for a visit. The moment the newcomer touches down, the other jumps three feet into the air, like a child surprised on a teeter-totter. It makes me laugh to watch them.

From the tip of a nodding stalk of bluestem, a red-winged blackbird sings. And sings again. In near darkness, two pheasant cocks erupt onto the road, fighting. It's mostly sound and fury, with a few flying feathers, until one gives a shriek and bolts into the tallgrass.

Fort Niobrara, where the big bluestem nods, is a 19,123-acre wildlife refuge that straddles the Niobrara River in northern Nebraska. Once there was an Army fort here, with troopers and horses and rumors of hostile Indians, but the only battles the troopers ever fought were against boredom. In 1912, J. W. Gilbert, owner of a private game park in Nebraska, offered the federal government 6 bison, 17 elk, and several deer if land could be made available for them. The old fort was chosen. The refuge has since been expanded, and a herd of Texas longhorn cattle was added in 1936.

I came back to Fort Niobrara in the morning to see the bison, now numbering about 225. They were bigger than I had expected; one bull peered easily over the top of my car as I contemplated his kneecaps. But when he looked me in the eye, his gaze was gentle and shy, as if he were embarrassed by his size.

Later I tried to stay out of the way as refuge manager Robert Ellis and four of his staff, on horseback and communicating by walkie-talkie, rounded up the herd and moved it to fresh pasture. The bison ran with ponderous heft, beards wagging, tongues lolling, clouds of flies hovering around them. Roused, a bull would gallop awhile, then slow to a canter, then to a walk, then stop for a quick wallow before moving on.

The bison galloping at Fort Niobrara naturally made me think of the days, not so long ago, when millions of those great beasts surged across the prairies—armadas of animals in seas of grass. The sight of them must have been staggering, and the first settlers, emerging from the eastern forests onto the broad prairies, were unprepared.

Midwestern nature writer John Madson speaks of this in *Where the Sky Began:* "The newcomers brought no real knowledge of grasslands; it is doubtful that any had seen the open steppes of Eurasia, and few had even heard of that region. They surely knew nothing of African veldt, South American pampas, or Australian lowlands. To those first European explorers and colonists, grassland

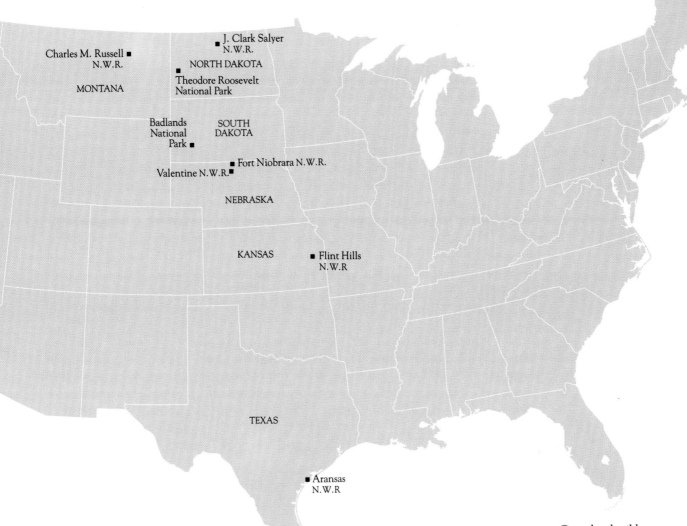

Charles M. Russell ■
N.W.R.

MONTANA

■ J. Clark Salyer
N.W.R.

NORTH DAKOTA
■
Theodore Roosevelt
National Park

Badlands
National
Park ■

SOUTH
DAKOTA

Valentine N.W.R.■
■ Fort Niobrara N.W.R.

NEBRASKA

KANSAS   ■ Flint Hills
N.W.R

TEXAS

■ Aransas
N.W.R

probably meant snug meadows, deer parks, and pastures safe behind fence and wall. They had no basis for even imagining wild fields through which a horseman might ride westward for a month or more, sometimes traveling for days without sight of trees."

Some, like explorer Louis Jolliet in 1673, recognized the potential of the prairies: ". . . no better soil can be found, either for corn, for vines, or for any other fruit whatever." Others, thinking the absence of trees indicated infertility, dismissed the prairies as worthless.

Settlers also found conditions on the prairies that were outside their experience. The solitude could be overwhelming, and some retreated into the familiar forests. Washington Irving, born in New York, visited the plains in the 1830s and wrote: "To one unaccustomed to it, there is something inexpressibly lonely in the solitude of the prairie. . . . We have the consciousness of being far, far beyond the bounds of human habitation. . . ."

Prairie weather, too, daunted the newcomers. Blizzards buried them in drifting snows; tornadoes fell on them like bombs from black skies; droughts destroyed their crops; the heat of summer tortured them. John Madson writes: "I can think of no purer form of hell than threshing oats in the old way, and

Grassland wilderness once blanketed about a million square miles of central North America—roughly a ninth of the continent. During the 1800s the federal government sold off or gave away most of the prairies, and homesteaders plowed the frontier. Cities and suburbs later paved over more prairie, and now little of the natural ecosystem remains. Scant federal holdings preserve some grasslands, mostly on wildlife refuges.

stacking straw under the blower of a steam-driven threshing machine on a July afternoon in central Iowa or Nebraska."

Three distinct types of prairie—tallgrass, mixed grass, and shortgrass—ran in three broad belts from north to south through the heartland. The tallgrass of the easternmost prairie grew 12 feet high in places. It merged with the shorter mixed prairie of the Dakotas, Nebraska, and Kansas. West of the 100th meridian were the Great Plains, where the grasses were only ankle high.

Though the vegetation has changed dramatically since pioneer days, the essential character of the three belts has not. The tall corn grows in Iowa; the middle section produces mid-height wheat; and cattle instead of bison now graze the shortgrass of the Great Plains.

For half a century, beginning around 1820, the federal government was financed largely by the sale of midwestern land, at an average price of $1.25 an acre. By 1890 most of that land had been settled and plowed, and today there are only a few federal areas left in the prairie heartland—a scattering of wildlife refuges, Theodore Roosevelt and Badlands National Parks, and some national forests and grasslands. The government acquired many of these areas soon after the Dust Bowl years of the 1930s, when the land had deteriorated and the farmers had moved away.

Virgin prairie, prairie that has never been plowed, exists only in patches. But the lakes, ponds, potholes, river bottoms, marshes, and sloughs of the Midwest and the Great Plains are the breeding grounds of birds—especially waterfowl—that flock to wildlife refuges throughout the country. Ducks and geese flow like tides up and down the Central flyway. At its southern end, on Aransas Refuge in Texas, winters a species that perhaps never numbered more than 1,500, and now survives only as an endangered remnant: the whooping crane.

Whooping cranes—at five feet the tallest of North American birds—used to nest in the sloughs of Iowa, Illinois, Minnesota, and eastern North Dakota, but with settlement much of their habitat disappeared, and the great white birds were killed for food and sport. The final prairie nesting of a whooping crane in the United States came in 1894 at Eagle Lake, Iowa. Thirty years later, the last whooper nest had vanished from the prairies of Canada, too, and the species seemed doomed. In the 1930s a few were spotted on the coast of Texas, and in 1937 Aransas was designated a migratory waterfowl refuge, where cranes and other wildlife would also be protected. It wasn't until 1954 that the whoopers' breeding grounds in northern Canada were discovered, some 2,500 miles from Aransas.

The worldwide population of whooping cranes reached a low of 23 in 1941, and despite efforts by the Fish and Wildlife Service and conservationists, it reached that low again in 1954. Since then, there has been a gradual increase—to 80 birds, both captive and wild, in 1971, and about 140 today.

Lying on a peninsula northeast of Corpus Christi, the 55,000-acre refuge is slowly being shaped by the tides and storms of the Gulf of Mexico. Grasses, live oaks, and red bay thickets anchor the sandy soil. Tidal marshes and long, narrow ponds are home to alligators and other animals. Deer and javelinas inhabit the live oak savannas. More than 350 species of birds have been sighted at Aransas, the largest count for any wildlife refuge.

I visited Aransas in early April, when the staff was on standby for a moment's notice departure. In two small planes and a couple of trucks, they were going to follow the whoopers north on their spring migration. They hoped to learn more about the hazards the birds face on their long journey, and to map their route and resting spots.

In the visitor center, a display case held letters from youngsters who had visited the refuge. One little boy, whose ambition exceeded his understanding, had written: "Please send me a picture of every animal in the world."

I didn't see every animal in the world at Aransas, but I did see whooping cranes. I joined about a hundred birders aboard *Whooping Crane*, Captain Francis "Brownie" Brown's launch, which makes several trips a week during the season to the whoopers' feeding grounds. Gulls by the hundred followed along as we chugged away from the pier and into the Gulf Intracoastal Waterway. We lined the railings and crowded onto benches, and the gulls wheeled by, begging for popcorn. Brownie, microphone in hand, called our attention to other birds—cormorants, pelicans, laughing gulls—and kept up a running commentary: "There's snakes in them grasses. Big snakes. Bad snakes. Mean snakes. It makes my hair stand right up on end whenever I tell about them snakes."

We began spotting whoopers, white punctuation marks in green paragraphs of marsh grasses. Engine off, we glided within a hundred feet of a feeding pair. They had red blazes of bare skin on their crowns, and startlingly black face masks. Majestic creatures, they stalked through the grass with slow deliberation. One lunged and came up with a small, wriggling snake, which it stood upon and pecked at. The cranes darted their yellow eyes at each other, but ignored us.

Ashore again, I explored among the willows, live oaks, persimmons, and false-buckeyes of Heron Flats, a lush world overgrown with trumpet vines, mustang grape, and Spanish moss. A rustling in the leaves made me stop, and I watched an armadillo approach, a little armored vehicle of a mammal. When it sensed or saw me, it paused and seemed to ponder in a slow, antediluvian way, then shuffled off.

From an observation tower I scanned a far shore through my binoculars. I was watching a pair of whooping cranes feeding in the distance when a black shape intruded into my field of vision: A barge was gliding past the birds, not 50 yards beyond them.

It is the barges, filled with crude oil and benzene, carbon tetrachloride, hydrochloric acid, and other caustic chemicals, that worry environmentalists—and refuge manager Frank Johnson. As I talked with him in his office, a cardinal outside pecked and chirped and fluttered at its reflection in the window.

"When the government bought the land for the refuge in 1937, it didn't acquire the mineral rights, so we have a good deal of energy development here," Frank said. "There are about 50 oil and gas wells on the refuge or in the waters just offshore."

Bird-lovers are driven nearly frantic by the fear that, after years of effort and the expenditure of millions of dollars, the whooping cranes could all be destroyed by one serious spill or leak fouling the waters of the refuge and killing the marine life the birds feed on.

"Most of the oil companies working on the refuge go to great lengths to cooperate with us in protecting the birds," Frank told me. "They often postpone the drilling of new wells until the birds have migrated north."

Until recently, the dredging for oyster shells nearby also bothered friends of the whoopers. Tons of the shells were used each year in the cement and paper industries of Texas, as well as in roadbeds. The dredging operations, which crept ever closer to the refuge boundary, were halted in the early 1980s for economic reasons, but could resume at any time. In addition, muck dredged from the Intracoastal Waterway has been dumped on the whoopers' habitat.

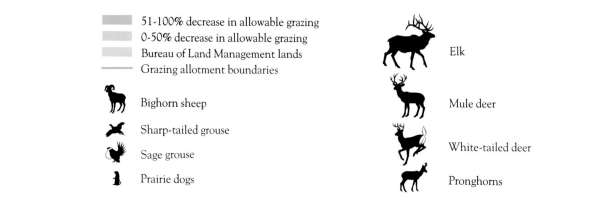

51-100% decrease in allowable grazing
0-50% decrease in allowable grazing
Bureau of Land Management lands
Grazing allotment boundaries

Bighorn sheep

Sharp-tailed grouse

Sage grouse

Prairie dogs

Elk

Mule deer

White-tailed deer

Pronghorns

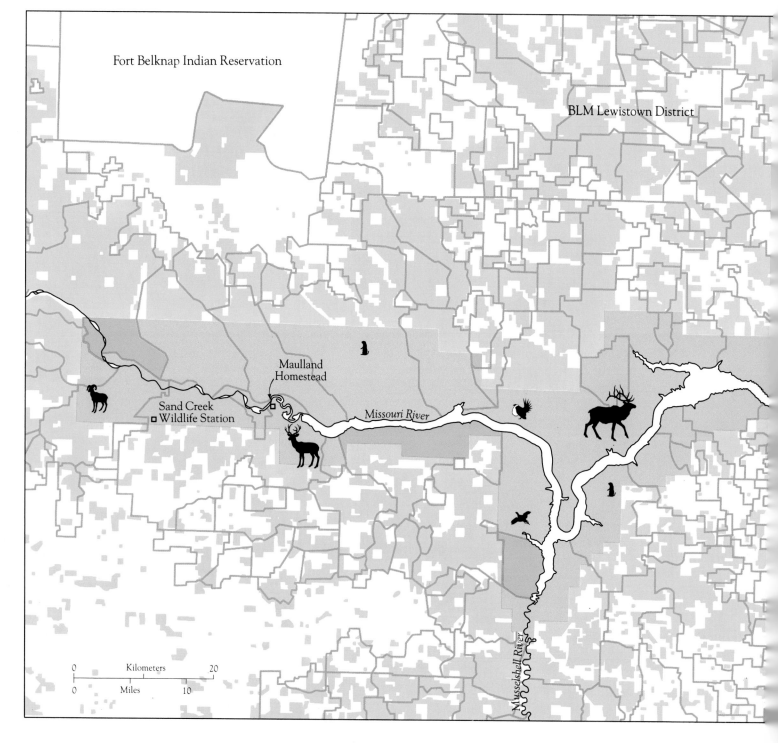

Fort Belknap Indian Reservation

BLM Lewistown District

Maulland
Homestead

Sand Creek
Wildlife Station

Missouri River

Kilometers

0   20

0   Miles

10

Musselshell River

Bordering the Missouri River for 125 miles, Charles M. Russell National Wildlife Refuge encompasses immense Fort Peck Lake, forested river bottoms, rugged badlands, and shortgrass prairie—more than a million acres in northeastern Montana. Grazing allotments pattern the region like pieces of a jigsaw puzzle, for area ranchers lease grazing privileges from the refuge (in blue) as well as from the Bureau of Land Management, which administers adjacent public lands (in gold). Reversing previous policy, a federal court ruled in 1983 that wildlife would take precedence over livestock within the refuge. To provide more suitable habitat for elk, pronghorns, deer, grouse, and the many other animals on the refuge, management plans to reduce domestic grazing by a total of 33 percent, with only excess forage available to livestock. This pleases conservationists but angers ranchers—a situation not uncommon in the plains states, where the government must balance the needs of wildlife with those of agriculture.

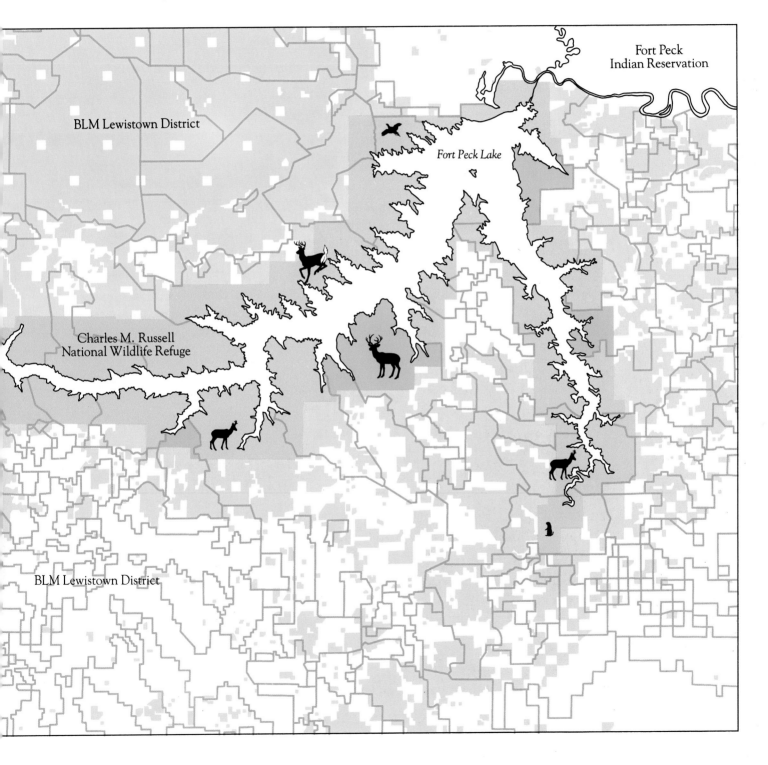

Fort Peck
Indian Reservation

BLM Lewistown District

Fort Peck Lake

Charles M. Russell
National Wildlife Refuge

BLM Lewistown District

Another issue at Aransas is the acquisition by Texas of a 19,000-acre chunk of Matagorda Island, just across the bay from the refuge. Matagorda was a bombing range until the 1970s, when the Air Force stopped the activity in deference to the cranes, a few of which were seen wintering on the island. Texas, perennially short of recreation areas for its growing population, released a plan in 1975 for developing Matagorda. It included a road and bus system, a ferry service, parking lots, dredged boat channels, camping areas, stands and blinds for hunters, other public-use facilities, corn and wheat fields for deer, and cultivated plots for doves. Environmentalists envisioned a Coney Island in the midst of their whooping cranes. The Texas Parks and Wildlife Department has since recanted, and now guarantees that development will be kept to a minimum and the birds' welfare carefully protected. But some environmentalists, including Steve Parcells of Defenders of Wildlife, are skeptical.

"Last year Congress ratified a 'memorandum of understanding' between the state of Texas and the Fish and Wildlife Service," Steve told me. "The 19,000 acres will be managed by Texas, but under Fish and Wildlife guidelines. State officials are working on a management plan now. I toured Matagorda with them a couple of months ago, along with other environmentalists, and I'm afraid some of our fears were confirmed. A lot of the Texas Parks and Wildlife people come from a pretty strong tradition of managing for game species—that is, for hunters. That's natural, because most of their revenue comes from hunters and fishermen. But we found they were planning to introduce exotic plant species for game birds, things quail and turkey like. All this to make the hunting better.

"They were initially willing to listen to our ideas. They weren't antagonistic, but it just hadn't occurred to them to do it any other way. They said, 'Tell us what to do. We'll give it a try.' However, the pressures to manage Matagorda for game species rather than natural wildlife diversity will be tremendous.

"It's the hunting I'm worried about. Any time you start hunting around an endangered species like the whooping crane, I get jittery. I have a hard time accepting the idea of hunting on *any* wildlife refuge. It seems a contradiction in terms. This land is supposedly *their* land.

"So I'm leery of the new arrangement, but I'm willing to wait and see. We'll be keeping an eye on them, and we'll go to court if necessary."

As a student at the University of Michigan back in 1979, Steve Parcells wrote a thesis titled "Preservation versus Development: A Proposed Tallgrass Prairie National Park in the Flint Hills Region." It helped fan a fire that had been flickering in eastern Kansas for 40 years.

George Catlin, painter and interpreter of Indian life, may have been the first to conceive the idea of a prairie park. In 1841 he wrote that the prairies should be "preserved in their pristine beauty and wildness, in a *magnificent park,* where the world could see for ages to come, the native Indian in his classic attire, galloping his wild horse . . . amid the fleeting herds of elks and buffaloes."

If a national prairie preserve is ever established, it will likely be in the Flint Hills region of Kansas and the Osage Hills of Oklahoma. Of the 400,000 square miles of tallgrass prairie that once existed in the Midwest, only about 4,000—one percent—survive, mostly in a strip running from northeastern Kansas to northeastern Oklahoma. Limestone and chert beneath the shallow soil have made this area ideal for grazing but unsuitable for farming, so much of it has never been plowed. The deep, spreading roots of the big grasses have always ensured new growth after fires. Though decades of grazing have certainly had an impact on the Flint Hills, the region is still as close to its original state as any large prairie in the country.

After the invention of barbed wire, stone fence posts were quarried here. Texas cattlemen found it a perfect area for fattening their animals before selling them at the railhead in Abilene; a cow could gain 300 or 400 pounds in one summer of grazing. Settlement dispossessed the resident Indians and coincided with the big land grants to the railroads, which at one time owned about a fifth of Kansas. Homesteaders ended up with small holdings along rivers and creeks, while huge blocks of pastureland, bought from the railroads or from speculators, passed into the hands of corporations. It's a pattern that persists in the region today, with many small ranchers owning a little land, and a few agribusinesses owning a lot.

Steve summed up the park issue for me: "You can look at the proposal for a prairie national park from two perspectives. One is that the park would threaten the economy and the way of life in the Flint Hills region. The other is that the Flint Hills bluestem pastures are already being threatened by increasing development and changing management practices, and a park would preserve at least a portion of the tallgrass prairie in its natural state."

Without some sort of protection, Steve predicts, the remaining tallgrass prairie will be destroyed by agriculture, energy development, dams and reservoirs, urban sprawl, the effects of fertilizers on prairie vegetation, and the indifference of absentee landlords. A park of 60,000 acres, he says, could preserve a viable prairie ecosystem, and it would comprise just over one percent of the Flint Hills—or one-eighth of one percent of Kansas.

Opponents, many of them in the Kansas Grassroots Association, say that the federal government has a long history of mismanaging land, and so the prairie is safer in private hands. They also claim a national park would force families to move and would attract to the easy-going, folksy plains the sort of honkytonk development that has sprung up around other national parks. So far, they've argued their case effectively: Several bills that would have created a prairie national park have died in Congress during the past decade or so.

While I was in the neighborhood, I stopped by Flint Hills National Wildlife Refuge on the Neosho River. Hartford, the little town where the refuge has its headquarters, is rimmed by dikes, for the Neosho, which runs into the nearby John Redmond Reservoir, floods every spring. That's fine for the refuge—birds love marshes and ponds—but sometimes it's hard on the farmers. Mark Heisinger, burly assistant manager, said, "Occasionally we get a fall or summer flood that will take out entire crops and put the farmers back on square one. It's really up to Mother Nature and the Corps of Engineers, which some people seem to think are the same thing."

When I explored the refuge, the river was thick and dark with silt, but firmly within its banks. Turtles and beavers carved V's in the sleepy current, and a great blue heron lifted off from a dead tree in the middle of a shallow pond. A rabbit was hunkered down beside the road as if waiting for a bus. It was hot, and the three cars in the parking lot were nosed into the one shady spot, like cattle beneath the only tree in an open field. Farmers, sealed off in the air-conditioned cabs of their tractors, raised boiling clouds of dust as they harrowed their fields. The riverbanks were all black mud and pale dead trees. At a wooded pond, turtles heard me coming and belly-flopped into the dark water a second before I spotted them. Cicadas buzzed in the trees.

"We're a feeding and resting area for waterfowl," Mark told me, "and we'll feed them and rest them if they come through. But if they don't reproduce up north, we can't feed them here. The problem is the loss of wetlands in the prairie pothole region of North and South Dakota. They're being drained and put into farmland. Like I said, if they can't produce waterfowl up there, there's no sense us growing feed for them down here."

I headed north to see what Mark was talking about.

*I*n Devils Lake, North Dakota, in the heart of the pothole region, I found David Janes, a Fish and Wildlife employee who runs the Devils Lake Wetland Management District. "It's an administrative unit," he told me. "It covers eight counties in northeastern North Dakota, roughly 10,000 square miles, the same size as Maryland."

About 10,000 years ago, when a vast ice sheet reached down from Canada into the Midwest, huge chunks of ice that broke off its forward edge were pressed deep into the earth by the weight of the advancing glacier. When the ice retreated, the buried chunks melted, creating millions of tiny lakes known as potholes. They extend from south-central Canada across a corner of Montana and into the Dakotas, Minnesota, and Iowa. The prairie pothole region is a rich nesting ground for millions of ducks and other waterfowl.

When the first European settlers reached America, there were perhaps 215 million acres of wetlands here. Today there are about half that many. They have been ditched, dredged, drained, filled, and converted to farmland. Beyond their importance to waterfowl, wetlands help control flooding and erosion, retain sediments and nutrients that would otherwise end up downstream, recharge groundwater, and provide habitat for furbearers, nongame wildlife, and non-migratory birds. And they're pretty. Between 400 and 500 thousand acres of wetlands are destroyed in the United States every year. It's David Janes's job to try to stop the destruction in his district.

We spent an afternoon driving around the district, through endless fields of small grains—wheat, barley, flax—as well as sunflowers. Dotted randomly upon them were little pools, some no more than a quarter acre in size. Cattails grew around them; multitudes of waterfowl placidly bobbed upon them; and phalaropes, godwits, and sandpipers were feeding beside them.

"Farms here average about a thousand acres," said Dave, "and many financially pressed farmers would like to drain and level every square foot to put in more crops. They all have contractor's levels and think they're engineers."

The disappearance of the wetlands here can be slowed in two ways: by acquiring the land in fee simple—that is, by buying it outright, which is expensive; or by an easement program. A farmer will sell to the Fish and Wildlife Service a wetland easement, which is basically a contract: The farmer agrees, for a price, not to drain, fill, or level his pothole.

"We pay fair market value for the easement, based on acreage and the vulnerability of the wetland," Dave explained. "There's a one-time reimbursement, and the easement is perpetual, even if the land changes hands.

"The farmers have very real needs, and we have very real needs. They don't always mesh. It gets heated. People get excited when they see a farmer being bullied by the Feds. But a contract is a contract. What we're trying to do is maintain natural cover, which the farmers call weeds. It's not just a local or state responsibility. It's a national—an *inter*national—responsibility.

"Because of current government policy, we're not acquiring many easements right now. Even though there are several hundred farmers who would like to sell them to us. In the meantime, the draining goes on. The state estimates it's losing 20,000 acres of wetlands every year. That's a fearful amount."

We drove slowly past Traynor Lake—or Traynor Slough. "There's some disagreement about that," said Dave. "If it's a slough, the farmer can drain it; if it's a lake, he can't. I guess I shouldn't be too hard on the farmers," he said. "I like farmers." He grinned at me. "Some of my best friends are farmers."

Before draining a pothole, a farmer must apply to his county water board for permission. The water boards are made up largely of other farmers, which, according to Earl DeGroot of the state's North Central Planning Council, "is like putting a committee of foxes in charge of the hen house."

Earlier, Earl had told me, "The water boards are set up by counties, but water doesn't concern itself with political boundaries. It flows from one county to another. The boards should be established on a watershed basis."

"Suppose a farmer gets permission from his county board to drain an area," said Dave. "The water may flow down the watershed onto his neighbor's property. But maybe the neighbor is under an easement contract, so he can't drain. Yet here comes all this water. . . ."

The town of Devils Lake itself is threatened. Since reaching a low in 1940, the lake has been rising and is currently coming up at the rate of 18 inches a year; soon the water will be lapping at doorsteps. Farmers say it's simply a hundred-year cycle that's raising the water; conservationists blame the hundreds of tons of water rushing out of former wetlands. Whatever the reason, the Corps of Engineers has been called in to determine what should be done.

"It's not only the waterfowl that are important here, it's also the land base," said Dave. "Give me a parking lot and I'll produce ducks for you. I'll turn out ducks faster than you can shoot them. But is that the habitat you want?"

The next day, a Sunday, I drove to nearby Sheyenne Lake Refuge, a rich waterfowl habitat that will be destroyed if a massive water management scheme—the Garrison Diversion Unit—goes through. Giant white summer clouds drifted overhead as I sat by the lake. It was a rackety spot, with insects buzzing, frogs croaking, birds singing in the cattails. There were a lot of ducks on the lake, some trailing fuzzy little ducklings like pull toys.

I remembered what Dave had said—"It gets heated"—and thought of all the other people like him I had met: good-hearted, concerned, overworked, underpaid, tolerant of misunderstandings and interference. And abuse.

Earlier in his career, in another part of the country, Dave had been in a similar situation, with angry local people lined up against the Fish and Wildlife Service. "We held a public meeting to let them know what we were up to," he told me, "and to give them a chance to express themselves. One woman stood up and came to the microphone, and I remember what she said. She said, 'I brought my 84-year-old mother and my teenage son here to show them democracy in action, and you have really showed me.' She started crying. All the cameras in the room turned on her. She pointed at me. 'Are you married?' she asked. 'Yes,' I said. 'Do you have any children?' she said. 'Yes, ma'am, I do,' I said. 'Well,' she said, and I'll never forget this. She said, 'Well, I hope they can sleep at night knowing what their daddy does for a living.'"

Farther west, on the Great Plains in Montana, Charles M. Russell National Wildlife Refuge has also had its share of controversy. Named for the famed cowboy artist and usually referred to as CMR, the refuge stretches 125 miles up the Missouri River from Fort Peck Dam. Its boundaries enclose about 1,100,000 acres, of which 249,000 are water in a huge reservoir. CMR is mostly native shortgrass prairies, forested coulees, river bottoms, and the badlands and breaks so often portrayed in the works of its namesake artist.

A flight over the refuge and the BLM lands surrounding it provided a strange perspective: Prairie dog burrows, little mounds of earth with holes in the middle, looked like miniature missile silos; and missile silos, housing Minuteman IIIs among the sagebrush and greasewood, looked like enormous, high-tech prairie dog mounds—with concrete doors. Seasonal streams in the hills had been dammed to create stock ponds. Deer grazed in a burned-over forested area, and eight elk peered up at us from one of the ponds. We circled a butte, as flat and green on top as a golf course, and counted a dozen Rocky Mountain bighorn sheep, out of approximately 60 on the refuge.

Native elk had disappeared from the breaks by the early 1900s. Then in the 1950s about 160 elk from Yellowstone National Park were released in the CMR area, and now this reintroduced species is doing very well. Attempts to introduce Rocky Mountain bighorns have met with varying success, but today the sheep are holding their own.

It is these animals—the sheep, the elk, the deer, and others as well— that figure so poignantly in the controversy at CMR.

We landed at Lewistown—"the least busy airport in the U. S.," according to the pilot. I strolled the sun-struck streets, where every pickup had a rifle slung across the rear window, and nearly every man had a little round bulge in the back pocket of his jeans—a can of Skoal or Copenhagen. I found the refuge headquarters and met there with assistant manager Larry Malone.

Patiently, Larry led me through the complex history of CMR and helped me understand the tangled state of affairs the refuge finds itself in today. "Back in the '30s, after the Fort Peck Dam and reservoir project had begun, an executive order by FDR created a game range here, under the old Biological Survey, Fish and Wildlife's predecessor. The survey people would look after the wildlife and the BLM would handle the grazing rights. So between 1936 and 1976 CMR was jointly managed. The arrangement never really worked very well. There was inevitable competition between the cattle and the wildlife."

In the late 1970s the area's designation was changed from range to refuge, and CMR was placed wholly under the Fish and Wildlife Service. "But about 60 percent of the available grazing was being allocated for cattle, and 40 percent for wildlife," Larry said. "Under the law, we're supposed to manage the refuge for wildlife. So we prepared a draft environmental impact statement proposing to reverse the grazing ratio. Other uses are allowed on the refuge, as long as they're compatible with wildlife. A 60-40 AUM is not compatible."

An AUM, Larry explained, is an Animal Unit Month, the amount of forage one cow, half a horse, or five sheep will eat in a month's time. The Interior Department, the Department of Agriculture, and private landowners all lease grazing privileges to ranchers on the basis of so much per AUM.

"We're trying to cut the grazing for cattle by about 33 percent," Larry went on. "This has met with fierce resistance from the ranchers, naturally. They took us to court, arguing that, even though the refuge was now managed solely by Fish and Wildlife, Congress had intended for cattle grazing always to take precedence over wildlife."

To the astonishment of environmentalists and the Fish and Wildlife Service, a local district judge ruled in favor of the ranchers. They were further angered, but not surprised, when Interior, under Secretary James Watt, refused to appeal the decision. The Justice Department and several environmental groups appealed jointly on their own, and in October 1983 the U. S. Court of Appeals for the Ninth Circuit overturned the decision, ruling that "wildlife has priority in access to the forage resources of the Range. . . ."

"So now we're going to try to shift the balance in favor of the wildlife," Larry said. "Some ranchers' allotments will be cut considerably more than a third, and some won't be cut at all. It depends on how good the soil and vegetation are on a particular allotment. I'm afraid a few will be put completely out of business. If they don't have grazing rights on federal lands, they just won't be able to make it. On the refuge, we figure it takes about 12 acres for one AUM, so in order to graze 300 head, which is about the minimum for making a living here, you need access to 3,600 acres. And that's just the minimum.

"There's another difficulty with the ranchers. We classify most of CMR as 'good' to 'excellent' range. Basically. But that's for livestock. It's difficult to explain to a rancher that range conditions for cattle and for wildlife are very different. What's excellent for cattle may be worthless for grouse, for instance. Cattle trim grass right down to the ground, like a golf course. That leaves nowhere for a grouse to nest or get away from predators. On the other hand, range that is no good for cattle may be just the ticket for prairie dogs.

"Finally, there's the matter of the rates we charge for grazing. The BLM and the Forest Service set their rates by a complicated formula that fluctuates with the cost and price of beef. We base our rates on fair market value. Every three years we survey people who are leasing grazing. We find out what they're charging and what benefits go along with the grazing. The lessor may provide all the fencing, for instance, or water and salt. So we compare their rates and benefits with ours and arrive at a fair price based on that. Right now, the BLM and the Forest Service are charging $1.37 per AUM. We're charging $4.61. Some private land is going for as much as $13. So there's quite a variation, and ranchers can't understand why government agencies have two different systems."

Larry turned me over to Jim McCollum, the tall and rangy manager of the Sand Creek Wildlife Station, and we spent a blistering day touring the western end of CMR. Jim brought along a thermometer—which read 103°F by midafternoon—and a big insulated jug of ice water that saved my life several times.

There were a lot of prairie dogs out, despite the heat. They stood like bowling pins and turned their heads to watch as we drove by. We descended to a river bottom along the Missouri. Abandoned log buildings—the remains of the old Maulland homestead—seemed to crouch in the grass, beaten down by the sun. They were solid structures, leaning only a little. In the main house, cracked linoleum still covered the floor, and tattered curtains hung listless in the quiet. There was a cobweb across the door, and it was cool inside. Outside, a sharp-shinned hawk took off with a deer mouse in its talons.

We drove through the thousand-acre Manning prairie dog town. "How many prairie dogs here?" I asked Jim. He shook his head. "We count prairie dogs by the acre."

Jim showed me the difference between range that was in good condition—with healthy growths of western wheatgrass and yellow sweet clover—and overgrazed areas, thick with greasewood and sagebrush. There should be more of the former at CMR in years to come.

We stopped to watch a flock of mountain plovers feeding in the grass. There were a dozen of the brown-and-white birds, the most Jim had ever seen in one place. When they flew away, one youngster was left behind, wandering in circles, looking confused, chirping plaintively.

Jim, perhaps with more on his mind than just plovers, said, "That's what you get for not paying attention."

*S*till shedding his winter coat, a bull bison feeds on spring grasses at Fort Niobrara. Great herds of bison dominated the plains until excessive hunting drastically reduced their numbers from an estimated 60 million to fewer than 1,000 in the United States by the 1890s. Conservationists advocated their protection, and today approximately 55,000 bison live in refuges and parks and on ranches. Fort Niobrara maintains a herd of 225 on 19,000 acres of native prairie. Among the world's most productive ecosystems, grasslands support a rich variety of animal life. Above, a lark sparrow perches on dried sunflowers at Nebraska's Valentine Refuge.

PRECEDING PAGES: A yellow-headed blackbird flits among grasses of the genus Phragmites *fringing a prairie wetland on Valentine.*

robing the bottom for clams and crabs, whooping cranes feed in the shallow waters of Aransas National Wildlife Refuge on the coast of Texas. Perhaps the world's best known endangered species, the whooping crane has come to symbolize man's attempts to preserve vanishing wildlife. Teetering on the edge of extinction, the whooper population shrank to fewer than 25 birds in the 1940s and '50s; today their number has increased to about 140. In 1936 biologists discovered the birds' wintering grounds in brackish marshes near the Gulf of Mexico, and the following year the federal government established Aransas to protect their fragile habitat. Not until 1954 did scientists find the cranes' summer breeding grounds—2,500 miles away in northwestern Canada. Now a tracking system follows the whoopers during their twice-yearly migrations. Sightings reported to Canadian and U. S. agencies help clear the way, sometimes resulting in diversion of air traffic and suspension of hunting along the whooping cranes' flight path.

ajesty in motion, whooping cranes fly over Sundown Bay, a favorite feeding area within Aransas National Wildlife Refuge. The birds have an average wingspan of seven and a half feet. Moving their wings with slow, powerful strokes, they display a stately elegance in the air. But aside from annual migrations totaling about 5,000 miles, whooping cranes generally spend little time on the wing, usually taking flight only to escape danger, defend their territories, or find a new feeding area. Whoopers pass most of the day wading through marshy shallows in search of food. More than 350 species of birds have been counted at Aransas— the most ever sighted on any refuge. Located on the Central flyway, Aransas serves as a major staging area where thousands upon thousands of migrating birds stop to rest and feed. At left, a great blue heron stalks prey at the water's edge.

*S*haggy with cattails and bordered by live oaks, Big Tree Marsh provides a freshwater home for ducks, alligators, and raccoons. A variety of vegetation zones—freshwater and saltwater marshes, savannas, and live oak forests—supports a large menagerie of animal life within Aransas's 54,829 acres. The white-tailed deer below, one of about 3,000 on the refuge, lives at the forest's edge, close to cover and the low bushes it browses. Each fall, the refuge holds a ten-day archery hunt. In 1983, 4,670 bow hunters succeeded in shooting 42 deer and 15 feral pigs.

N.G.S. PHOTOGRAPHER BATES LITTLEHALES

155

*S*inuous maze of salt marshes, lakes, and streams mirrors the setting sun at Aransas. The broad channel

of the Gulf Intracoastal Waterway—in upper left corner—slices through the refuge for about 15 miles. Above, a tugboat pushes a barge along this coastal highway. At least 20 barges a day transport oil, gas, toxic chemicals, and other materials through the waterway. Whooping cranes feed in the shallows just 50 yards from passing barges. Several oil spills have already occurred, but were contained quickly enough so that the cranes' habitat escaped damage. The threat of a serious accident continues to worry refuge officials, who point out that waters must remain productive and clean to ensure the whoopers' survival.

*P*rairie cordgrass bends with the wind on a 20-acre patch of tallgrass prairie at Flint Hills National Wildlife Refuge in Kansas. Plowed and planted, the rich, dark soils of the Midwest sprouted America's "corn belt," and today less than one percent of the original tallgrass prairie remains. On previously farmed land, refuge management has reintroduced such species as Indian grass (opposite, left) for wildlife habitat. In unspoiled fields white asters grow among stands of big bluestem. Conservationists hope to have 60,000 acres of virgin tallgrass in the nearby Flint Hills set aside as the nation's first prairie preserve.

159

*B*lackening the land, a slow-burning fire destroys woody plants that could turn a prairie into forest. The deeply rooted perennial grasses withstand the heat, and in just a few weeks this field at Konza Prairie in Kansas will grow back thick and green. Researchers here use controlled burns to simulate and study the prairie of presettlement times, when lightning periodically ignited the grasslands and Indians deliberately set fires to attract bison to the regrowth. Managed by Kansas State University, the Konza is owned by the Nature Conservancy, a private organization that acquires prairies and other lands for preservation and research. The task of protecting the fragile prairie ecosystem falls largely to private groups, universities, and individuals. A preservationist in Illinois (below) gathers tallgrass seeds by the bagful and handful for the planting of future prairies.

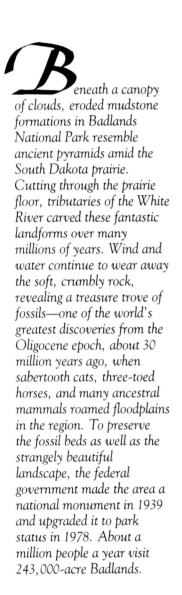

Beneath a canopy of clouds, eroded mudstone formations in Badlands National Park resemble ancient pyramids amid the South Dakota prairie. Cutting through the prairie floor, tributaries of the White River carved these fantastic landforms over many millions of years. Wind and water continue to wear away the soft, crumbly rock, revealing a treasure trove of fossils—one of the world's greatest discoveries from the Oligocene epoch, about 30 million years ago, when sabertooth cats, three-toed horses, and many ancestral mammals roamed floodplains in the region. To preserve the fossil beds as well as the strangely beautiful landscape, the federal government made the area a national monument in 1939 and upgraded it to park status in 1978. About a million people a year visit 243,000-acre Badlands.

*R*ecalling scenes by famed western artist Charles M. Russell, cowhands for the Two Crow Ranch in Montana herd cattle during fall roundup. The ranch owners run about 400 head on private lands as well as on range leased from Charles M. Russell Refuge and the Bureau of Land Management (see map, pages 138-9). Livestock overgrazing, however, alters the natural vegetation of shortgrass prairie. Cattle trample the grasses and nibble them down to stubble, making the range unsuitable for many kinds of native wildlife.

FOLLOWING PAGES: With a full moon rising, the meandering Missouri looks much as it did when Lewis and Clark camped along its banks in 1805-06. The bison, grizzlies, and wolves have vanished, but elk and bighorn sheep have been reintroduced. Along with mule deer, they roam the green bottomlands and pine-studded Missouri Breaks on CMR.

esting on the open prairie, a mountain plover guards its clutch of spotted eggs. Below, Jim McCollum, an assistant manager at Charles M. Russell, points out mountain plovers to a tour group from the Yellowstone Valley Audubon Society. "On the refuge, mountain plovers tend to build nests in prairie dog towns," says Jim (kneeling) as the group gathers around him. "Prairie dogs nibble down the grasses around their burrows. By keeping the vegetation cropped very short, they help maintain the bare ground where plovers like to nest."

*W*edged among grain fields, J. Clark Salyer National Wildlife Refuge lies in the prairie pothole region of North Dakota, one of the most productive breeding areas for migratory waterfowl in the United States. Scattered through the Dakotas, Minnesota, Iowa, and south-central Canada, thousands of shallow ponds called potholes provide food and nesting cover essential to the breeding birds. Many farmers drain potholes (dark oval areas in foreground) to plant the fertile land. In a process called level ditching, a farmer digs a deep trench (below) to concentrate the water in a small area and open up the surrounding land for cultivation. But the resulting ditch does not supply the vegetation and invertebrate life that waterfowl need.

*S*now geese by the thousand flock to the lakes, marshes, and potholes of the northern prairies each spring and fall during yearly migrations. To prevent further destruction of wetlands and loss of valuable waterfowl habitats, the Fish and Wildlife Service buys easements from private landowners, paying them not to drain, fill, level, or burn their wetlands. On a farm near J. Clark Salyer Refuge (below), Franklin's gulls rest on a marsh between feeding forays into nearby croplands; the marsh is under easement to Fish and Wildlife.

FOLLOWING PAGES: Delicate harebells nod in the sunlit prairie of North Dakota's Theodore Roosevelt National Park. In the 1880s the young Roosevelt ranched here amid the badlands of the Little Missouri River. As President, he passionately championed the cause of conservation, proposing 5 national parks and 18 national monuments, and establishing the country's first wildlife refuge—then adding 54 more. TR set aside 230 million acres in all—leaving a living legacy of his love for the outdoors and preserving much of America's natural heritage.

Land of

Cloud-darkened peaks of the Teton Range jut above silvery waters and wooded islands of Jackson Lake in Wyoming's Grand Teton National Park.

Sierras and Peaks

*T*he national parks are being loved to death. That view may have been first held, if not actually uttered, on August 27, 1915. On that day, a group of Shriners was being conveyed by tallyho coach through Yellowstone National Park. They met an automobile, a 1911 Winton, the first the stage driver had ever seen. It frightened his horses, and he later said, "This park as I have known it and loved it is as dead as a dodo."

The same lament may be heard across the land today as the parks continue to change. Some call the changes evolution; others, destruction.

National parks are an American innovation, but born more of happenstance than design. When Thoreau and Emerson began expounding the glories of nature in the 1840s, most Americans had no idea what they were talking about. Nature was an enemy to be combated. Mountains were not eloquent expressions of the Creator's grandeur, but rather roughhewn barriers to progress. The forest primeval was potential farmland, waiting for the plow. There was no hint of a movement to preserve scenic areas on a national basis.

Then, in the middle of the Civil War, with no debate and little fanfare, President Lincoln signed a bill transferring jurisdiction over Yosemite Valley to the state of California, an arrangement that lasted less than 30 years. The bill stipulated that the lands "shall be held for public use, resort and recreation." Californians like to claim that Yosemite was thus the first national park, but that honor is generally considered to belong to Yellowstone.

Most of the earliest witnesses to the marvels of Yellowstone were thought to be liars—and many of them were, spinning tall tales of petrified birds perching on petrified trees, singing petrified songs. Gradually, as expeditions returned from the Yellowstone territory with reliable eyewitness accounts, the area was recognized as an incomparable wonderland deserving of protection. On March 1, 1872, President Ulysses S. Grant signed the bill setting aside two million acres as "a public park or pleasuring ground for the benefit and enjoyment of the people." But Congress provided no funds for the new park, and the superintendent, until he grew disgusted and resumed his work as a bank examiner in Minnesota, served without salary or staff. Poachers and vandals had free run of the park until 1886, when a troop of U. S. Cavalry arrived to assume responsibility. The Army did the job for 30 years, and did it well, according to John Muir, who wrote that "every pine tree is waving its arms for joy." Muir fought for and achieved national park status for Yosemite in 1890. Two other parks—Sequoia and General Grant (later part of Kings Canyon)—were established that same year to protect California's giant sequoias.

President Theodore Roosevelt broadened the base by setting aside areas noteworthy less for their scenic wonders than for their historical or scientific importance. The first of these, called national monuments, included Devils Tower in Wyoming, Montezuma Castle in Arizona, and El Morro in New Mexico.

So the parks and the monuments came along, one at a time, but there was no Park Service to manage them. Some were the responsibility of the Interior Department, some of Agriculture, and some of the War Department. There was no policy for administering them, and personnel came and went.

In 1912 President William H. Taft, urged on by a group of park enthusiasts, notified Congress that "I earnestly recommend the establishment of a Bureau of National Parks." To oversee those parks already managed by Interior, a remarkable man, Stephen T. Mather, was brought to Washington as an assistant to the Secretary. Millionaire philanthropist, former reporter, onetime salesman for Twenty Mule Team Borax, avid outdoorsman, Mather lobbied tirelessly for the parks. In 1915 he organized a junket into Yosemite and Sequoia for a group of influential journalists, artists, scientists, and public officials. Pampered and coddled, they were given new and comfortable sleeping bags and air mattresses. A renowned Chinese camp cook provided daily fresh-baked bread and lavish dinners served on linen tablecloths. The trip paid publicity dividends for years. Editor Gilbert H. Grosvenor, one of the party, devoted an entire issue of NATIONAL GEOGRAPHIC to the parks some months later, and on August 25, 1916, President Woodrow Wilson signed the legislation establishing the National Park Service.

Today the agency oversees some 80 million acres constituting 335 parks. They have a bewildering array of designations—monuments, preserves, battlefields, parkways, trails—but Park Service people tend to call them all parks.

In the beginning, many were remote from urban centers. But the world is a smaller place today, and what were once distant seas of wilderness are now islands in oceans of development. While superintendents once worried most about problems within the parks—poachers, souvenir hunters, and the like— today they also ponder threats outside their boundaries—urban sprawl, mineral exploration, air pollution. The 1980 *State of the Parks* report noted that some of the larger, more famous parks, such as Yellowstone, Glacier, and Yosemite, "were at one time pristine areas surrounded and protected by vast wilderness regions. Today, with their surrounding buffer zones gradually disappearing, many of these parks are experiencing significant and widespread adverse effects associated with external encroachment." More than 60 percent of the parks reported scenic degradation, and 45 percent had detected threats to the quality of their air. Nearly all the superintendents of the Rocky Mountain parks warned that, because of pollution near their domains, they could no longer guarantee visitors clean air and good visibility. This "adjacent lands" issue, as it's called, affects many parks, including Grand Teton in northwestern Wyoming.

Two of Grand Teton's most perplexing problems—aside from the 3,500 acres of private property inside the park, aside from nearby oil and gas exploration, aside from development on the borders, aside from controversies over snowmobiles and dams—two of the most perplexing involve airplanes and elk.

Airplanes have for years used the Jackson Hole Airport within the park. In the days of small, propeller-driven aircraft, no one minded much, but today the meadows echo with the roar of jets taking off and landing. The airport had been scheduled to close in the 1990s, when its permit expired, but in 1983 Interior Secretary James Watt extended the permit at least 30 years, though requiring stronger noise-abatement procedures.

"The average city tourist probably doesn't notice the noise unless you call his attention to it," said Ed Riddell, a photographer-environmentalist who has lived in the Jackson area for ten years. "But even if only a small percentage of the visitors come for solitude and tranquillity, I think a national park is one place where they are entitled to it, and they're just not getting it here."

The elk are another matter. The whole Teton Park-Jackson Hole complex lies in the midst of huge, historic elk populations. The National Elk Refuge was established in 1912 to protect the elk, whose winter habitat was being disturbed and lost to development. Today, large herds still migrate through the park to the refuge. Since 1950 the Park Service has been required by law to issue hunting permits as part of an overall plan to manage what has been called "one of the most complex wildlife problems in the West." Each year several hundred elk are shot within Grand Teton.

"The elk are sitting ducks," said Ed. "Since they migrate in herds, it's

"Land of sierras and peaks," the western mountains hold some of the country's most spectacular treasures. In 1872, with the establishment of Yellowstone, the federal government created the world's first national park, land set aside strictly for conservation and for "the enjoyment of the people." The crown jewels of the National Park System, Yellowstone, Yosemite, Glacier, and Grand Teton draw many millions of visitors annually. Overcrowding and general wear and tear, as well as pollution and pressures from outside, pose serious threats to these parks. Other federal holdings in the Sierra Nevada and northern Rockies include immense forests managed for multiple use—recreation, wildlife habitats, and resource development. The Bureau of Land Management also administers parts of the region, among them the shores of Mono Lake in California and the Snake River Birds of Prey Area in Idaho.

hard for a hunter to get a clear shot at a single animal. He doesn't know what he's hit until the herd moves on. The hunt isn't sporting—and is it really needed?"

Often people who visit the Tetons continue on to Yellowstone National Park just to the north. I followed along, trailing mammoth recreational vehicles that lumbered up hills like circus elephants. RVs have become more elaborate in the last few years. With bikes strapped to the front, boats overturned on top, family cars in tow, they reminded me of affluent refugees fleeing catastrophe with all their worldly possessions.

I trailed them to Old Faithful, where, on benches rimming the famous geyser, we wilted like daisies in the sun. When Old Faithful began sputtering and gurgling, we muttered our disappointment, thinking that was all there was to it. But when it finally erupted in earnest, we oohed and ahhed like spectators at a fireworks display. The roar of the geyser was nearly drowned out by the click and clatter of hundreds of camera shutters, and I wondered how many times Old Faithful had been photographed in the last hundred years.

Look at a map and you'd think Yellowstone could hardly be better protected, buffered as it is on every side by federal land. Running clockwise around it from the top are Gallatin National Forest, Custer National Forest, the North Absaroka Wilderness, Shoshone National Forest, the Washakie Wilderness, the Teton Wilderness, Bridger-Teton National Forest, Grand Teton National Park, and Targhee National Forest.

But look again.

Man-drawn boundaries have carved up an entire ecosystem, and now that ecosystem is the heart in a body of mining and energy development. Much of the federal land around the park is under lease application for oil and gas exploration, including 300,000 acres of the Washakie Wilderness. Mining interests crowd the park from three directions. A year-round ski resort and two power lines threaten nearby grizzly bear habitat. But what most alarms many people is the possibility of geothermal development in Targhee National Forest just to the west of the park. About 100,000 acres of private, state, and federal land are under lease application. The nearest well would be about 13 miles from Old Faithful. The question everyone asks is: What would this do to Old Faithful and Yellowstone's other geothermal features? The universal answer is: We don't know.

Three hundred miles west of Old Faithful, along the Snake River, there's a sight as impressive, in its way, as the renowned geyser. There, raptors leap from cliffside aeries and ride warm gusts of dry desert air over neighboring tablelands in search of prey. Ornithologists say that the Snake River Birds of Prey Area south of Boise has the densest concentration of nesting raptors in the world, at least 800 pairs representing 14 different species. That includes perhaps 5 percent of the world population of prairie falcons, beautiful relatives of the equally splendid peregrine falcon. Golden eagles, great horned owls, ferruginous hawks, red-tailed hawks, burrowing owls, marsh hawks, American kestrels, and long- and short-eared owls also nest here. Bald eagles use the area as winter habitat, and ospreys migrate through.

Birds of Prey has grown over the years, not always with unanimous approval. Because of the large population of raptors, Secretary of the Interior Rogers Morton in 1971 designated nearly 27,000 acres of public land along 33 miles of river as a natural area, extending it back half a mile from the canyon rims. The next year the BLM initiated probably the most intensive study of raptors the world has ever seen, and it was immediately apparent that the natural area was too small. The birds searched for prey farther from the river than expected. Their bedroom was being protected, several people pointed out, but not their pantry. So in 1974 the BLM established the Snake River Birds of Prey Study Area, encompassing the natural area, 278,000 acres of public land, and adjacent private and state lands. But even that acreage was inadequate for a complete study of the birds' hunting ranges, and today the area has been enlarged to include 483,000 acres of public land.

In 1975 Mike Kochert, a young BLM biologist with experience among the wolves and moose of Michigan's Isle Royale, had been put in charge of what would become a comprehensive research effort that lasted four years. It was aimed at determining the minimum amount of land required to maintain both the nesting population of birds and the ecosystem needed to support them.

I went on a day-trip with Mike and assistant research leader Karen Steenhof to band a couple of golden eagles in a nest overlooking pasture and river. We climbed through shrubby grassland to the boulders atop the bluff, where Mike donned the paraphernalia of a rock-climber—ropes, harness, carabiners, gloves, helmet—and walked backward off the cliff. By craning I could see, 20 feet down, a nest with two eagles in it. Mike stuffed them into a canvas bag, sent them up, then rejoined us on top. Unpacked from the bag and set on their big yellow feet, the eagles—despite being perfectly robust—were a sorry-looking pair. They had aged beyond the downy state, but had not yet acquired their golden brown flight feathers. About the size of chickens, scruffy and ragged, they nonetheless did their best to look like eagles, scowling with a fierceness that was daunting. Then one would waver, totter, and topple forward onto its chest, an undignified lump of scraggly feathers.

One seemed to like having its throat and the back of its head stroked, and I obliged. It stood, swaying unsteadily, blinking, its beak agape, while

I smoothed its ruffled feathers and murmured praise of its beauty and courage.

Mike and Karen gave each bird a quick physical, checking its mouth, eyes, crop, and feathers, then secured it in a plastic bag to be weighed. One was 3.7 kilograms, the other 3.5—about 8 pounds.

"This is excellent terrain for raptors," Mike told me after returning the eagles to their nest. "They use thermals like elevators to lift themselves out of the canyon and onto the grasslands where they hunt. The most prolific species of prey animals, and the one that constitutes about 70 percent of the prairie falcon's diet, is the Townsend ground squirrel."

As we drove across the rolling countryside, we'd see the little creatures scurrying alongside the road, one eye cocked heavenward, where doom hovered on swift wings. My heart went out to them. To be labeled a "high-calorie rodent" by biologists seems bad enough, but to be the favored prey of a skyful of taloned fury seems downright unfair.

It was during the years of Mike's research that the phrase "sagebrush rebellion" began appearing in newspapers. This was an attempt by western farmers, ranchers, and developers to have federal lands transferred to the states to be managed or disposed of by them as they saw fit. Proponents argued that eastern states were not saddled with extensive federal holdings, so why should the West be; that the federal government had a long history of mismanaging land; that local people were more apt to make wise management decisions than officials in faraway Washington; that their use of the land for grazing and farming over several generations gave them a proprietary interest in it and a right to it.

Under two settlement laws—the Desert Land Act of 1877 and the Carey Act of 1894—farmers can still buy some federal land at $1.25 an acre, if they irrigate it within three years. About 160,000 acres within Birds of Prey have been converted to private irrigated farmland this way, and another 100,000 are under application. But one of Secretary Cecil Andrus's last actions—in November 1980—was to withdraw Birds of Prey from application, selection, entry, or patent to private ownership. He said, in effect: No more conversion of federal land to private ownership in Birds of Prey. Sagebrush Rebellion, Inc., filed suit against the Interior Department to have the ruling overturned, and the case is still pending. As Mike noted, "The wheels of justice grind exceeding slow."

The reason for Mike's concern: "We've found that intensive irrigated agriculture isn't compatible with ground squirrels. The more intensive agriculture, the fewer ground squirrels. The fewer ground squirrels, the fewer prairie falcons. In a good ground squirrel year, 200 pairs of prairie falcons capture and eat about 50,000 squirrels during the 6-week nesting season. Add to that the other predators—badgers, snakes, coyotes, ravens, other raptors—and you can see that it takes a lot of ground squirrels to keep this area cooking."

The 1980 *State of the Parks* report listed Glacier in northwestern Montana as our most threatened national park. Many have argued that the survey the report was based on gave an inaccurate picture because of the varying degrees of experience, veracity, and thoroughness of the individuals who filled it out. Even so, many people who thought Glacier was remote and unspoiled were shocked to learn it had so many problems. As in other parks, most are external threats caused by oil, gas, and coal development, livestock trespass, logging, and highway, power-line, and railroad construction. A complication for Glacier that other parks don't share is the proximity of the Canadian border. How can the United States control impacts that originate in another country?

Gary Gregory, resource manager for Glacier, talked with me in his office. "As far as short-term threats go, we're most concerned about the Cabin Creek Coal Mine six miles north of the park, in British Columbia. There's a mountain—*two* mountains, actually—of coal there that will be strip-mined down to pits a thousand feet deep and a mile wide. The mine itself probably won't affect us much, but there are things associated with it that will.

"First, there'll be a washing and drying process, fired by coal burned on site. So we'll be getting some sulfur dioxide and particulates in our air. Second, it's located on the North Fork of the Flathead River. They'll be putting in some settling ponds on the floodplain there, and a flood would carry acids and other pollutants into the river. It's a breeding ground for our native cutthroat and bull trout, both very sensitive species and important components of our ecosystem. Third, there'll just be more people in the area, which will disturb not only Glacier but the whole larger ecosystem. Even if we put a triple fence around the park, we wouldn't be protected. Some of the animals here range outside Glacier as well. Grizzlies, Rocky Mountain gray wolves, elk—these have migration corridors adjoining the park."

Many environmentalists suspect that the Canadians would be more responsive to our environmental complaints if we would be more serious about tackling the problem of acid rain.

The animals migrating into and out of Glacier will face another hazard: The highway entering the park from the west will soon be widened from two lanes to four. "Animals can get across a two-lane highway OK," said Gary, "but they have trouble with four lanes. Grizzlies are especially vulnerable. Glacier contains only about 20 percent of the bears' northern habitat. They need the entire ecosystem. It's probable that if the grizzly didn't have the habitat outside Glacier, it wouldn't be able to survive in the park alone. So a four-lane highway is bad news for grizzlies.

"The problems began years ago when the first national parks were established," Gary continued. "Many of the boundaries are just lines on a map. They should have been drawn according to ecosystems, but people in those days didn't understand what ecosystems were. That knowledge has come just in the last few years. We think we're doing the right things now, but I'm sure we're going to learn things in the next 10 to 20 years that will make people wonder what on earth we were up to. It would be naive to think we have all the answers now."

A few miles to the west of Glacier, in Kootenai National Forest, a handful of grizzly bears is at the center of a controversy that illustrates the difficulties of reconciling different laws and policies, all intended to govern the use of federal lands.

The Kootenai is more than two million acres of stream-rich forest—largely fir, larch, spruce, and pine. Running down its center is the 95,000-acre Cabinet Mountains Wilderness, prime habitat for probably no more than 15 grizzlies. You'd think these threatened animals would be safe here.

Although the Wilderness Act of 1964 prohibits many things in wilderness areas—roads, power lines, mechanical equipment, airplanes—it does not prohibit mining. Mineral exploration and the patenting of claims were specifically permitted until December 31, 1983. And validated claims can be worked any time after that date. The Endangered Species Act of 1973 requires federal agencies to use "all procedures and methods necessary" to protect listed species, but a court has never ruled on a clash between mining and a threatened animal.

At least two companies may be mining silver and copper in the Cabinet Mountains Wilderness for the next 20 years.

*Artificial boundaries
drawn by man carve the
Yellowstone ecosystem
into a hodgepodge of park,
forest, refuge, and private
lands. Protected only in
federal areas, wide-
ranging elk and grizzly
bears find their habitat
and food supplies
disrupted. Elk,
summering in mountain
pastures, migrate to lower
elevations when snow
covers their forage. Some
7,500 of these animals
winter in the National Elk
Refuge, where the Fish
and Wildlife Service
provides supplemental
feed—alfalfa pellets—to
expand the capacity of the
range. Grizzlies, a
threatened species, may
roam a hundred miles a
week seeking the grubs,
berries, and small animals
they eat. The 1969 closing
of Yellowstone National
Park's garbage dumps
deprived the bears of a
major food source.*

Forest wildlife biologist Alan Christensen—a Robert Redford look-alike—met with me in his office in Libby, a little Montana town dedicated to hunting, fishing, and logging. I asked him how the Cabinet bears were doing.

"I wish we really knew," he said. "I vacillate between optimism and pessimism. In the broad view, grizzlies obviously aren't doing very well or they wouldn't be listed as threatened. On the other hand, the bears are receiving a lot more management emphasis now than they were five or ten years ago. We're being much more careful about how we lay out timber sales or roads, for instance, or when and how we allow mineral exploration to occur. We don't know of any deaths among the Cabinet bears, and we *do* know that reproduction is taking place. Given their mobility, grizzlies have a real knack for finding each other during the mating season.

"But look at the pressures on the habitat. We've got oil and gas development, hard-rock mineral extraction, a timber program being pushed to produce more timber, a proposed ski complex, hunting, trout fishing. How can we keep bear habitat relatively undisturbed and still meet all these other needs?"

Another issue involving forests worries Alan as much as the plight of the grizzlies: the disappearance throughout the United States of old-growth timber. "A lot of wildlife prefer old-growth habitat," he told me, " and when you eliminate that habitat, you eliminate those animals. But as a biologist I'm uncomfortable focusing on one animal and saying, 'We've got to have *that* habitat for *this* species.' Old-growth habitat is important in itself.

"The Forest Service is clearing old growth to produce timber. Generally, old-growth sites are biologically productive—good soil, good water, and so forth. Loggers like them because there's a tremendous return. So the Forest Service over the years has focused on old-growth stands. Under current management practices, nearly all old growth will be gone—I mean *gone*—in the next 20 years. Are we going to be patient enough to wait hundreds of years for more old-growth stands? Probably not. So we're facing the extinction of a habitat. You can't put a 300-year-old tree back where you found it. Only time can do that.

"I logged for a couple of years while I was in college, and to walk up to a 300-year-old tree with a chain saw and in 10 minutes have it felled—it bothered me. To think that the tree could stand for centuries and survive everything—drought, fire, insects, wind, disease—everything except me."

The crisp, cool air of northern Montana beckoned from the hilltops, and on a Saturday morning I joined a couple of Forest Service men and their wives on a firewood-cutting trip. Forty minutes from Libby, after winding across gurgling streams and up green hillsides and past deer bounding alongside the road, we came to a small clear-cut. A few tall seed trees had been left standing, and brush and scrub had been bulldozed into piles. A larch tree several hundred years old had been left lying—fair game for firewood hunters—and the foursome attacked it with chain saws and axes. I had envisioned a morning of sitting on a stump communing with nature while they worked, but it was not to be: There were extra gloves and an ax, and soon I was whacking away at chunks of tree, trying to reduce them to fireplace size. It was a happy morning, a carefree break, but three days later I was still feeling the effects of splitting that larch.

The trip also prompted more questions: I was puzzled by the number of logging roads angling off into the forest, and later heard that roads have become something of an issue within the Forest Service. Under the Wilderness Act, the agency reviewed those areas in its holdings that had been previously classified as "primitive." Then the Forest Service decided to review its remaining roadless areas. This effort was called RARE, for Roadless Areas Review and Evaluation. In 1972 the agency recommended 12 million acres for wilderness study, all of them

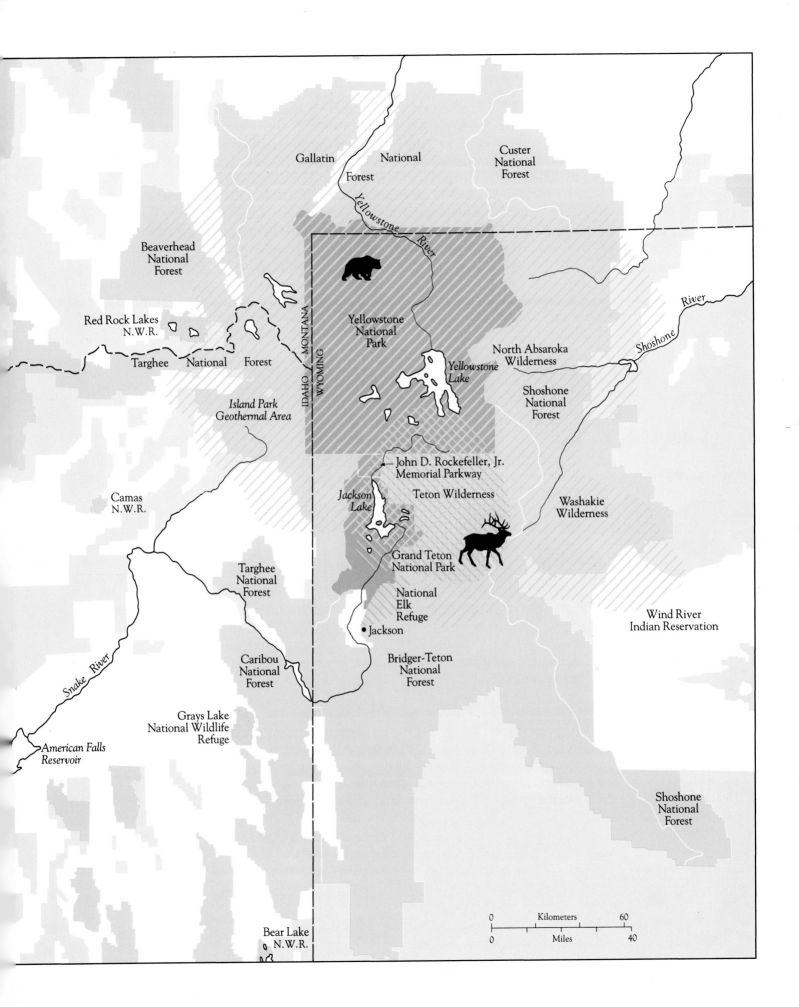

Gallatin National Forest

Custer National Forest

Beaverhead National Forest

Yellowstone River

Red Rock Lakes N.W.R.

IDAHO MONTANA

WYOMING

Targhee National Forest

Island Park Geothermal Area

Yellowstone National Park

Yellowstone Lake

North Absaroka Wilderness

Shoshone River

Shoshone National Forest

Camas N.W.R.

John D. Rockefeller, Jr. Memorial Parkway

Jackson Lake

Teton Wilderness

Washakie Wilderness

Targhee National Forest

Grand Teton National Park

National Elk Refuge

Wind River Indian Reservation

Snake River

Jackson

Bridger-Teton National Forest

Caribou National Forest

Grays Lake National Wildlife Refuge

American Falls Reservoir

Shoshone National Forest

Bear Lake N.W.R.

0	Kilometers	60
0	Miles	40

in the West. Another study in the late '70s—RARE II—recommended more wilderness areas, but left environmental organizations still dissatisfied.

A California court ruled in 1983 that the planning process that had produced RARE II was "insufficient," and, though the ruling applied only to California forests, it was sufficient to kill RARE II. Now the roadless areas are once again being studied, as "part of the ongoing reevaluation process in conjunction with the master plans for forest management now being prepared." In other words—but not words that the Forest Service likes to use or hear—RARE III.

Suppose you're the Forest Service. You've had to deal with the "roadless areas" issue for years. But if you build some roads in your roadless areas, the problem disappears. That's what some critics say has been happening.

One employee I talked with in the Kootenai said: "When I came here ten years ago there were two engineers in each of the forest's seven districts charged with building roads. A total of 14. Today there are a hundred full-time engineers doing nothing *but* building roads. It used to be that a logger would buy rights to a timber sale, then the Forest Service would build a road to the site. Now the Forest Service builds roads to the sites before the timber is sold. There are about 7,000 miles of roads in the Kootenai, and we'll double that in a couple of years. Our stated policy, even on paper, is to 'road the unroaded.'"

He showed me the 1982 *Regional Goals and Regional Forester's Directions*, published by the Forest Service. It said, in part, "First priority for the allocation of the public works road construction funds . . . will be given to Forest project proposals which provide cost-effective access to commercial timber stands in unroaded areas." He also showed me the 1983 budget for the Kootenai. Five and a half million dollars, almost 25 percent of the forest's budget, was to be devoted to road construction.

"National forests in the West are not pristine woodlands full of animals," he said. "They are big green machines, geared to producing timber."

A road of a different sort—a 338-mile-long aqueduct—drew me to another trouble spot, this time in California. Just east of Yosemite, on the downslope of the Sierra Nevada, lies Mono Lake. Its salty waters sustain trillions of brine shrimp, which in turn feed hundreds of thousands of birds. As many as 40,000 California gulls nest on the lava-built islands.

In 1930 the people of Los Angeles approved a $38,000,000 bond issue for constructing dams, reservoirs, and a tunnel near Mono Lake, as part of the Los Angeles Aqueduct. In 1941 the city began diverting water from four of the lake's five major feeder streams into the aqueduct, and the lake began to fall. In 1970 a second aqueduct increased the diversions from 70,000 to about 100,000 acre-feet a year, and the lake fell even faster. In 1978 the Mono Lake Committee was organized to defend it. By 1979 a land bridge had formed between one of the major nesting islands and the shore, allowing coyotes access to the gull nests. The gulls abandoned the island, and no chicks survived. That same year, a California interagency task force recommended stabilizing the lake at its 1970 level. The Los Angeles Department of Water and Power refused to sign the recommendation. By 1981 Mono Lake had dropped nearly 44 feet—*forty-four feet*—below its 1940 level, and the salinity of the lake had doubled. The summer of 1981 was one of the hottest in years, and virtually every gull that fledged—about 25,000 in all—died; the possible causes of this catastrophe are still under study. "Unless diversions are curtailed," the committee warned, "salinity will poison Mono Lake's unique ecosystem, and our children will inherit a sterile, chemical sump."

Mono Lake was being allowed to deteriorate so that the City of Angels could meet its water needs. In 1983 Mono Lake finally won a victory. The California Supreme Court reaffirmed the public interest in protecting natural resources, and it now looks as though Los Angeles might have to relinquish at least some of the water it diverts from the lake's tributary streams.

As the lake fell, it exposed ghostly islands of tufa, porous calcium carbonate formed when springwater brought up calcium that interacted with Mono's chemicals and coalesced into towers. It's a bizarre landscape.

The shoreline is the subject of a controversy between California and the BLM. The state owns the lake and its bed, but the federal government owns most of the land around the lake. As the water level dropped, the shoreline widened. Who owns the new land? About 75 percent of the shoreline is claimed by both. They'll manage it cooperatively until the courts settle the question.

What especially intrigued me about Mono Lake was the committee that seems on the verge of triumphing over a powerful, distant municipality. In Lee Vining, the little California town on the western shore of Mono, I looked up the young couple largely responsible—David and Sally Gaines. I found them in their backyard. David, bearded and thoughtful, had scattered about him the fittings and elbows and pipes of a new bathtub he was about to install in a house he's renovating next door in his spare time. Sally was hoeing the garden. Their new baby girl, Vireo, crawled from one to the other, gurgling. Back in 1978 David and Sally, pretty much on their own, took on a corporate giant, the Los Angeles Department of Water and Power, whose budget of two billion dollars a year is larger than some countries'. I was interested in why and how they had done it.

"I had heard of Mono Lake years ago," said David. "In fact, I first visited it in the '60s. But it wasn't until I spent an entire summer here, in 1976, working on an inventory of natural areas in Mono Country, that I really became aware of the threat to the lake. I began to think about what the lake would look like if it dropped another 40 feet. But we didn't do anything till two years later. I guess we were waiting for someone else to."

Sally said, "Remember? It was a drought year, and the Sierra Club thought maybe that wasn't the best time to try to get water away from L. A."

"So we started forming a committee," said David.

Sally said, "We didn't even know what officers were called. We said, 'Let's see. There's always, like, a president, and there's some kind of secretary.' We didn't know anything. Really innocent. We came to town to look for a place to rent, because we were camping out and had no phone. So it was hard to do business. That first year we ran the committee from home. There was a constant stream of people in and out. Hectic."

"Since then the committee has been my full-time job," said David. "That first fall I spent three or four months traveling around the state, giving slide shows and talks on Mono Lake. It was crucial for getting funds and support. We'd pass the hat and use the donations to buy the gas to get to the next talk. We also started a newsletter, with a list of two or three hundred names. We've published 25 issues so far and have about 6,000 members."

"We had a couple of lucky breaks, too," said Sally. "A law firm donated a quarter of a million dollars' worth of legal work to the committee for the lawsuit against L. A. Water and Power. A printer did all our printing free for the first two years. The California chapter of the Audubon Society voted Mono Lake its number one conservation priority one year. That got us national attention."

"When we had to incorporate to take part in the lawsuit," David said, "the lawyer asked to see all our financial records. We had them in a shoebox. We started paying ourselves $75 a month late in 1979, and increased it to the minimum wage in 1980. Now we start full-time staffers out at $900 a month and pay ourselves the same."

I asked them if they would fight the same fight today, at another spot. They exchanged smiles. Finally David answered, "Only if it was a place that moved me as much as Mono Lake. Remember, I have a family now. Those early years were rough. I worked 70, 80 hours a week—writing newsletters, giving slide shows, conducting field trips to the lake, running the information center, and talking, talking, talking. For three years I had no personal life at all."

That's what it sometimes takes to be an environmental activist.

Perhaps the world's most famous environmental activist had his heart broken just a few miles west of Mono Lake. When John Muir lost his battle to halt the damming of Hetch Hetchy Valley in Yosemite National Park, his friends said, his health and spirit failed, and he was dead within a year. Born in Scotland in 1838, Muir came to America in 1849 and began tramping the wilderness areas of his new country. He later helped found the Sierra Club to lobby for the protection of Yosemite Valley, and when San Francisco needed water and began casting covetous eyes on the exquisite Hetch Hetchy, Muir threw himself into the fray. "Dam Hetch Hetchy!" he wrote. "As well dam for water-tanks the people's cathedrals and churches, for no holier temple has ever been consecrated by the heart of man." Gifford Pinchot disagreed, and testified before a House committee that "the delight of the few men and women who would yearly go into the Hetch Hetchy Valley" should not eclipse the national need "to take every part of the land and its resources and put it to that use in which it will best serve the most people."

Many U. S. senators were baffled by the national uproar over Hetch Hetchy, the first environmental issue to generate any controversy. Before the dam bill reached a vote, many received hundreds of angry letters from constituents opposing construction. At the end of six days of debate, Senator Thomas B. Reed of Missouri addressed the chamber: "The Senate . . . has devoted a full week of time to discussing the disposition of about two square miles of land . . . It is merely proposed to put water on those two square miles. Over that trivial matter, the business of the country is halted, the Senate goes into profound debate, the country is thrown into a condition of hysteria, and one would imagine that chaos and old night were about to descend upon the land." The bill was passed in 1913, the dam was built, and Hetch Hetchy Valley became a lake.

My first stop in Yosemite, as is the case for practically everyone, was Yosemite Village. It's the major area of hotels, lodges, campgrounds, restaurants, and shops, and I busied myself buying T-shirts and postcards. A street band made an unearthly racket outside a general store selling everything from beer to bumper stickers to bicycle tires. There were thousands of people shopping and eating. Walking among them, dodging pets and backpacks, I happened to look up, above the tourists and shops—and caught my breath. Rising around us was the most sublime, most astonishing scenery I had ever seen. A waterfall tumbled from a granite cliff, turning to mist as it fell. Forested mountains climbed toward a dazzling sky puffed with clouds. I was in a bowl of granite and trees. But the most fascinating thing was this: No one was paying any attention to it. We were all caught up in the shopping-mall atmosphere of Yosemite Village. Surely, I thought, this is not the kind of experience John Muir had in mind for us.

In the early days of the national parks, businesses scrambled to supply lodging and food for the visitors. Some concessionaires have been around longer than the parks. The Yosemite Park and Curry Company, for example, was established 22 years before the Park Service. Stephen Mather brought some order through a system of "regulated monopolies"—private enterprise providing services inside the parks but only under Park Service supervision. Today more than 430 concessionaires operate in the parks, offering everything from raft trips to campsites. Some are subsidiaries of giant companies; Yosemite Park and Curry, for instance, is owned by MCA, Inc., an entertainment conglomerate. Some environmentalists say that the concessionaires are interested only in profiting from the parks, that their structures and services detract from the natural features, and that they ought to be moved to the outskirts.

The congestion of Yosemite has long been an issue. In the early 1900s, James Bryce, Great Britain's ambassador to the United States, commented on a proposal to allow automobiles in the park: "If Adam had known what harm the serpent was going to work, he would have tried to prevent him from finding lodgment in Eden; and if you were to realize what the result of the automobile will be in that wonderful, that incomparable Valley, you will keep it out. . . ." But the automobile was let in, and for years Yosemite was a chaos.

I talked with Harold Reynolds, who had been coming to Yosemite from southern California for many years. "There were times," he said, "when you literally couldn't move in here. There was no check-in at the entrances, and no reservations for campsites. You could park your car wherever you could find a spot and throw up a tent or two. In the morning there might be a hundred people within 25 feet of you. These meadows around us? They used to be full of parked cars and tents. There were cars parked along the roads. *In* the roads. People's tent ropes actually crossed. We joked about sharing tent pegs. People would hang blankets around their site for a little bit of privacy. Let's face it. You can only put so much peanut butter between two slices of bread."

Things are much better now, with reserved campsites, and shuttle buses that eliminate a lot of the cars. But it's still crowded.

"What we have here," Richard Riegelhuth, chief of resources management, told me, "is an old park, with tremendous scenery and a marvelous climate, near heavily populated areas, and it's being loved to death. That's not the kind of threat you can do much about.

"Another thing that sometimes frustrates resource managers is the way funds are allocated. A couple of years ago we found a peregrine falcon nesting on the face of one of our cliffs. I asked for $11,000 to monitor it through the nesting season. The response was, 'Eleven thousand dollars for a *bird?*' At the same time, they'll spend a lot of money to design and build a roadside parking turnout, often at the one spot where it's necessary to cut down a big oak tree.

"You always hear about the big glamour threats," Richard said. "Strip-mining, or nuclear waste repositories. But I think the little things can be serious problems, too. Problems that are going to go on and on, and take real effort and money and imagination to solve."

Effort. Money. Imagination. It will take all three to bring happy solutions to the dilemmas facing the "land of sierras and peaks." Effort to ensure the safety of Old Faithful and the Montana grizzlies; money to preserve and protect Grand Teton; imagination to solve the continuing water problems of Mono Lake. But despite the worries that exist in that splendid part of the country, I like to think, on gloomy days when the problems begin to seem insolvable, that maybe somewhere in the sunshine of Idaho there's a golden eagle with dim memories of gentle human hands, climbing thermals into a clean blue sky.

*G*rand Teton, at 13,766 feet the highest peak in its namesake park, rears above Lake Solitude at the head of Cascade Canyon. Snowfields lingering into September on shaded slopes feed this backcountry tarn, a ten-mile trek from the nearest road. Even isolated places such as this feel the pressure of large numbers of visitors; some 80,000 people a year hike the canyon trail, and rangers estimate that 20,000 of them reach Lake Solitude. In the early 1970s, when the fragile alpine environment showed signs of overuse, the Park Service closed camping sites here. Now, with only day use allowed, the area is recovering.

uck-and-rail fence wanders about a onetime cowboy's cabin in a grove of aspens; today the rustic structure serves as a stable and tack room for horses that transport tools and supplies for trail maintenance. The Park Service tries to acquire similar inholdings—islands of private land—inside Grand Teton; development outside presents a far greater threat. Housing projects such as the one advertised at bottom mushroom on the park's fringes. The roar of jetliners using Jackson Hole Airport (below) echoes for miles across the rugged landscape. The federal government has imposed some restrictions on aircraft noise and overflights of the park.

String Lake mirrors the grandeur of peaks known as the Cathedral Group on a peaceful August morning in Grand Teton. Lodgepole pines, interspersed with aspens, cover the lower slopes. Financier John D. Rockefeller, Jr., thought the Tetons "quite the grandest and most spectacular mountains I have ever seen." Much of the park consists of land he purchased in the 1920s and donated to the federal government. Below, an American white pelican cruises the Oxbow Bend of the Snake River, a few miles downstream of Jackson Lake. Flocks of these large water birds nest to the north in Yellowstone National Park. Pelicans may fly more than a hundred miles a day in search of the fish they feed their young.

olumn of boiling water jets 130 feet above an icy landscape as the world's best-known geyser, Old Faithful, erupts in Yellowstone National Park. Algae—microscopic plants—color terraces (left) and fluted mounds (below) of snowy calcium carbonate deposited by Mammoth Hot Springs a few miles inside the park. Only 5 miles from Yellowstone's western edge, and 13 miles from Old Faithful, lies Island Park Geothermal Area in Targhee National Forest. Developers would like to tap the water and steam of its hot springs to generate electricity, but so far the Forest Service has denied their lease applications.

FOLLOWING PAGES: Steam from Lower Geyser Basin creates a billowy backdrop for bison grazing near the Firehole River.

*E*legance
afloat, a trumpeter swan
glides past snowy banks of
the Yellowstone River.
Millions of these birds
once existed throughout
North America. Hunted
commercially for feathers,
the species nearly
vanished; by 1931 only
35 known birds remained
in the lower 48. Now
protected, their numbers
have risen to about 1,500,
but they no longer
migrate. Yellowstone's hot
springs and geysers keep
many streams ice-free,
making winter more
tolerable for elk and
grizzlies as well as swans.

201

*S*pellbound visitors observe and photograph a moose as it feeds in a Yellowstone meadow. Large animals such as moose, elk, and grizzlies provide one of the park's greatest attractions, but the increasing numbers of people who come to see them disturb both the animals and the habitats essential to their existence. Below, scientists from federal and state agencies examine a tranquilized grizzly and her two cubs; the mother wears a radio collar that enables the researchers to track her movements. They trapped her after she killed at least four sheep on leased grazing lands outside the park. The study team later flew the bears by helicopter to a remote area of Yellowstone and released them.

Thundering over the Upper Falls (opposite), the Yellowstone River plummets 308 feet into the Grand Canyon of the Yellowstone. Downriver, a rainbow arcs through mist rising from the Lower Falls. Drawn by such scenic beauty, by wildlife, and by geysers and hot springs, 20,000 people visit Yellowstone National Park on a typical summer day.

asalt-topped cliffs rise 800 feet above the Snake River in southwestern Idaho's Snake River Birds of Prey Area. Here, craggy ledges provide homes for 800

pairs of raptors, including prairie falcons and golden eagles. Since 1971, the Department of the Interior has protected nesting sites along the river; however, irrigated fields of sugar beets, potatoes, and other crops on privately owned land bordering the banks (above) have displaced ground squirrels, rabbits, and gophers the birds eat. In 1975 the BLM began a four-year study of the birds and stopped processing applications for homesteading in the research area. In 1980 the Secretary of the Interior proposed the establishment of a national conservation area incorporating 483,000 acres of public land, enough to guarantee sufficient nesting sites and prey. By mid-1984, Congress had not yet acted on the proposal.

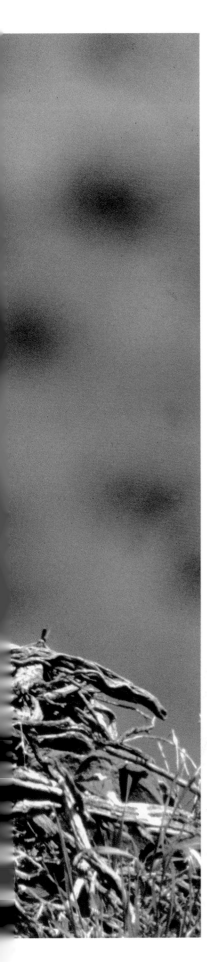

*S*ettling onto its nest, a ferruginous hawk brings a Townsend ground squirrel to its young. Carcasses of other ground squirrels litter the mound of branches. Rappelling to a ledge a hundred feet above the Snake River, BLM research leader Michael Kochert (right) lifts a seven-week-old golden eagle from its aerie for examination, weighing, and banding. Too young to fly, the eight-pound bird (below) already displays a strong beak and sharp talons. Researchers engaged in this study of raptors—perhaps the most intensive ever undertaken— have determined that a number of hawks, eagles, and falcons banded as nestlings in the Snake River Birds of Prey Area have returned there to raise their own young.

*D*rums of poisons—hazardous industrial wastes—await burial in a huge trench on private land near Birds of Prey. Crates behind a truck (opposite, upper) hold transformers contaminated by dangerous chemicals known as PCBs. More than 90 percent of the wastes at this 120-acre landfill (opposite, lower) come from outside Idaho. In 1983 the Environmental Protection Agency fined the operating company $194,000 for violations including illegal burial of liquid wastes, and ordered it to clean up the site and improve safety procedures. EPA, state, and county officials have increased their monitoring activities here. Toxic waste disposal has become one of the nation's most critical environmental problems—and one of the hardest to solve.

*C*raggy slopes catch the sun's last rays above St. Mary Lake in Glacier National Park, an ice-carved wonderland in the Rockies of northwestern Montana. "No words can describe the grandeur and majesty of these mountains," said conservationist George Grinnell, an early proponent of the park. Created in 1910, Glacier encompasses 1,584 square miles of jumbled peaks, glaciated valleys, countless waterfalls, and more than 650 snow-fed lakes. Called "absolutely unfit for cultivation or habitation" during a Senate debate on its establishment, the park now feels the squeeze of commercial interests that increasingly crowd its perimeter. Oil and gas extraction, logging, coal mining, housing construction, and ski resorts could have irreversible impacts on its environment. A federal study in 1980 listed Glacier as our most threatened national park.

213

*H*igh adventure: Steep terrain and an approaching storm confront hikers on the Highline Trail in Glacier. Below, the group listens as park naturalist Bob Jacobs describes plant and animal life along the way. A hiker's paradise, Glacier boasts nearly 750 miles of trails through some of America's most dramatic scenery. At upper elevations, 50 glaciers—remnants of the Ice Age—still scour and shape the land as they recede. Rocky Mountain bighorn sheep (bottom) race across the snowy surface of Swiftcurrent Glacier.

Like phantoms, evergreens emerge from clouds in one of Glacier's high forests. Fierce winds have twisted branches into grotesque shapes. Conifers dominate the park's rumpled landscape, though vegetation zones range from prairie at the lowest elevations to alpine meadows on the upper slopes, where wild flowers burst forth in profusion during the brief, three-month growing season. Bright yellow blossoms of glacier lilies (below) unfold during snowmelt in June. The plants' starchy bulbs make good eating for the park's 200 resident grizzly bears. Glacier and Yellowstone— and adjacent wild lands— are among the few areas within the lower 48 states where the threatened grizzly still roams.

*F*orest primeval: Trees remain safe from the chain saw in hundred-acre Ross Creek Cedar Grove, a virgin stand of western conifers and giant red cedars—many of them more than 400 years old—in Kootenai National Forest. Old-growth timber provides ideal habitat for a variety of wildlife. The female spruce grouse (above) will hatch a brood of 8 to 12 in a nest she builds on the forest floor. The Kootenai encompasses more than two million acres of mountainous woodlands in Montana and Idaho. The government sells timber on 10 percent of the forest to logging companies.

PRECEDING PAGES: Scorched skeletons of Douglas firs frame a mountaintop view of the Kootenai. The Cabinet Mountains command the horizon. The Forest Service uses controlled burns and timber harvesting to create conditions once caused naturally by wildfires. Clear-cutting by commercial loggers, however, takes big bites out of this mixed forest of larch, pine, spruce, and fir.

221

$\mathcal{A}$ mid spires of evergreens, a diesel-powered drill bores for copper and silver in the Cabinet Mountains Wilderness, 95,000 acres in the heart of Kootenai National Forest. On the drill rig, John Balla (above, at center), an exploration manager for a company called ASARCO, checks core samples brought up from a depth of more than 300 feet. A cross section of the two-inch cylinder reveals quartz flecked with blue bornite—iron sulfide containing copper and traces of silver. Mineral exploration in Cabinet Mountains has outraged conservationists, who argue that mining conflicts with the intended purpose of a designated wilderness, defined by Congress in the Wilderness Act of 1964 as a pristine area "where man himself is a visitor who does not remain." The act specifically allows exploration and development of valid existing claims as long as the wilderness character of the area is maintained.

*M*other moose and her month-old twin calves canter through a clearing in the Kootenai. Researcher Randy Matchett (opposite) tracks their movements with a radio receiver that picks up signals transmitted from a collar around the cow's neck. Such studies permit biologists to learn how logging affects moose habitat. In winter moose usually retreat to high, heavily wooded slopes; in summer they descend to lakes and streams, wading chest-deep in the water to feed on aquatic plants. In open areas such as the one below—clear-cut years ago and slowly growing back—they find twigs, leaves, bark, and shrubs to browse. Data on their behavior help the Forest Service to minimize the impact of logging on the Kootenai's 1,500 moose.

Their bark startlingly white against deep forest greens, slender aspens encircle a marshy pond. Kootenai Indians, former inhabitants of these wet woodlands, lived a bountiful life fishing for trout, hunting game, and gathering wild foods such as sweet strawberries (below), huckleberries, and currants. Today people fish and hunt here for sport. Hikers, campers, boaters, snowmobilers, and cross-country skiers also enjoy the recreational offerings of the Kootenai. Forest Service employees work to accommodate visitors as well as to manage and protect resident wildlife. Adhering to the concept of multiple use, they also oversee logging, mining, and other resource development. The need to balance often divergent activities and to set priorities presents a continuing challenge to the staffs of all the national forests.

Reflecting a blue California sky, Mono Lake spreads beneath snow-draped peaks of the Sierra Nevada. Negit Island, an ancient volcanic crater, wears a crusty ring of alkali deposited as the mineral-laden waters of the lake receded. Mono Lake supports few life-forms besides tiny brine shrimp, chief food of the 40,000 California gulls that nest here each spring. In recent years the number of fledglings has declined drastically, and many environmentalists believe the reason lies in the falling water level. Since 1941 the city of Los Angeles has diverted four of the lake's five major feeder streams for domestic use. By 1982 the level of the lake had dropped 46 feet and the salinity of the water had doubled. Heavy spring runoff in 1983 and 1984 caused a rise—at least temporarily.

FOLLOWING PAGES: Completely submerged about 20 years ago, islands of tufa dot Mono Lake. They formed as fresh water bubbled up from springs in the lake bed, mixed with chemicals in the lake, and coalesced into columns of porous calcium carbonate.

229

"*It sways and sings in the wind, clad in gauzy, sun-sifted spray, half falling, half floating...,*" wrote John Muir of ethereal Bridalveil Falls. Plunging 620 feet into Yosemite Valley, its foamy white waters rush toward the Merced River, flooding stream banks during spring thaw (below). Muir first glimpsed the valley in 1869, declaring, "No temple made by hands can compare...." Enthralled by the beauty he found here, Muir spent more than ten years exploring the Sierra Nevada and surrounding ranges. Yosemite National Park, established in 1890, embraces 1,187 square miles of Muir's "glorious wilderness." Naturalist, poet, and guiding light of the early conservation movement, John Muir helped found the Sierra Club, one of many organizations that strive to preserve our natural heritage.

FOLLOWING PAGES: *Weathered over the years, ponderosa pines lie like sleeping giants in an untrodden field of bear clover. As he wandered through the mountains, Muir often stopped in flower-spangled meadows he called "bee pastures" to collect specimens or sketch them in his notebooks. With more than 2.5 million visitors a year, Yosemite today must cope with such people-caused problems as littering, vandalism, and traffic jams. The Park Service has initiated a free shuttle-bus service and has closed some concessions and lodges to help ease congestion.*

*G*ranite ramparts guard the approach to Yosemite Valley from Bridalveil Meadow. On a camping trip here in the spring of 1903, President Theodore Roosevelt and John Muir discussed the need to "preserve remnants of American wilderness." Pioneering conservationists, both recognized the importance of protecting scenic resources—from glacier-carved valleys to fragile wild flowers. The wild hyacinth (top) decorates hillsides from February to May. Exotics have taken hold here, among them sheep sorrel, with red-flecked stalks, and grass of the genus Agrostis (center). Named for famed explorer William Clark, Clarkia rhomboidea opens its showy pink petals at nightfall. The mariposa lily (below) grows from a bulb that Indians roasted as a delicacy.

FOLLOWING PAGES: Like spiders on a thread, two climbers scale the massive face of El Capitan, a granite monolith that soars 3,604 feet above Yosemite Valley. Cut and polished by ancient glaciers, the vertical walls of Yosemite challenge expert climbers from around the world. During good weather, several climbing parties at a time may be seen attempting the sheer rocks of El Capitan.

Land of

Haloed by morning light, spiny teddy bear chollas march across the Sonoran Desert at Cabeza Prieta National Wildlife Refuge in southwestern Arizona.

Sweet-air'd Plateaus

oices. In the enchanted Southwest, I heard them everywhere. Voices of reason, and voices at odds; frustrated voices of environmentalists and developers; eager voices of boaters and birders and biologists; disillusioned voices, talking in the night; ancient voices, speaking from the past in enigmatic scrawls and shards; snarling voices of heavy machinery, stripping coal; and the pure, floating voices of birds and children.

Silence, a kind of voice, pervades the Arizona desert, where the United States Air Force sometimes speaks in hammerblow claps from the sky.

I was sitting in a van with James Fisher, then manager of Cabeza Prieta National Wildlife Refuge in the southwestern part of the state. Only the pinging of the cooling engine broke the quiet. Jim was telling me about Cabeza Prieta, established in 1939 to protect the desert bighorn sheep; it also protects the extremely rare Sonoran pronghorn. "There's only a handful of these pronghorns left," he said, "here and in Mexico. We have a herd of about 125, we think. And probably about 250 bighorn sheep. Though they're both hard to count accurately." He spoke softly, as people do in the desert. "Other wildlife is more numerous. Like it or not, we have six species of rattlesnake here. . . ."

A sonic boom, a double thunderclap that came out of nowhere, lifted me off my seat and rattled the windows. A jackrabbit leaped into the air, did a half gainer, bit himself on the tail, and hit the ground running.

"*Good grief!*" I yelled.

Jim grinned at me. "About a third of the refuge is used by the Air Force as an air-to-air gunnery range, so we get some jet traffic overhead."

Later we saw some of the targets, darts the size of large kites, planted nose first in the desert. They looked, from a distance, like giant silver flowers. One plane tows a target while another shoots at it. The riddled dart is then released to fall in a designated area on the Air Force's range outside the refuge. When one occasionally lands inside, it's because the cable has snapped.

"The Air Force has generally been a good neighbor," Jim said, "and we get along fine with them. There's even some speculation that they help protect the animals, since much of the gunnery range is off limits to visitors. The sonic booms don't seem to bother the sheep or the pronghorns, and the few darts that drop from the sky are unlikely ever to hit anything."

Jim and I spent a couple of days exploring Cabeza Prieta, driving the sandy tracks that pass for roads there. We didn't see any pronghorns or sheep—visitors seldom do—but birds were plentiful. A red-tailed hawk sat in a paloverde tree, whose greenish bark looked hand-polished. Tumbleweeds were smashed against a fence like prisoners desperate to escape. Saguaro cactuses lifted spiny arms, and prickly teddy bear chollas looked deceptively cuddly.

For a while we followed El Camino del Diablo, The Devil's Highway, an early route across the desert to California. Pioneer graves, rimmed with stones, survive there from gold rush days. Between 1850 and 1860 about 20,000 people, mostly prospectors, took this route, and 400 to 600 died in the attempt.

We slept that night under desert stars at Buckhorn Tank, one of twelve water holes used by the bighorn sheep. We awoke to jets screaming into the sunrise and a weather front moving through. Later in the day it kicked up a fierce little dust storm that reduced visibility to a couple of feet and brought fine-grained sand sifting into the van.

Another desert drive offered visibility seemingly to the edge of the world. The Black Rock Desert, a Bureau of Land Management holding in northwestern Nevada, is shaped like a lopsided Y. Its total area is nearly a thousand square miles, and the southern end is an alkaline playa made up of silt—from an ancient lake—that in places is a mile deep. It's possible to drive out onto the playa near Gerlach, turn left, and proceed in a perfectly straight line on a perfectly flat surface for 25 miles. It begins to seem, as the flat playa unrolls like a carpet beneath your wheels, that the car is motionless and the land moving.

"Miles and miles of nothing at all," said Lynn Clemons of the Winnemucca BLM office. As recreation planner, Lynn deals with the diverse voices demanding a piece of the Black Rock. "Environmentalists want the east arm of the desert declared a wilderness area," he told me. "Some want the playa as well. But rock hounds and ORVers don't want us to take any action that will restrict their freedom to drive anywhere they please. History buffs want us to protect the scenic integrity of the old Applegate-Lassen Trail, one of the emigrant routes to California and Oregon. About half of the gold seekers in 1849 used this trail across the Black Rock, and it's essentially unchanged today. Oil, natural gas, and geothermal developers want permits to explore for energy resources. Ranchers don't want anything done that would interfere with their grazing."

The Black Rock's latest controversy involved high-speed vehicles out on the playa. A British team called Project Thrust first attempted to set a new world land speed record there in the fall of 1982. They managed 590 miles an hour, some 30 mph short of the record, and asked to try again in 1983. The Nevada Outdoor Recreation Association, founded in 1958 by former BLM employee Charlie Watson as a public land advocacy group, claimed that rocket cars were inappropriate in such a scenic area and initially protested the issuing of permits. Project Thrust got the go-ahead it needed, and on October 4, 1983, Richard Noble set a new record of 633.468 miles an hour.

"The Bonneville Salt Flats in Utah have been flooded the last few years," said Lynn. "Environmentalists worry that Project Thrust has set a precedent, that the Black Rock playa will soon be filled with rocketing vehicles."

In the playa area, little orange ribbons on stakes marked mining claims. Wild horses ambled in single file across the scrubby flats, and cattle browsed here and there. "This is 60/40 country," said Lynn. "It takes 60 acres to support one cow going 40 miles an hour with her mouth wide open."

In Winnemucca I talked with Gerald Brandvold, BLM area manager. "Eighty-six percent of Nevada is federal land," he told me. "Any one of the six BLM district managers oversees a territory larger than Massachusetts."

But before there was a BLM, there was a GLO—General Land Office—created by Congress in 1812 to handle the disposition of the public domain. Eventually there were 349 land offices in 31 states, though not all were operating at the same time. Business boomed. In his history of the BLM, Marion Clawson, one of its former directors, tells of a young man who worked in a South Dakota land office in the late 19th century: "In the morning, when it was time for the office to open, all the other employees lined up behind the counter. He, being the youngest and most agile, would unlock the outside door for the public to enter, then run back and vault over the counter before he could be trampled underfoot in the ensuing rush. For the whole day, public land-seekers crowded the counter, pushing, shoving, trying to obtain the maps and tract books, shouting, even fighting. . . . And this went on, week after week, without letup." The phrase "doing a land-office business" survives from those days.

In later years, the GLO became riddled with incompetent political appointees and out of step with a changing nation. The Grazing Service, which managed rangelands, also found itself in trouble: A move to increase grazing fees

Defying an early traveler's prediction that much of it would remain "forever unvisited," the rugged, arid Southwest lures millions of visitors each year. The federal government controls the lion's share of the land—ranging from more than four-fifths of Nevada to a third of New Mexico. Those states, along with Arizona and Utah, contain nearly a fourth of all Park Service lands outside Alaska. Their national parks, recreation areas, and other park reserves protect countless scenic, archaeological, and historical treasures. Besides parks, forests, and wildlife refuges, federal lands here include vast BLM holdings such as the Black Rock Desert in Nevada. In the Four Corners area, the public domain encompasses basins, escarpments, and canyons of the Colorado Plateau. The region's principal river, the Colorado, has created America's most acclaimed natural wonder— the Grand Canyon.

in the 1940s so angered ranchers that Congress slashed the service's appropriation—to the point where the agency couldn't function.

Thus was the ground prepared for a new agency, the Bureau of Land Management, established in 1946 to perform the work of both the GLO and the Grazing Service. There are now 11 state BLM offices in the West and Alaska, and 55 district offices. The BLM is responsible for 342 million acres of public land. About 175 million of these are in the lower 48 states, virtually all in the West. Nevada has the biggest block, 48 million of the state's 70 million acres. Large parts of Idaho, Utah, Oregon, Wyoming, California, and Arizona and smaller but still significant portions of Colorado, New Mexico, Montana, Washington, and the two Dakotas are still public domain.

These are the public lands that were left after the homesteaders, railroads, towns, the military, and everyone else had taken their pick—"the lands nobody wanted." The puzzle is: Why? The wealth found on BLM holdings is enormous. About half the nation's coal reserves are in the West, and of that amount 60 percent is on BLM land. Some 10 percent of the known oil and gas reserves, 80 percent of the high-grade oil shale, and 35 percent of the uranium reserves are on public land, in addition to huge deposits of non-energy minerals. About 60 million acres have potential for geothermal development. More than a billion board feet of timber are cut from BLM forests each year, and 21,000 ranchers graze cattle and sheep on 174 million acres of public range. Ninety archaeological and paleontological sites on BLM land are on the National Register of Historic Places. About 20 percent of the country's big game animals—moose, mule deer, and the like—roam public lands. The BLM oversees 17 million acres of wetlands, 15 million acres of riparian habitat, and 4 million surface acres of lakes and reservoirs. More than 200 million visitor-days are recorded on public land each year. It now seems that these are the lands *everybody* wants.

For 30 years after it was established, the BLM functioned without a proper definition of its role. Some 3,000 land-use laws had accumulated over the years, many at cross-purposes, and the BLM was supposed to make sense of them and oversee their application. Not until the passage of the Federal Land Policy and Management Act (FLPMA) in 1976 did the BLM have a clear mandate. FLPMA also settled for the time being a question that had been plaguing Congress: Should the remaining public lands be retained and managed by the federal government—or disposed of? The answer, according to FLPMA: retained.

Though the BLM's budget has been increased and its staff enlarged, its men and women are still thinly scattered over their enormous domain. Another BLM site in Nevada illustrates the problem. Leviathan Cave, named for the huge opening in its roof, lies 7,800 feet up a mountainside south of Ely. It's far away from anywhere, remote even by western standards. People who visit the cave—and there have been only a few hundred since it first became generally known in the 1950s—must want very badly to reach it, for the climb from the sagebrush flats to the entrance can be a grueling, daylong scramble.

I explored Leviathan with some BLM and Park Service people and saw evidence that others had been there before us. The two Indian wickiups—huts—that once stood in the entrance room had been scavenged and used for firewood. In the Pendant Room, with its riotous growth of formations, stalagmites and stalactites had been broken off and hauled away by souvenir hunters.

"It's easy to see the damage that's been done in just the 30 years since the first recorded visit," Wayne Lowman, BLM area manager, told me later. "Obviously, the cave's natural systems can't keep pace with the potential wear and tear of visitors. So the question is: How can the cave be protected and preserved and still be made available for enjoyment by the public? We certainly can't afford to staff it full time. We're considering several options, like restricting the number of visitors or working out special arrangements with user groups."

To some in the BLM, "underground" means more than just caves. In the Southwest, especially, men and women at odds with official Washington quietly work to circumvent policies they see as destructive of the lands they're charged with managing. One of them, a young outdoor recreation planner, agreed to talk with me, but only in his home, after hours.

He talked at length about the BLM, about its traditional conservatism—"It's OK for the staff to belong to the National Rifle Association or to cattlemen's groups, but if I should put a Sierra Club sticker on my car. . . ."—and about how politicized he thought the agency had become. He told me of personnel shuffled about or promoted, either as punishment or reward; of the way district managers emphasize some programs—grazing, for instance—and de-emphasize others—such as recreation—by the judicious shifting of funds. "About a tenth of my time is actually spent on outdoor recreation," he told me. "Recreation is at the bottom of the funding totem pole."

He talked about the process of selecting potential wilderness areas in Utah—a scandal to environmentalists in the Southwest. "In response to FLPMA, it was up to every BLM district outside Alaska to review its holdings for wilderness characteristics and then recommend areas for possible inclusion in the wilderness system. In Utah the BLM did an intensive inventory of more than 5 million acres and in 1980 proposed 2.6 million acres of wilderness study areas. In 1981 conservation groups filed an appeal on almost a million additional acres, and the BLM was ordered to reconsider 825,000 of them. Eventually the study areas totaled 3.1 million acres. The BLM has made a preliminary recommendation that 1.7 million be considered for wilderness designation.

"Why the huge disparity in acreages? One reason is that some managers are more interested in grazing. They're a bunch of vicarious cowboys. Roughly 4 percent of the beef that ends up on American tables comes from cattle that graze on public lands. Yet we spend enormous sums on grazing. We put in water catchments that may cost thousands of dollars apiece and build miles and miles of fencing just to maintain a cowboy culture and tax shelters for the wealthy."

Another BLM employee told me about the role he had played in the controversial inventory. "We'd go out by helicopter every morning, get dropped off at the top of a canyon, and work our way down to the mouth. We saw some terrific country. But the inventory process in Utah went haywire. You have to realize that BLM managers were under a lot of local political pressure at the time. And we were under a lot of pressure to make our recommendations agree with decisions that had already been made. Environmentalists claimed that units were dropped because they were too hilly, or too steep, or too hot. They said one was dropped because it was too flat! There was no vegetative screening on it to provide the 'outstanding opportunity for solitude' the Wilderness Act requires."

Potential wilderness—what the BLM calls a wilderness study area—is open to certain activities such as mineral exploration and development. But the BLM must manage it to preserve its wilderness values until Congress decides if it will receive wilderness designation. "It's a 'Catch-22' situation," said Dick Carter of the Utah Wilderness Association. "The BLM is supposed to protect wilderness values, but it can also allow mineral activity. The real fear environmentalists have is that *Congress* won't consider an area if mineral development has occurred there. Congress can't designate an area as wilderness if it no longer meets the definition set forth in the Wilderness Act."

"What you see in the Arizona Strip exists nowhere else on earth," Sherm Cawley of the Arizona chapter of the Sierra Club told me. "The whole area could be one enormous national park." The Arizona Strip is that section of the state north and west of the Grand Canyon and the Colorado River, about half of it BLM and Forest Service land. "There are two issues there," Sherm said, "wilderness and energy development."

At the eastern end of the Arizona Strip, astride the Utah-Arizona border, I found the Paria Canyon Wilderness Area, perhaps the most spectacular piece of BLM property in the country.

Rod "Skip" Schipper showed me around. Skip had been a summer employee of both the BLM and the Park Service. "The BLM is more casual," he told me. "In the Park Service we had to wear V-neck T-shirts so that little patch of white cotton wouldn't show at our throats. The BLM doesn't worry about that sort of thing." For the last three summers Skip had worked at Paria Canyon.

We strolled one cool November afternoon across sand dunes and sandstone outcroppings, up little ridges and down talus slopes. After a while we came to Skip's favorite part of the canyon, a fantasyland that was outside anything I had ever experienced. Geology had run amok, with a sort of let's-try-everything-once exuberance that was breathtaking. Layers of solid rock dipped and swirled like partially mixed cake batter. There were layers of rock in rainbow tints: green, yellow, pink, red. *Purple!* Over eons, wind and water had played with stone, sculpturing arches and rounding off corners, carving bowls and sanding rough edges. "If I could figure out a way to live here all year, I'd do it," said Skip. I later learned that he has.

I went for a helicopter ride over the Arizona Strip with Pam Hill, public relations representative of Energy Fuels Nuclear, a uranium exploration and mining company. As we racketed across miles of rolling, sagebrush-covered desert, she told me about EFN's interest in the Strip. "We've targeted about 200 spots here where we think we're likely to find uranium," she said.

We circled one of EFN's drill sites—the Pigeon Mine—with its temporary buildings, roads, and single drilling rig. We passed, too, over the rim of Kanab Canyon, part of the Kanab Creek Wilderness Study Area just north of the Grand Canyon. "We had proposed doing some test drilling here. It would have involved drilling a shaft eight feet across and a thousand feet deep. We estimate there are one to three million pounds of high-grade uranium on the site."

An environmental group, the Southwest Resource Council, fought EFN hard on this one, and, even though the company had a legal right to proceed, it decided to wait until Congress had defined the status of Kanab Creek.

In the end, the voice of reason in the Arizona Strip came from Energy Fuels Nuclear. Sherm Cawley told me about it over lunch in Phoenix. "There were about 775,000 acres of potential wilderness in the Strip, the same area where EFN was exploring for uranium. They could see the handwriting on the wall. With conservationists going to war with the BLM, the wilderness selection process was going to drag on and on. So they approached us—a coalition of environmental groups—in the fall of 1982 and said: 'Listen, we're wondering if there isn't a better way to do this. It's going to take *years*. Can't we all sit down together and come to an agreement on which areas should be wilderness and which shouldn't?' And that's what we did. We told them which areas *we* absolutely had to have, and they told us which areas *they* absolutely had to have, and we came to immediate and mutual agreement on two-thirds of them, and managed to work out compromises on the others.

"The bill we prepared for Congress is one of the most important compromises worked out by industry and conservationists. We're very encouraged by the process, and it couldn't have happened without a concerned company."

In April 1984 the House of Representatives passed the Arizona Strip Wilderness Bill, and Senate passage is expected soon. The bill will add 395,000 acres of BLM and Forest Service lands to the wilderness system, and return 675,000 acres to multiple-use status.

Voices become more strident in eastern Utah, where the Department of Energy is investigating the possibility of constructing a repository for nuclear waste on the right flank of Canyonlands National Park. Environmentalists are appalled; most local businessmen are for it; the BLM is trying to walk a tightrope between them; the park is "concerned."

Mary Plumb, young and enthusiastic public affairs officer with the BLM in Moab, began the story for me: "The DOE—Department of Energy—is responsible for finding a place to store high-level nuclear waste from commercial reactors. They've decided that the best solution is to bury it, and they're studying three types of geologic formations: basalt, tuff, and salt. Three salt areas are being considered, and one of them is here at Gibson Dome in the Paradox Basin. In 1978 it became known that they were considering a site on BLM land just 4,000 feet from Canyonlands, and things began to get controversial. Some say the testing the DOE has to do before it can make a final decision will have an impact on the park—noise, drilling rigs, truck traffic, people—and some are arguing that the DOE should be required to do an environmental impact statement. The BLM feels that's not necessary for the temporary testing phase."

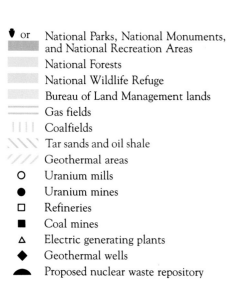

or National Parks, National Monuments, and National Recreation Areas

National Forests

National Wildlife Refuge

Bureau of Land Management lands

Gas fields

Coalfields

Tar sands and oil shale

Geothermal areas

○ Uranium mills

● Uranium mines

□ Refineries

■ Coal mines

△ Electric generating plants

◆ Geothermal wells

◗ Proposed nuclear waste repository

A "profitless locality," Army officer J. C. Ives called the canyon country of the Southwest in 1858. Today the discovery of energy sources such as uranium, coal, gas, and oil—particularly in the Four Corners area and the Arizona Strip—promises profits undreamed of a century ago. Private companies hope to locate and extract natural resources here, primarily on BLM and other federal lands. Profits will not come without controversy and hard choices. Vast coalfields such as Kaiparowits Plateau in Utah and the San Juan Basin in New Mexico, Colorado, and Utah lie next to some of our best known national parks and other wild lands as well. Oil-bearing tar sands underlie parts of the Glen Canyon Recreation Area. Coal mining and power plants have already marred some scenic areas and have polluted once pristine air; uranium mines pit the landscape. Energy projects of all kinds compete with agricultural and urban users for the region's limited water supply.

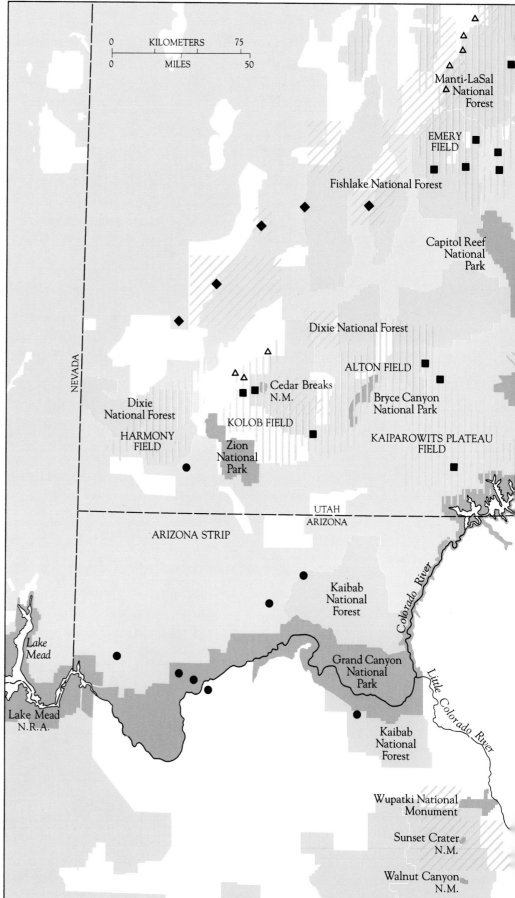

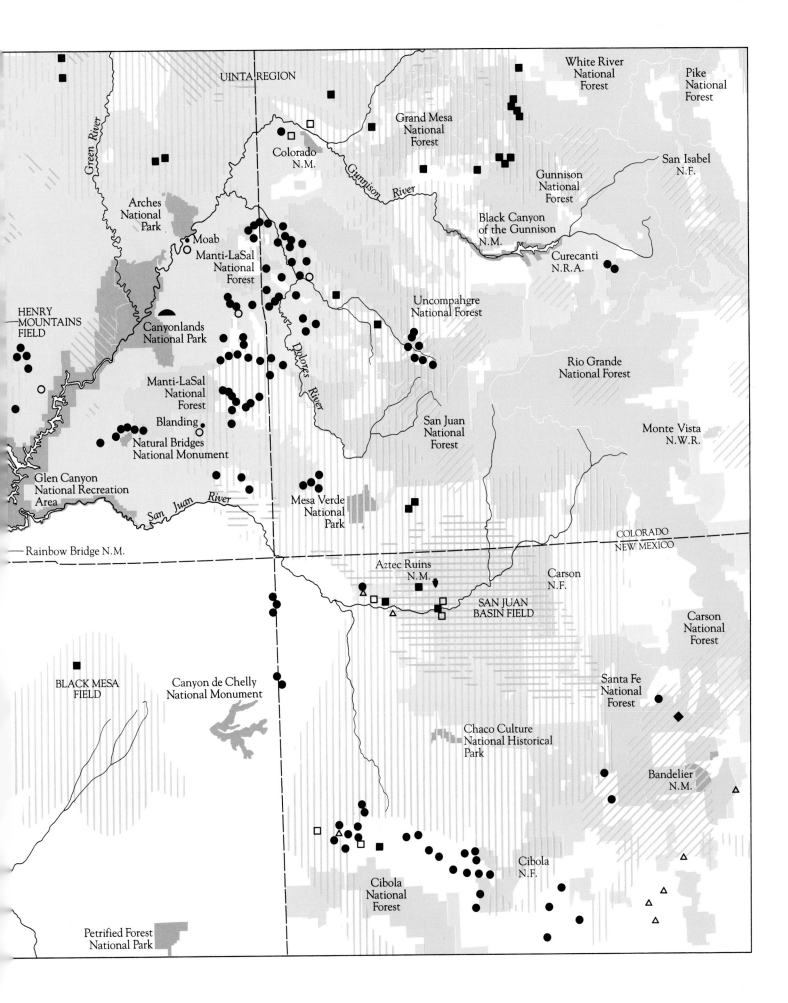

UINTA REGION

White River
National
Forest

Pike
National
Forest

Grand Mesa
National
Forest

Colorado
N.M.

San Isabel
N.F.

Gunnison River

Gunnison
National
Forest

Arches
National
Park

Moab

Black Canyon
of the Gunnison
N.M.

Curecanti
N.R.A.

Manti-LaSal
National
Forest

HENRY
MOUNTAINS
FIELD

Uncompahgre
National
Forest

Rio Grande
National
Forest

Canyonlands
National Park

Dolores River

Manti-LaSal
National
Forest

San Juan
National
Forest

Monte Vista
N.W.R.

Blanding

Natural Bridges
National Monument

Glen Canyon
National Recreation
Area

San Juan River

Mesa Verde
National
Park

COLORADO
NEW MEXICO

Rainbow Bridge N.M.

Aztec Ruins
N.M.

Carson
N.F.

Carson
National
Forest

SAN JUAN
BASIN FIELD

BLACK MESA
FIELD

Canyon de Chelly
National Monument

Santa Fe
National
Forest

Chaco Culture
National Historical
Park

Bandelier
N.M.

Cibola
National
Forest

Cibola
N.F.

Petrified Forest
National Park

If approved, the storage facility would be under construction for five to seven years, employing a work force of around 1,800 during that time and an operating force of 900. "It would be open for 30 years," Mary said, "and then they'd close it up. They're looking at Utah Indian rock art for some kind of symbol they could put on the closed repository so that if someone came along after 2,000 years, there'd be something to tell him that the place was dangerous."

Cal Black, chairman of the San Juan County Commission, favors the repository. "I don't say there are no risks involved," he told me, "but if the studies show that the area is geologically and technologically suitable, and transportation and safety questions can be addressed satisfactorily, then I say go ahead. For two reasons: It would be good for the community economically, and nuclear energy is the power source of the future. We've been mining and milling uranium here for many years; why shouldn't we put it back in the ground here? Like somebody said, if the park's the problem, then move the park."

Rather than move the park, Gordon Anderson, Colorado Plateau representative of Friends of the Earth, supports a plan that would enlarge it and take in the site of the repository. "The boundaries should be moved back to encompass the whole rim-to-rim ecosystem, which is the case at the Grand Canyon." He ticked off some of the threats to the area the repository represents. "Much of the construction activity would be heard within the park, and from certain overlooks you would see the railroad used to haul the waste to the site. That railroad would cross the Colorado, so think what a spill there would do."

The DOE is taking a hard look at both the location and the management of the repository. It's studying the aquifer—the water-bearing stratum—to see if there is any possibility of contamination. It's exploring ways to contain and control the pile of excavated salt, which would be 32 feet high and cover 50 acres. And it's developing storage canisters that will last a thousand years.

Pete Parry, superintendent of Canyonlands, can only express concern to the DOE about impacts on the park; most of the activity will be outside its boundaries. "The silence in the park's backcountry is overwhelming," he told me. "It's like being in a soundproof room. Obviously, 1,800 workmen drilling and blasting less than a mile away would affect that. And to study the underground hydrology, scientists may have to drill some test holes *within* the park. We won't like it, but it may be one of those issues of national security that takes precedence over everything else."

According to Sam Taylor, editor of the Moab *Times-Independent*, Moab residents favor continued testing by two to one. "People here feel that they have been betrayed by the Park Service. When the park was first pushed, back in the early '60s, people had visions of tourist dollars pouring in. The Park Service published a booklet proposing paved roads to visitor centers in the park, trails, campgrounds, restaurants, boat-launching facilities, lodging. But in 1977 the Park Service decided to leave the park undeveloped. Last year there were 100,000 visitors to the park, 400,000 short of what was projected for ten years ago. So people here in Moab feel they are being asked to jeopardize their economic future to protect a park that has contributed to the woeful state of their economic past. No wonder they're fed up."

The Department of Energy won't make its final site selection before 1987, and anytime between now and then it may drop Gibson Dome from consideration. Or it may not.

Northeast of Tucson, Arizona, along a stream few people have heard of and even fewer have seen, voices become agitated. The 630-mile-long Gila River, which rises in southwestern New Mexico, writhes like a sidewinder across southern Arizona to join the Colorado near Yuma. A 15-mile-long canyon in its midsection—the Gila River Box—is being considered for inclusion in the wilderness system. Rafters float the stream in spring; ORVers drive its bed in summer during low water; birders come, especially to its tributary Eagle Creek, to watch for rare black hawks; the BLM manages it for multiple use, which includes grazing and mining; and the Army Corps of Engineers has its eye on a possible site for a dam that would halt downstream flooding.

I floated the Gila with Jim Blair and Arizona environmentalist Thor Lane, and I remember mostly the birds. There was never a time during the daylight hours of the three-day trip when I couldn't hear birds. They chirped in bushes and sang from cliffs, warbled in treetops and whistled along the banks. Swallows backed out of their cliffside nests like little feathered cars.

Tamarisk and mesquite grew along the banks, and wild flowers bloomed on sandy terraces and among pale driftwood. Little brown lizards darted across the hot sand like blown leaves. The river was full of grit and twigs.

A poisonous Gila monster, an appropriate sight on the Gila River, moved along the bank. It was maybe 18 inches long and lumbered over rocks and logs like Godzilla. We stopped and surrounded it. It seemed to be made up of parts from other animals: face of a turtle, tongue of a snake, eyes of a cat. It had a blunt tail shaped like a hot dog. Its skin was patterned with orange and black bumps, like BBs. When it tired of our attention, it dozed off, its slow pulse thumping at its throat.

Along the Gila River, voices ricochet like rifle bullets off canyon walls. Steve Knox, BLM wilderness coordinator: "There are so darn many uses for the Gila Box, and unfortunately they conflict. We originally recommended a portion of the Gila Box for wilderness status, but we knew we had ORV use there, and we decided that use was significant. A wilderness designation would preclude use by ORVers. We feel we can manage the area for both ORV use and wilderness uses such as hiking and rafting. So we changed our minds and recommended nonwilderness."

Tony Goodman, who makes and sells ORVs in Safford: "There's not one thing we damage up there. Nothing. I've been going up the Gila since I was 15. If they make it a wilderness area, they'll have to lock me out."

Heaton Underhill, senior research scientist with the Park Service: "The main problem with multiple-use management in this area has been overgrazing. There's no question it's been overgrazed. Look at those hillsides! Cattle eat the young cottonwood sprouts, so the cottonwoods, which are vital habitat for birds, are disappearing. There are no cottonwoods along this stretch of the Gila less than 40 years old."

Les Rosenkrance, BLM district manager: "I don't see anything in the Gila Box that isn't protected under existing law. We can protect the hawks and other wildlife by careful management, by doing some cottonwood replanting, by closing the area during critical nesting periods. Everybody seems to get in an adversary role. The Gila Box is ideal for multiple use. You've got rafters who can use it only during high water, ORVers who can use it only during low water. They *can't* use it at the same time."

Dan Fischer of the Safford District BLM Public Lands Advisory Council: "I don't like to see federal issues influenced by local pressures. The BLM office in Safford is full of good and informed people, but they get a lot of pressure from locals. These are federal lands and they should be federally managed. Les

Rosenkrance says he can close the area during critical times, but the next district manager may be less sensitive to the total environment."

W. L. Minckley, professor of zoology at Arizona State University: "The Gila is significant because it provides a transition corridor between the Chihuahuan and the Sonoran Deserts. Stabilization by damming spells death for rivers of this kind. They need flash floods to eliminate exotic plants and animals and to enhance native species. Damming changes them so much that the native biota is largely displaced. There are only two or three of these wild desert rivers left, and I think we can afford to protect 15 miles of one."

Bob Witzeman of the Audubon Society: "Dams proposed for the Gila are outrageous pork-barrel travesties to provide more water for more of the same kinds of surplus crops that we now pay people not to grow."

Charlie Watson of the Nevada Outdoor Recreation Association: "The BLM nonwilderness recommendation is a death sentence for the Gila Box."

Les Rosenkrance: "I'm not going to argue with you, Charlie. Your mind is made up."

Across the line in New Mexico, the voices are confused. I'm convinced that no one in the country has fully grasped all the conflicting interests, environmental predicaments, state and federal laws and regulations—complications surrounded by entanglements in labyrinths of convolutions —involved in the coal-leasing situation in that state.

Simply put, the San Juan Basin, which extends from northwestern New Mexico into Colorado and Utah, is an area of some 26,000 square miles of largely BLM, state, and Navajo land. Within it are three wilderness study areas; about a thousand fossil-rich sites where paleontologists pick and probe; some 250,000 archaeological sites associated with the last 12,000 years of Native American history in the area; Chaco Culture National Historical Park; and two billion tons of coal, some of which will soon be leased for strip-mining.

One of the BLM wilderness study areas, the Bisti, is an otherworldly landscape of bizarre shapes—badlands eroded and carved from beds of shale and sandstone. Just to the south is an area called the Fossil Forest, and I visited it with a BLM paleontologist, Mike O'Neill. Petrified wood lay scattered about, and from the flanks of sandstone mounds and hillocks protruded the bones of long-vanished creatures.

"The San Juan Basin is important to a paleontologist because it's one of the few places in the world where there is almost complete continuity of geologic structures," said Mike. "You can start south of here and walk north through the Cretaceous period—the age of dinosaurs—and into the Paleocene epoch, the beginning of the age of mammals."

One of Mike's duties with the BLM is to devise "mitigation procedures"—methods of lessening the impacts of mining on the fossil beds. "Most of the mitigation will have to be done before the mining begins—survey, inventory, data collection, that kind of thing. Once the mining starts sometime after 1990, blasting will destroy the sequence of deposits, and bulldozers will remove them from their context. We have to consider economic realities: It's not very practical to close down a dragline so a paleontologist can excavate a bone."

But before the coal can be mined, qualified surface owners must be located and their consent obtained. That task, seemingly hopeless, falls to the BLM. Many of the owners are Navajos. I talked with one—Eugene Harrison—at a public meeting in Farmington called by the BLM to answer questions about the proposed coal leasing. He had a handful of maps, brochures, and forms. Eugene and his family may be relocated when the mining begins. There are pluses in that—they would be nearer a highway, a school, a store, and have electricity in their new home—but also minuses. Unmarked Navajo sacred areas and burial sites are scattered throughout the basin. And Eugene would have to give up his home. "The Indians say, 'Why so fast?' The mining companies say, 'Why so slow?' " he told me.

A Navajo named Danny Charlie is employed by the BLM as a Navajo coordinator. "The Harrisons—like a lot of other Navajo families—have been living here for years on public land," he said. "They're in what the BLM calls a 'checkerboard area' because of the different kinds of land ownership. But they've lived there so long they consider the land their own."

Huddled in the midst of all this is Chaco Culture National Historical Park, site of Pueblo Bonito and other archaeological ruins famous throughout the world. Coal mining may occur on three sides of Chaco Canyon. Erosion, air and noise pollution, tremors caused by blasting, truck and rail traffic, power lines—these are only the most obvious worries of the park's managers.

About a thousand years ago, a people skilled in building and pottery developed a harmonious culture in this sun-drenched canyon. They built flat-roofed pueblos beneath the canyon walls, with round, semisubterranean chambers. By the early 1100s some 7,000 people lived here, hunting, trading, and tending a complex irrigation system that watered farmland on the canyon floor. In the mid-1100s they began abandoning Chaco. Drought, erosion, or soil depletion may have made the site uninhabitable, and by the late 1200s the canyon had been returned to the silent desert and the endless sun.

In a cold wind near Pueblo Bonito, I sat and talked with park archaeologist Randy Morrison, now with the Bureau of Indian Affairs in Arizona.

"It appears now that Chaco Canyon, with its 3,700 sites, is merely the center of a far-flung Chacoan culture," he told me. "In the last few years we've been discovering roads the Indians built to other sites. At first we tried to fit them into neat packages, theorizing that they just went to 'resource areas'—forests or quarries. But it's clear now that they went much farther; in fact, went to *places*. Some portions were beautifully constructed, paved with cobblestones, complete with gutters. They run to other communities, right up to big houses, in one side and out the other. We've found about 90 of these communities in the San Juan Basin, an area approximately the size of West Virginia. It's as if we just discovered West Virginia with nobody in it."

The roads and their associated communities lie atop great beds of coal.

I prowled the ruins of Chaco, trying to imagine it as it once was—a bustling place, much like a small town today. The wind whistled through doors and windows and around walls. Wooden beams protruded from masonry, and great round chambers, ten feet deep, were filled with mystery and patches of dry grass.

I sat and leaned against a wall in the sunlight, out of the wind, and got out my pen and notebook. A family of Navajo tourists arrived, mom and dad and a clutch of children. They dispersed through the ruins, and I could hear them calling to one another in their melodious tongue. The children were playing hide-and-seek. I thought: Other voices in other days have sounded here before them; other children played noisy games here a thousand years ago. The sunlight shone through the clear plastic of my pen, which, acting as a prism, cast a spectrum of colors onto the white paper in my lap. So, with childish cries echoing off the ancient walls and a sliver of rainbow dancing at my knuckle, I sat in the sun and wrote: *Voices. In the enchanted Southwest, I heard them everywhere.*

FOLLOWING PAGES: *Familiar symbols of the Sonoran Desert, saguaros tower over other cactuses and shrubs at the edge of the Cabeza Prieta Mountains. In the 19th century, traders, settlers, and gold seekers traveled El Camino del Diablo—The Devil's Highway—across this nearly waterless expanse, now part of Cabeza Prieta Refuge. Luke Air Force Range overlies most of the 860,000-acre wildlife preserve on the Arizona-Mexico border. Since its creation in 1939, Cabeza Prieta has protected desert bighorn sheep and rare Sonoran pronghorns.*

"*W*here life is difficult it seems to acquire a higher value." These words of Southwestern writer Edward Abbey could well apply to Cabeza Prieta's plants and animals. Opposite, a male house finch peers from a creosote bush, which responds to moisture with yellow flowers and cottony seed balls. The ocotillo (top, center) sheds its leaves in dry periods. The white prickly poppy grows on sandy valley floors. Showy blooms of buckhorn cholla (top, right) and calico cactus open in spring. A leafcutter ant totes an ocotillo leaf, which it will use to grow the fungus it feeds on.

*D*ropped after gunnery practice, a 16-foot wood-and-aluminum dart target pierces the desert floor at Cabeza Prieta. In another part of the refuge, a yearling bighorn ram and his younger sibling gaze from a rocky slope. Since World War II, servicemen have trained on the gunnery range that takes in Cabeza Prieta. The Air Force believes that aircraft noise —and the few darts that fall here—have no adverse effect on wildlife. By limiting mining, hunting, and off-road vehicle use, the military actually may help preserve the Sonoran habitat. With federal and state agencies and the University of Arizona, the Air Force seeks to develop a management plan for maintaining the environmental integrity of the entire range.

ainbow of banded calcite arches above a visitor at Leviathan Cave in east-central Nevada. A spelunker rappels through the 180-foot-wide opening that gives the cavern its name. Leviathan and other remote caves present special management problems: Inexperienced or ill-equipped visitors may injure themselves or damage delicate rock formations.

PRECEDING PAGES: Dwarfed by Leviathan's huge entrance room—600 feet long—a hiker scales a pile of debris that fell from the ceiling long ago. To preserve the natural values of the area, the BLM recommends wilderness designation for the mountain range in which Leviathan lies.

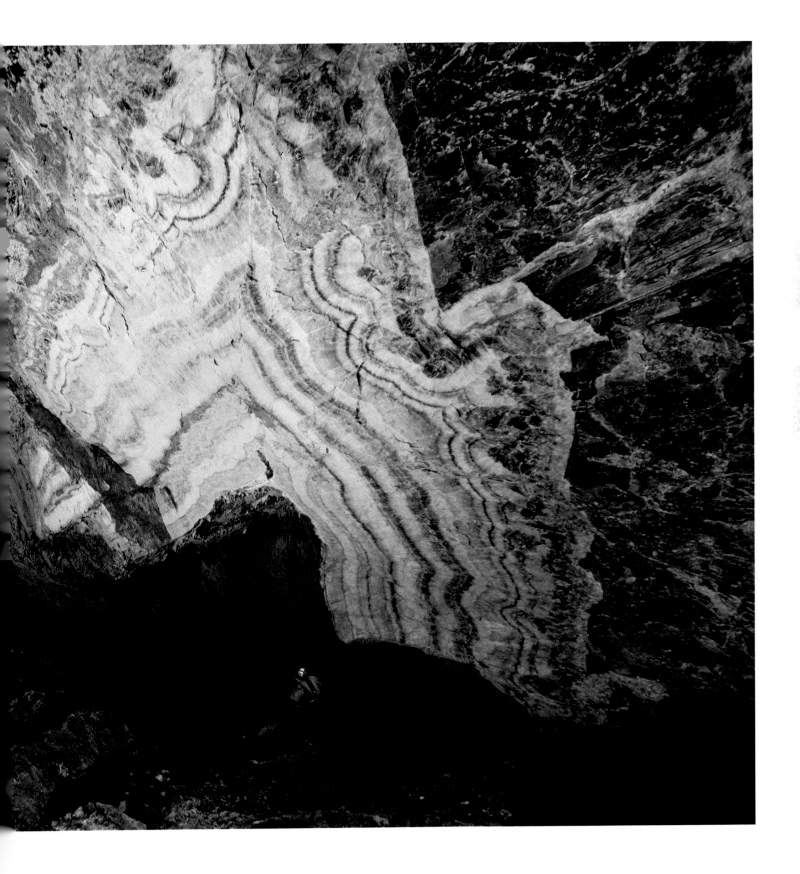

*F*ree as the wind, wild horses gallop across BLM land near the Black Rock Desert in northwestern Nevada. A wary kit fox, mother of seven pups, checks for danger outside her den. Ears pricked, a three-day-old pronghorn kid nestles amid sagebrush. Charged with protecting the animals' habitat, the BLM also must contend with mining, grazing, and other interests seeking to develop the Black Rock. Conservationists fear the impact of such uses on lands being considered for wilderness designation.

FOLLOWING PAGES: Summer rain clouds darken the sky over the Black Rock playa—the dry bed of prehistoric Lake Lahontan.

TONY DIEBOLD (ABOVE AND TOP)

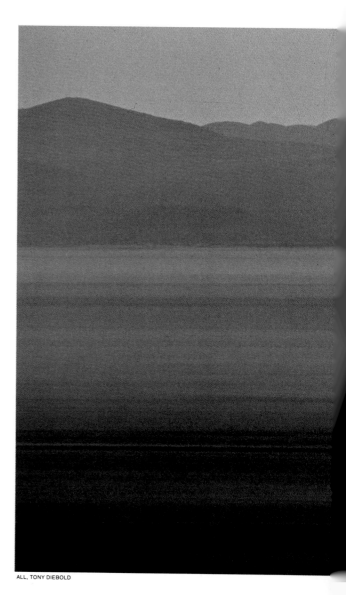

*T*railing plumes of dust and exhaust, Thrust 2 jets across the Black Rock Desert. Before a test run, a crew (above) checks systems in the 4-ton, 34,000-horsepower vehicle. Afterward they inspect them again.

British driver Richard Noble set a world land speed record of 633.468 miles an hour on October 4, 1983. Metal wheels, safer than rubber, cut into the surface of the playa (opposite, bottom), but winter rains erased the tracks. The Black Rock playa is one of only a few known places flat and empty enough for such tests. Environmentalists think the precedent-setting run might bring an influx of cars and ORVs—off-road vehicles—that could damage the terrain.

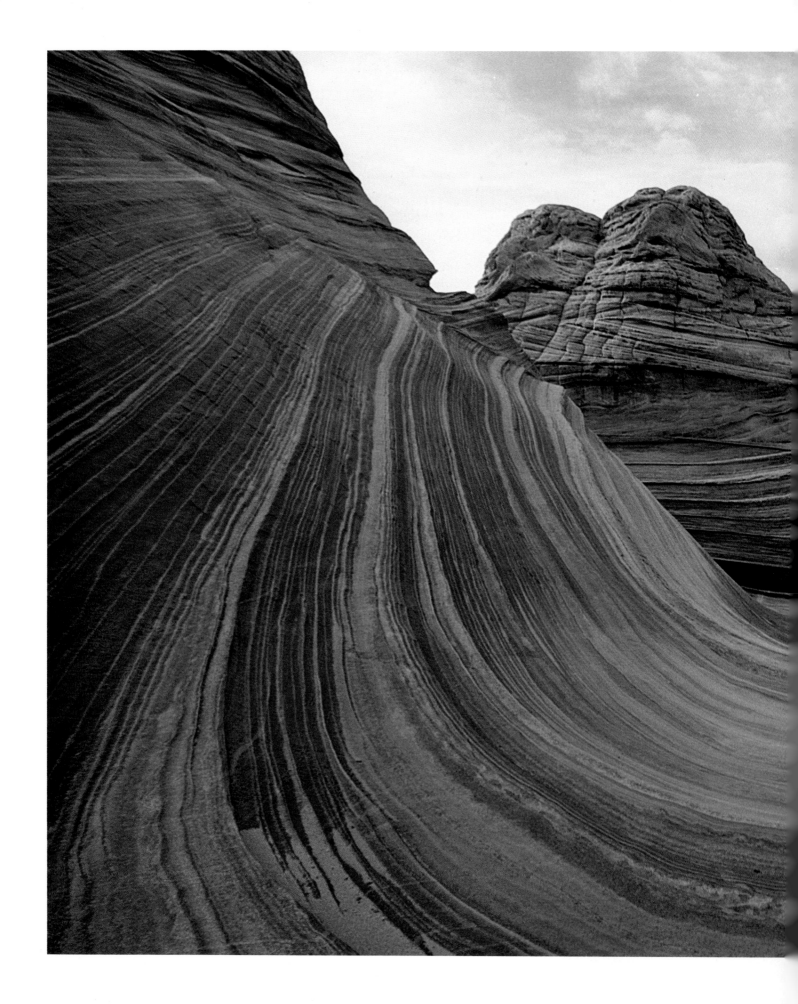

rillers bore for uranium ore at the Pigeon Mine near Kanab Creek, a few miles north of the Grand Canyon in the Arizona Strip. Mining companies active here promise no lasting harm to BLM lands. Environmental groups worry that uranium waste could contaminate groundwater and creeks such as Kanab that flow into the Colorado River.

At another site nearby, miner Jim Pehrson wields a Geiger counter to measure radiation and to grade a load of ore. When processed, the gray-black ore (above) will yield uranium oxide, or yellowcake. Environmentalists and mining and agricultural interests have reached an unusual compromise over public lands in the Arizona Strip. Congress will set aside 675,000 acres here for multiple use—and 395,000 as wilderness.

PRECEDING PAGES: Rising and falling in sinuous curves, sandstone formations epitomize the beauty and solitude of the Southwest's unspoiled lands.

"*It seems as much of heaven as of earth,*" *said naturalist John Burroughs of the Grand Canyon. Sunrise gilds Wotans Throne, seen here from the North Rim. Below, a mule deer browses juniper needles on the South Rim. The mile-deep gorge attracts nearly 2.5 million visitors a year. Besides heavy use, other pressures threaten the 1,218,375-acre national park. A haze of pollution—from copper smelters and coal-burning power plants, and even from Los Angeles— frequently veils once crystal-clear vistas. Hydroelectric interests, urban and agricultural users, wildlife defenders, and white-water boaters engage in a tug-of-war over the waters of the Colorado River. Proposals to build dams right in the heart of the canyon keep resurfacing. "Leave it as it is," President Theodore Roosevelt advised in 1903. "You cannot improve on it. The ages have been at work on it, and man can only mar it."*

*S*tone pestle and mortars ground into bedrock mark where people known as the Salado pounded acorns and beans into meal. They lived along the upper Gila River in eastern Arizona more than 700 years ago. Turbid with spring runoff, the river courses through the Gila Box (opposite), a remote gorge on BLM land. Archaeological sites, a nesting area for raptors, and habitat for rare fish species all lie within the Gila Box, which also attracts rafters and ORV users. Its scales as intricate as Indian beadwork, one of the Gila's namesake ''monster'' lizards makes an unusual daytime appearance. A dam proposed for this section could flood out wildlife habitats and tame one of the last stretches of free-flowing water in Arizona. Many advocate wilderness or wild and scenic river designation for the Gila Box.

DAVID MUENCH

*C*liffside alcove in Utah's Canyonlands National Park shelters ruins of a granary where Anasazi Indians stored their crops. Mostly primitive backcountry, the 337,570-acre park holds a wealth of ancient cliff dwellings and pictographs. Its red sandstone formations include Angel Arch (below); a gigantic figure with folded wings leans against the buttress. The Department of Energy is considering a site less than a mile from the park's eastern boundary for a high-level nuclear waste repository. On a 66,000-acre tract near the western edge, companies hope to extract oil from tar sands.

PRECEDING PAGES: Canyonland's Monument Basin spreads below Grand View Point.

BOTH, DAVID MUENCH

*W*ide eyes and outstretched arms seem to extend a greeting across the centuries in a rock painting found near the Green River in southeast Utah. A snake slithers above the elongated figure, and a fantastic beast hovers to one side. The work at left depicts two humanlike figures. Hunter-gatherers who lived in this area before A.D. 500 probably intended to show beings imbued with supernatural powers. Vandals chiseled out sections of a petroglyph of bighorn sheep (below) in a BLM area near Canyonlands. "One vandal can destroy a painting in a few minutes," says Polly Schaafsma, noted authority on rock art. A greater threat may come with coal mining and other development in the region. Schaafsma adds, "Bulldozers destroy on a broad scale."

Casa Rinconada reveals architectural skills of a culture that reached its zenith in Chaco Canyon during the 12th century. The 63-foot-wide structure in Chaco Culture National Historical Park in northwestern New Mexico served as a ceremonial center for the Anasazi people. Below, wooden joists called vigas protrude from a carefully crafted masonry wall at Pueblo Bonito.

PRECEDING PAGES:
Beneath a sheer mesa wall, Pueblo Bonito fans out over two and a half acres. Strip-mining here in the San Juan Basin could destroy ruins of outlying communities and threaten Pueblo Bonito itself with massive erosion.

old bands of sandstone and darker shale stripe the Bisti Badlands in New Mexico's San Juan Basin. Uranium, oil, gas, and billions of tons of coal lie beneath the region, once a lush river delta where dinosaurs roamed. Fossil beds here provide data about events that led to the disappearance of dinosaurs and the dominance of mammals. Now mining corporations compete with scientists to unearth the treasures of this eerie landscape.

A particularly rich area called the Fossil Forest has yielded remains of several prehistoric animals new to science. BLM paleontologist Mike O'Neill (below) uses a brush and probe to expose a limb bone of a large dinosaur. He and his colleagues work to develop faster, more efficient salvage techniques before the fossils fall victim to coal operations by the end of the century. Opponents say mining would consume quantities of scarce water, and they doubt the land could ever be reclaimed. Even if it could, New Mexico would have lost some of the strange rock formations that helped earn it the nickname "Land of Enchantment."

ouble spans of Grosvenor Arch soar 152 feet on BLM land in southern Utah. Below, water spills over Navajo sandstone on its way to the Virgin River in Zion National Park. Coal mining proposed for the area may encroach on Zion and other natural treasures.

FOLLOWING PAGES: Limestone hoodoos in Utah's Bryce Canyon National Park glow in late afternoon sunlight. Mining companies want to strip the Alton coalfield near the southern boundary of Bryce, one of the most spectacular of the Southwest's red-rock canyon regions.

290

Glinting in the sunset, Pacific waters recede from craggy sea stacks and a wave-carved arch along a deserted coastal stretch in Washington's Olympic National Park.

Land of

the Western Sea

"This we know. The earth does not belong to man; man belongs to the earth. This we know. . . . Man did not weave the web of life, he is merely a strand in it. Whatever he does to the web, he does to himself." These words are attributed to Chief Seattle, a friend to early settlers around Puget Sound. He understood the subtle marriage of man and nature, as did other Native Americans. Whites, by and large, had to be taught.

An early teacher, George Perkins Marsh, published a landmark book called *Man and Nature* in 1864, two years before the death of Chief Seattle. In it he defined the principles of what we now call ecology—the interrelationship of living things and their environment. More than a century ago he wrote, ". . . the earth is fast becoming an unfit home for its noblest inhabitant." He abhorred the destruction of the natural world: ". . . man is everywhere a disturbing agent. Wherever he plants his foot, the harmonies of nature are turned to discords." Gifford Pinchot called the book "epoch-making," and historian Lewis Mumford considered it "the fountainhead of the conservation movement."

The history of that movement in the United States is largely a history of people, articulate students of man and nature. Thoreau and Emerson saw the handiwork of the Creator in nature, and John Burroughs approached nature with "sympathy and tenderness." John James Audubon's monumental works on the birds and quadrupeds of North America delighted and inspired generations of budding naturalists. Geologist John Wesley Powell introduced Americans to the harsh beauty of the arid West. George Bird Grinnell edited the magazine *Forest and Stream*, which in 1886 proposed an "Audubon Society," and founded, with Teddy Roosevelt and others, the Boone and Crockett Club to promote the study, protection, and controlled hunting of wild game. Elliott Coues, a founder of the American Ornithologists' Union, produced nearly a thousand papers and monographs on wildlife. The eloquent Joseph Wood Krutch was, in the words of critic Mark Van Doren, "a prophet crying in the wilderness of man's brutality to the very world on which his own existence depends." William Beebe, explorer of the ocean depths, linked the past and present: Born 12 years after the Civil War, he lived to befriend Rachel Carson, author of *The Sea Around Us* and *Silent Spring*. In 1949 Aldo Leopold wrote in his classic *Sand County Almanac*, "We abuse land because we regard it as a commodity belonging to us. When we see land as a community to which we belong, we may begin to use it with love and respect." These spiritual descendants of Chief Seattle, and many others, raised the consciousness of Americans to the beauty and fragility of their land.

But to send soldiers into the field—and the courtroom—to fight the actual battles, organization was needed. The 1984 *Conservation Directory*, published by the National Wildlife Federation, lists more than 1,500 international, national, and state organizations, commissions, agencies, and citizens' groups that are concerned with the use and management of natural resources.

Probably the best known is the Sierra Club, founded in 1892 primarily for the exploration of the Sierra Nevada. Today its 350,000 members "explore, enjoy, and work to protect the wild places of the earth." A related but independent organization, the Sierra Club Legal Defense Fund, represents the club and other clients in environmental court cases.

Defenders of Wildlife—established in 1925 as the Anti-Steel-Trap League—works for the welfare of wild animals. Protection of wildlife habitat is a priority of the National Wildlife Federation, formed in 1936. The first has 57,000 members; the second, more than four million, mostly hunters and fishermen.

Two renowned naturalists, Aldo Leopold and Robert Marshall of the

Forest Service, helped found the Wilderness Society in 1935. For years it promoted legislative protection of wild areas, and was largely responsible for the passage of the Wilderness Act in 1964. Today its 105,000 members keep an eye on Congress and federal agencies as the selection of wilderness areas proceeds.

Organized in 1970, the 46,000-member Natural Resources Defense Council combines legal action, scientific research, and citizen education in its efforts to conserve the nation's resources and improve environmental quality. NRDC concentrates on issues such as land use, nuclear safety, and pollution.

The exclamation point of Earth First! suggests the radical tactics of that organization, founded in 1980. Its 7,000 members engage in civil disobedience, which in their case may involve illegal and even dangerous interference with development. The group's slogan—"No compromise in the defense of Mother Earth!"—rallies members to construction sites, where they lie in front of bulldozers or chain themselves to trucks.

The Nature Conservancy, established in 1951, identifies what it calls "ecologically significant natural areas" and often safeguards them through direct acquisition. Though it sometimes transfers lands to state and federal agencies, it manages more than 700 preserves itself. Set up in 1973, the Trust for Public Land finds ways to protect and expand parklands and other open spaces. Unlike the Nature Conservancy, its parent organization, the Trust always looks to public agencies to acquire and manage lands it has saved. Earthwatch, formed in 1970, has come up with a new approach: For a fee, citizens can participate as assistants in scientific research projects.

Although the interests of these and other organizations encompass the globe and everything on it, each group is intimately involved in the protection of our federal estate. Each, too, might take as its motto a statement by Allen H. Morgan of the Massachusetts Audubon Society: "What we save now is all we will ever save."

Chief Seattle would understand and agree. Near his homeland in the far northwest, across Puget Sound from Seattle, the Olympic Peninsula juts like a thumb from the corner of the country. On it, in five sections totaling 650,000 acres, is Olympic National Forest. It's shaped roughly like a big doughnut, with a few bites taken out, and in the middle is Olympic National Park, with Mount Olympus, nearly 8,000 feet high, at its center.

If, in Wisconsin, it had rained as if the world would end, on the Olympic Peninsula it rained as if the world *had* ended. Perpetual gray drizzle seeped from leaden skies as I explored. Horses steamed like lobsters in their paddocks, and sea gulls stood hunched and dripping in the lee of boulders. Some places here, especially on high western slopes, receive more than 200 inches of rain a year. That's more than 16 *feet!*

The Wilderness Society has long been interested in the area. When I spoke with Jean Durning, director of the northwest regional office, she was proud of the Washington State Wilderness Act. It will add about a million acres of Washington's national forest lands to the wilderness system, of which 93,000 acres are in Olympic National Forest.

But other issues worry Jean. Small hydroelectric projects proposed for the peninsula's many rivers might harm salmon and steelhead runs. In the national forest, "excessive attention is given to timber harvesting, especially stands of old growth." Clear-cutting, which the Forest Service calls "even-aged management," prevails on the Olympic Peninsula. "Douglas fir, the most common valuable tree around here, doesn't regenerate in shade; new seedlings need

Sea stacks and mountain peaks, glaciers and forests—all lie within federal lands on or near the coasts of Washington, Oregon, and California. With their magnificent scenery and great natural wealth, these areas have remained battlegrounds for conservationists and developers since the mid-1800s. Today federal holdings here preserve a lush rain forest on Washington's Olympic Peninsula, centuries-old redwoods in California, and herds of sea mammals in that state's Channel Islands. Providing open space for urban dwellers, Congress established San Francisco's Golden Gate National Recreation Area, one of the world's largest parks in a major metropolitan region. Olympic ranks among the most productive national forests, and virgin wilderness survives in Oregon's Siskiyou. Rugged mountains plunge to the sea in the BLM's King Range National Conservation Area.

space where there's sunshine to thrive. So the loggers clear-cut. Fortunately, the Forest Service now usually restricts clear-cuts to no more than 60 acres. But southeast of the park a special hundred-year contract with a timber company allows more clear-cutting than in any other area in the national forest system. The damage there is appalling."

Olympic National Forest is trying to grow trees faster than they are harvested. Virgil Allen, a 25-year veteran of the Forest Service, ran the Dennie Ahl Seed Orchard there. He showed me around his 115-acre domain, named for a former Forest Service employee, where genetically superior seeds are produced, collected, and shipped to nurseries. Since 1959, the orchard has produced 1,860 pounds of seeds, enough for 22 million trees. Orderly ranks of conifers of various ages marched across the orchard. Each tree had a number on it. New shoots were spliced onto tips. "Our goal is to grow all the seeds for all the seedlings for all the planting of all the species grown in Olympic National Forest," Virgil told me. He took apart a cone, peering through his bifocals, and showed me the seeds of a Douglas fir—a "Doug fir," he called it. They looked like sunflower seeds. He talked of "conelets" and "controlled crosses" and "progeny tests." "We get seven or eight ounces of seeds from a bushel of cones," he told me. "Occasionally we come across a supertree that produces 12 ounces per bushel."

Supertrees of awesome majesty grow farther down the coast, in northern California. There, more than a century of logging had reduced the once extensive old-growth redwood forests to mere remnants. Largely through the efforts of the Save-the-Redwoods League, these are now preserved in 31 state parks as well as Redwood National Park. It was established in 1968 to protect the finest remaining stands of *Sequoia sempervirens*, the world's tallest tree. But continued logging outside the park, especially along Redwood Creek, created problems of erosion and downstream sedimentation that threatened the trees within the park. So in 1978 Congress added another 48,000 acres, nearly doubling the park's size, and also established a 30,000-acre "park protection zone" upstream in the Redwood Creek watershed. There the Park Service works closely with private owners to minimize erosion from logging.

Much of the newly acquired parkland was in a sorry state, with miles of logging roads, logjams clogging streams, and erosion scars, washouts, and landslides on the hillsides. To remedy the situation, Congress authorized a 10- to 15-year rehabilitation program that will cost an estimated 33 million dollars.

The logging roads and skid trails are the biggest problems. About 300 miles of abandoned roads and 3,000 miles of tractor skid trails crisscross the area, blocking and diverting streams, causing landslides, and turning into muddy streams during rainstorms. As the roads are removed, hill slopes and stream banks are being regraded to the original contours and revegetated. It's a massive, expensive, time-consuming, labor-intensive project. Eventually, the newly planted trees will produce a landscape not unlike the original forests.

By far the largest investment is time. The first new redwood seedlings, six to twelve inches tall when they were set out in 1978, have now reached three to four feet. Five hundred years will pass before they attain the height of their felled ancestors, giants of 250 feet or more.

"The least dramatic aspect of the rehab project is the reforestation," said Mary Hektner, "because the trees grow so *slowly.*" I was in a Park Service pickup with Mary, Redwood's supervisory plant ecologist, and Don Reeser, head of the resource management division. Rain pattered on the roof, and fog drifted through the treetops. Trucks, heavy with redwood and fir logs cut from nearby private forestland, thundered out of the fog and roared by, dripping trails of bark and twigs onto the highway through the park.

Mary and Don showed me examples of the Park Service's rehab efforts. We stopped where an old logging road had once run across a steep slope. Its lower edge had been bulldozed up onto the roadbed and the contour restored. Straw had been spread across it, and redwood and fir seedlings planted here and there.

"The straw is the best method our geologists have found for controlling erosion quickly," said Mary. "We plant a variety of species. Alders, fast growers, start to build up the soil again. Many of these old roadbeds have practically no topsoil. We've planted shrubs, too. They form a ground cover and provide some shade. Young redwoods don't thrive in too much direct sunlight."

Mary stooped to measure the height and girth of a redwood seedling with a pair of calipers. Girth? One-eighth of an inch. "You have to be careful not to squeeze too hard," Mary said, "or you snip it in half.

"It's ironic. Our heavy equipment operators doing the restoration work are all local, and were the people who put in the roads in the first place. They'll say, 'Hey, I remember building this road!'" In 1982 the park rehabilitated 13 miles of roads, so Mary and Don and their staffs will be at it for a while yet.

The Redwood Highway, U. S. 101, which bisects the park, also provides access to the nearby King Range National Conservation Area. Remote and rugged—so rugged it forced the coastal highway 30 miles inland—the King Range is a spectacular meeting of sea and land. Warped and wrinkled mountains rise practically from the surf, reaching 4,000 feet just 3 miles inland. The conservation area measures 35 miles by 6, and the BLM administers it for "multiple use and sustained yield." Hunting, fishing, camping, and hiking coexist fairly peaceably with grazing, logging, and ORVs on a stretch of the beach. But on south-facing slopes deep in the mountains there grows a crop that defies control—marijuana. It has become one of the leading cash crops in the United States, with a street value of more than ten billion dollars a year. And California leads the nation in production, with more than 10 percent of the total. About half of that is grown on public lands. A raid by drug officials in 1983 on plots in the King Range yielded nearly 5,000 pounds. I was told that marijuana cultivation is so rampant that hardware stores in the area have trouble keeping plastic irrigation pipe in stock, and turkey manure goes for $30 a cubic yard. Hikers and fishermen have been threatened by growers guarding their illegal plantations.

I spent a couple of days—one rainy, one clear—in the King Range, and my guides were both with the BLM: Jack Lahr, the area manager, and Jim Decker, a young fish and wildlife biologist. We checked on a herd of Roosevelt elk. Once common in the area, the animals have recently been reintroduced. They lazed in lush grass near the beach. One, Mamie, stood watching us. All 17 have names. "We moved them here from Prairie Creek last February," said Jim. "They were a hundred pounds underweight, all but one were anemic, and they had parasites they'd picked up from cattle and sheep. We held them in an imprinting pen for a while, to get them used to the area, then let them go. I felt real proud, like a father. As you can see, they're doing beautifully."

Cows and sheep grazed on mountaintop meadows, and small, trim deer flicked their tails and bounced into the forest. "Whenever I bring an expert of some kind in here," said Jim, "a herpetologist, say, they always discover a subspecies or two that's new to them."

"When I first came here and saw the results of the logging," said Jack, "I was reminded of the strip-mined areas back in Pennsylvania, my home state."

"The mouth of the Mattole River used to be the number one steelhead river in California," said Jim. "Now when it rains, there's so much sediment you can't see to fish. It's mostly erosion from logging and rural development roads."

"Sometimes devastation like this can have one positive effect," said Jack. "People can clearly see the mistakes of the past. A few years ago, at a public meeting, a couple of old-time loggers got up and confessed their sins. It almost turned into a sort of revival meeting."

Along the banks of Nooning Creek, an area undergoing rehabilitation, we found a group of young people working in today's CCC—the California Conservation Corps. They were installing screens around fir seedlings to protect them from deer. Hooded and slickered against the drizzle, they looked like trolls out gathering mushrooms. One girl, from New York, said she had joined because she wanted "to see southern California. And here I am freezing in the rain up north." But she smiled as she said it.

Several were from San Francisco, 230 miles down the coast. That beautiful city is the site of an unusual component of the National Park System.

*T*he 26,000-acre Golden Gate National Recreation Area got its start partly because the Interior Department's Bureau of Outdoor Recreation couldn't decide what to do with Alcatraz Island. Its function as a federal prison had ended in 1963, and for nearly ten years it sat decaying on its fortress island in the middle of San Francisco Bay. A number of other parcels of land in and around San Francisco were in limbo, too. Some were being held by conservation organizations; some were surplus military holdings. Working with the Park Service, the bureau recommended they be combined in an 8,000-acre park.

Part of the 8,000 acres was former military land across the bay from San Francisco, in Marin County, where cattle grazed amid the chaparral on windy hills. Gulf-Reston had planned a new town of 25,000 there, but abandoned it in the face of strong local opposition. The Nature Conservancy had subsequently bought most of the land. When the General Services Administration proposed building an enormous archives storage facility on some surplus Army land near Lands End in San Francisco, more opposition erupted. A neighborhood group—People for a Golden Gate National Recreation Area—began lobbying for a park that would gather up and protect all those spare pieces of property. Letters went out, organizations were solicited for support, and in October 1972 Congress passed the bill establishing the recreation area.

Today the park includes everything from historic ships to a grove of redwoods, from windswept beaches to erstwhile Army buildings alive with experimental theater and restaurants, from the National Maritime Museum to bluffs and hills favored by hang gliders. And, of course, Alcatraz. Golden Gate is an odd park in one respect: Often you can't be certain whether you're in it. The various bits and pieces, cheek by jowl with the city, are an integral part of it.

The problems of the park are what you might imagine: some vandalism, some crime, some littering and overcrowding, some street people trying to move in. But probably the most severe problem involves funding: Golden Gate is fiendishly expensive to operate.

"We inherited about 300 structures when the park was formed," general superintendent Jack Davis told me in his office. I envied him his desk—an antique table from an old sailing ship—and his view, the lovely bay and hills of San Francisco. "We have buildings ranging from an old Civil War fort to obsolete Nike missile sites, from old Army barracks to an Art Deco bathhouse. Many are on the National Register of Historic Places, so we're legally mandated to preserve and protect them. That gets very expensive, when you consider the dilapidation of some of them." Alcatraz alone will cost ten million dollars to restore.

A number of historic ships float under the administrative umbrella of the GGNRA. Among them are *Wapama*, the last of some 225 steam schooners built on the West Coast to carry lumber from northern forests to San Francisco, and *Balclutha*, a square-rigged sailing ship launched in Scotland in 1886. Beginning in 1902, she hauled fishermen from San Francisco to Alaska and returned laden with their catch.

"To restore *Wapama* to her former state will cost about 5.3 million dollars," Jack told me. "*Balclutha* will be another 3 million, just to deal with basic structural problems. It costs about a million a year simply to take care of maintenance needs above the waterline. Our funding isn't keeping up with inflation, so we're looking more and more toward volunteers. Each historic ship has a number of them. One group put in about 30,000 hours of labor on an old Liberty ship that is moored in the park and was restored over the last few years."

Steve Hastings, tall and as straight as a schooner's mast and sporting luxuriant muttonchop whiskers from another era, took me to see *Wapama*. Steve works on ship reconstruction and maintenance for the National Maritime Museum, a part of the GGNRA. As we crossed the Bay Bridge to Oakland, Steve told me about his work. "Wooden ships were built to last 20 years and then be thrown away. They weren't meant to be taken apart and put back together again. That's why they're difficult to work on and why the cost is so terrific."

The cost of storing *Wapama* in a commercial dry dock until restoration could begin was excessive, so engineers sank a barge beneath her, refloated it, and lifted her out of the water. We found her, high and dry, at the water's edge. "*Wapama* could carry about 30 passengers and more than a million board feet of lumber," Steve said. Donning a yellow plastic hard hat, I followed him up and down planks and ladders into the bowels of the big ship, which is more than 200 feet long. The hold was gloomy and damp, and a little spooky, too. Dry rot at timber joists looked ominous. Up on deck, little three-tiered bunks and a small but elegant lounge had served passengers. There was a nice view of Oakland's inner harbor. Sea lions bobbed in the water, and brown pelicans sat meditating on boulders. The tide went out and an odor strong enough to power a freighter rose from the mud flats. Peevish sea gulls paced to and fro.

*T*he Western Sea that laps at the edge of California laps also at the five tiny isles of Channel Islands National Park, 25 miles off Santa Barbara. Eleven species of seabirds and a variety of pinnipeds—seals and sea lions—inhabit the surf-washed shore and the rocky heights.

A six-mile-wide swath of protected waters—Channel Islands National Marine Sanctuary—encircles the park, but beneath the ocean floor lie more deposits of our old friends, Oil and Gas. Many people here are touchy about oil; the 1969 spill in the Santa Barbara Channel damaged miles of California beaches.

The waters within three nautical miles of the Channel Islands belong to the state of California, so jurisdiction over the oil beneath the 1,250-square-nautical-mile marine sanctuary is divided between the state and the federal government. Until the discovery of offshore oil and gas, the question of who had rights to them never arose. It was hotly debated in the 1930s and '40s, after oil was discovered in the Gulf Coast tidelands, and the Supreme Court decided in favor of the federal government in 1947 and again in 1950. But in 1953 Congress passed legislation giving coastal states control of the waters within the three-mile limit, a range adopted by the United States in the 18th century. Beyond the three-mile limit, on the Outer Continental Shelf, the ocean floor is federal.

Many of the people who opposed giving the tidelands to the states feared a precedent would be set. Senator Estes Kefauver said, "I can see little or no difference in giving away the oil resources under the sea—because we say they are within a state's boundaries—and giving away any of the rest of the national wealth which happens to be located within a state's boundaries. . . . If we establish the principle that the national heritage can be given away today, there will be precious little of it left by the time our children have grown. . . ."

The Outer Continental Shelf made news again in July 1982, when Interior Secretary James Watt proposed offering 200 million acres a year for leasing; only about 22 million acres had been leased in the previous 30 years. Environmentalists and many coastal states rushed to the courts, but in June 1983 the U. S. Court of Appeals for the District of Columbia ruled in favor of the Interior Department's massive leasing program. Watt's successor, William P. Clark, has promised that Interior will decrease the amounts offered for leasing and work with states, industry, and environmentalists "to harvest the riches of the sea and under the sea, while protecting its grandeur and life-sustaining qualities."

So Channel Islands National Park finds itself in the middle of an ocean of oil and gas as well as salt water. And the marine sanctuary? "It is charged with balancing oil development with resource conservation," its manager, Carol Pillsbury, told me. "It's a brand-new program, compared to the Park Service, for instance. We're here to help people understand that the preservation of marine areas is as important as the preservation of terrestrial ones."

What about the threat of oil and gas development? "Our regulations

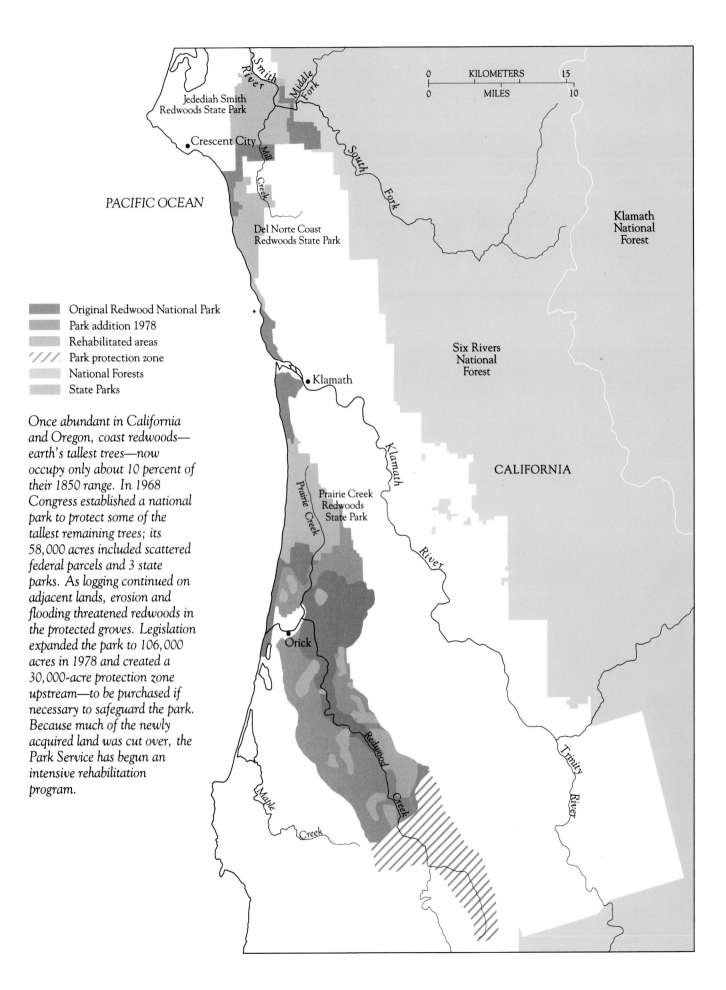

Original Redwood National Park
Park addition 1978
Rehabilitated areas
Park protection zone
National Forests
State Parks

Once abundant in California and Oregon, coast redwoods— earth's tallest trees—now occupy only about 10 percent of their 1850 range. In 1968 Congress established a national park to protect some of the tallest remaining trees; its 58,000 acres included scattered federal parcels and 3 state parks. As logging continued on adjacent lands, erosion and flooding threatened redwoods in the protected groves. Legislation expanded the park to 106,000 acres in 1978 and created a 30,000-acre protection zone upstream—to be purchased if necessary to safeguard the park. Because much of the newly acquired land was cut over, the Park Service has begun an intensive rehabilitation program.

PACIFIC OCEAN

Jedediah Smith Redwoods State Park

Crescent City

Smith River

Middle Fork

Mill Creek

South Fork

Del Norte Coast Redwoods State Park

Klamath

Klamath River

Prairie Creek

Prairie Creek Redwoods State Park

Orick

Maple Creek

Redwood Creek

KILOMETERS
0   15
0   10
MILES

Klamath National Forest

Six Rivers National Forest

CALIFORNIA

Trinity River

prohibit new development but allow drilling on seven existing leases within the sanctuary boundary. Because the designation of the sanctuary in 1980 called for multiple-use management, we're trying to sensitize all users to the importance of preserving the natural resources of the area. For example, we've been taking oil-company executives out and showing them the sanctuary. They're extremely impressed. It seems that every time we go, something exciting happens—dolphins ride the bow, or whales appear, and of course they see all the seals and seabirds. The beauty of the place speaks for itself."

West of the Channel Islands, across miles of ocean, waves lap at other islands, unique and beautiful: Hawaii. Two situations there interested me. In one, Mother Nature seems to be fighting human developers with fire; in the other, she seems overwhelmed by a long history of human interference.

On the big island of Hawaii, a group of businessmen proposes building a geothermal power plant next to Hawaii Volcanoes National Park to tap the sub-surface heat. The plant—actually five clustered together—would draw power from about 70 wells. Concerns about air, water, and noise pollution, the safety of several endangered bird and plant species, and potential impacts on the park have led to opposition from assorted individuals, community associations, and environmental groups. Attorney Ken Kupchak is handling the legal battles.

"We created a statewide land-use system here in Hawaii, the first state to do so. It was adopted in the early '60s. The state divided all its lands into four categories: conservation, rural, agricultural, and urban. The proposed power plant is on land zoned 'conservation,' and we're arguing that a power plant is inappropriate on such land. So far the State Land Board has tried to avoid the issue, and the legislature and the executive branch are proceeding to dismantle our once acclaimed land-use system."

Opponents have succeeded, however, in limiting the proposed activity, for the time being, to a 6,000-acre exploratory area, where proponents must prove that a viable geothermal resource exists.

"We've seen one prophecy come true," he told me. "When we finished hearings before the Land Board in late 1982, we said that our last witness would be Madam Pele, the volcano goddess." Pele was listening. "Kilauea began erupting in January of '83 and is still carrying on. By June of '84 more than 50 percent of the exploratory area had been covered with lava. There were seven well sites in there, and five of them have been buried. The site of one power plant is under lava. The average thickness of the flow is between 20 and 40 feet."

I went for a flight over the area with pilot Joe Enriquez, a young Hawaiian. In 1960 he was in his fifth-grade classroom when the eruption that buried the village of Kapoho began. "The walls started shaking and the windows cracking. The teacher yelled, 'Don't panic! Don't panic!' but she was the only one still in school." A broad blanket of forest unrolled beneath our plane, with a broad black gash, a congealed river of new lava, running through it. White smoke wafted from it, and small fires flickered at its edge where trees burned. We passed over a subdivision, where three houses lay beneath 30 feet of lava.

Is Madam Pele doing this? I asked Russ Apple, a retired Park Service historian who has lived in Hawaii since 1950. "Madam Pele is a very real presence in the minds of many Hawaiians," he told me. "There are offerings to Pele at every eruption by people hoping to placate her. The more conservative Hawaiians oppose any use of Pele's steam, so to speak. They're watching with a good deal of amusement as she wipes out all these well sites." But plans for the geothermal power plants are continuing.

Back in Honolulu, I made my way to the University of Hawaii, its busy campus full of bronzed students in shorts, sandals, and T-shirts. There I talked with Dr. Clifford Smith, associate professor of botany. In shorts, sandals, and a saucy red T-shirt, Dr. Smith was indistinguishable from his students—and angry about Hawaii's past.

Kauai
Kilauea Point
Administrative Site
Nihau
Oahu
Molokai
Maui
Haleakala
National Park
Lanai
Kahoolawe
Hawaii
Hawaii Volcanoes
National Park

"Hawaii is a pretty shameful example of man's desecration of plants and animals," he told me. "A third of all U. S. species that are now extinct became so in Hawaii. Nearly half the U. S. bird species listed by the Fish and Wildlife Service as threatened or endangered are Hawaiian. The islands are so isolated that very few colonizing organisms reached here, and the ones that did, generally speaking, had no predators and no diseases.

"The Hawaiians themselves, after they colonized the islands in the fourth century, had a terrific impact on the native flora and fauna. Probably half the species of birds here at the time were extirpated, just because of the disturbances to the lowland habitat. Many were flightless birds that had no defense against man. The Hawaiians also brought with them some aliens—a species of small pig, rats, lots of different kinds of plants.

"When Captain Cook and other Europeans arrived in the late 18th century, they introduced more animals, particularly ungulates—cattle, goats, sheep, more pigs. The idea was to use the islands as a sort of refueling station where ships could replenish their meat supplies. Since there were no predators, the populations of these animals just exploded. Native plants suffered because they had developed no resistance. There were no noxious substances in their leaves. Even the mints here don't have highly scented leaves if you crush them. Native plants have very few and pretty innocuous thorns. If you run across something really thorny in the forest, you can bet it's an alien."

Attempts to rectify the problems have sometimes backfired. Mongooses were introduced in 1883 to combat rats in the sugarcane fields. But the rats are largely nocturnal and the mongooses diurnal, so they seldom run into each other. Thus Hawaii is now plagued not only by rats, but also by mongooses, which prey on the eggs of such endangered birds as the nene and the dark-rumped petrel. A 1979 study determined that 40 percent of the petrel eggs and chicks in Haleakala National Park were destroyed by mongooses and feral cats and dogs.

According to Dr. Smith, wild goats were a severe problem in Hawaii Volcanoes National Park until the early '70s, when an aggressive superintendent started a program to eliminate them. "Unfortunately, it was called a 'goat eradication program,' and it met with a firestorm of opposition from hunters and conservationists. So the name was changed to 'native ecosystem restoration program,' and support was universal and wholehearted. While there were once 15,000 or 20,000 goats in the park, there are now fewer than a hundred."

The pigs, the earthworms, and the strawberry guava—these might be the elements of a riddle, but in fact they are the central players in a drama being enacted in the native rain forests of Maui.

Hawaii's federal domain embraces Haleakala National Park, famous for its immense crater, and Hawaii Volcanoes National Park, where both Mauna Loa and Kilauea erupted in 1984. During centuries of isolation, the Hawaiian Islands nurtured unique species in a fragile ecological web. But eventually Polynesians began cultivating the lowlands, and Europeans and Americans introduced domesticated animals, many of which ran wild. Unable to withstand such onslaughts, native plants and animals declined or perished. Today, a refuge on Kauai provides a secure nesting area for albatrosses, and in a reserve at Haleakala some island species tenuously survive.

"Before 1967, Haleakala National Park was just the crater district, the top of the mountain," Dr. Smith told me. "But in that year the Nature Conservancy sponsored an expedition into a steep valley west of the crater. It's a beautiful, pristine, and nearly impenetrable area. The Nature Conservancy bought half the valley, and they and the state, which owned the other half, presented it to the Park Service. The agency closed off the valley so that it would remain pristine, and for the next ten years very few people were allowed in there. There was another expedition in 1976, and they found that the whole forest was being opened up by pigs. A *real* problem.

"The Park Service sponsored a study in 1979, and found that the pigs' principal source of protein was earthworms! They were rooting up the forest searching for earthworms, themselves aliens.

"We next found that the strawberry guava, a small subtropical shrub that crowds out everything else, was invading the valley. During its fruiting season in November, the pigs were homing in on it. To them the fruit's a delicacy. They would wander off, carrying the seeds inside them. They hold the seeds for about 48 hours. And in 48 hours a pig can travel two or three miles. The pigs were moving up the valley searching for more strawberry guava, which they were in fact carrying with them, creating new plantings as they went."

The obvious solution seemed to be to fence them out, along with the wild goats, which browse almost all plants down to the ground. At Haleakala headquarters I asked superintendent Hugo Huntzinger about that. "First we're going to complete the fencing around the crater district of the park," he told me. "About 35 miles in very rugged terrain. Some slopes approach 85 degrees, practically straight up and down. We started seven years ago, using Sierra Club volunteers and college students. With the recent increase in funding we now hire regular park crews and will issue our first contract in 1984. But this costs an arm and a leg—between 40 and 60 thousand dollars a mile in the backcountry."

Superintendent Huntzinger said that in the rain forests in the eastern half of the park, where the pigs are spreading strawberry guava, the solution will be even more costly. "The forests are virtually impenetrable. We're going to try for two cross-valley fences to split Kipahulu Valley into three management units and then initiate intensive control efforts in the midsection. It's going to be one of the most difficult resource-management efforts ever attempted. The survival of an entire native ecosystem will be dependent upon the outcome."

The park's chief ranger, Barry Cooper, walked me down a hill to show me an experimental exclosure, an area of several acres fenced to prevent animals from entering. The idea is to leave the plot alone and see how the vegetation recovers and changes. To a layman, at first glance, it didn't look all that different from its surroundings, but Barry could detect, and point out to me, new growth, a healthier mix, and plants attaining a maturity they never achieve in the wild.

He told me a touching story, of a discovery at Hawaii Volcanoes that had tipped the park's management toward fencing. "In one of the test exclosures a plant came up, a small twining vine that had never been described before, a species new to science. Probably it grew from old seeds that had been stored in the soil for years. Goats had destroyed the ground cover, so the soil dried quickly after a rain, and the seeds didn't get enough moisture to germinate. As soon as the fence was up and the pressure from the goats relieved, a ground cover grew that provided shade and held moisture for the seeds, and the vine flourished."

In the grand scheme of things, one vine more or less may not matter much. Nevertheless, it nearly breaks my heart to think of that poor plant, waiting year after year to take its place in Chief Seattle's "web of life." Somehow it makes me hopeful. And I think it would make Chief Seattle hopeful, too.

*F*airy-tale realm of moss-draped trees and other lush plant life nestles in the Hoh, Quinault, and Queets Valleys of the Olympic Peninsula. Nearly continuous fog, a mild coastal climate, and 140 inches of rainfall a year nourish this temperate rain forest. Along the Hoh Valley's Hall of Mosses Trail (left), sword ferns unfurl their fronds beneath big-leaf maples; wispy club moss clings to branches. This unusual ecosystem has earned the park a place on the World Heritage List, which recognizes areas of unique value to mankind. Flowers of red columbine (below) bloom at higher elevations.

FOLLOWING PAGES: Sunset casts a rosy glow over 7,965-foot Mount Olympus. The wettest part of the contiguous United States, the Olympic Range annually receives some 200 inches of precipitation.

igh on a mountainside in Olympic National Forest, a logger saws an old-growth hemlock into 40-foot lengths. Stands of fir, hemlock, and cedar in 650,000-acre Olympic yield a yearly harvest ranked sixth in the national forests of the Northwest. Opposite, crews use steel cables attached to a yarding tower to lift logs up steep slopes. Trucks haul the timber to mills.

*C*hallenging the bulldozer: Members of Earth First!, a radical environmental group, block construction of the Bald Mountain Road in Oregon's Siskiyou National Forest. By cutting through this area and opening it to logging, the road prevents its inclusion in the adjacent 180,000-acre Kalmiopsis Wilderness. After finding the bulldozer stuck on a slope, the protesters celebrate (below). Josephine County sheriffs charged them with trespassing and arrested them (opposite, upper and lower). They spent a night in jail and received fines of $125 each and a year's probation. In July 1983, a court injunction halted construction until the Forest Service makes a recommendation based on further environmental studies.

ALL, DAVID J. CROSS

317

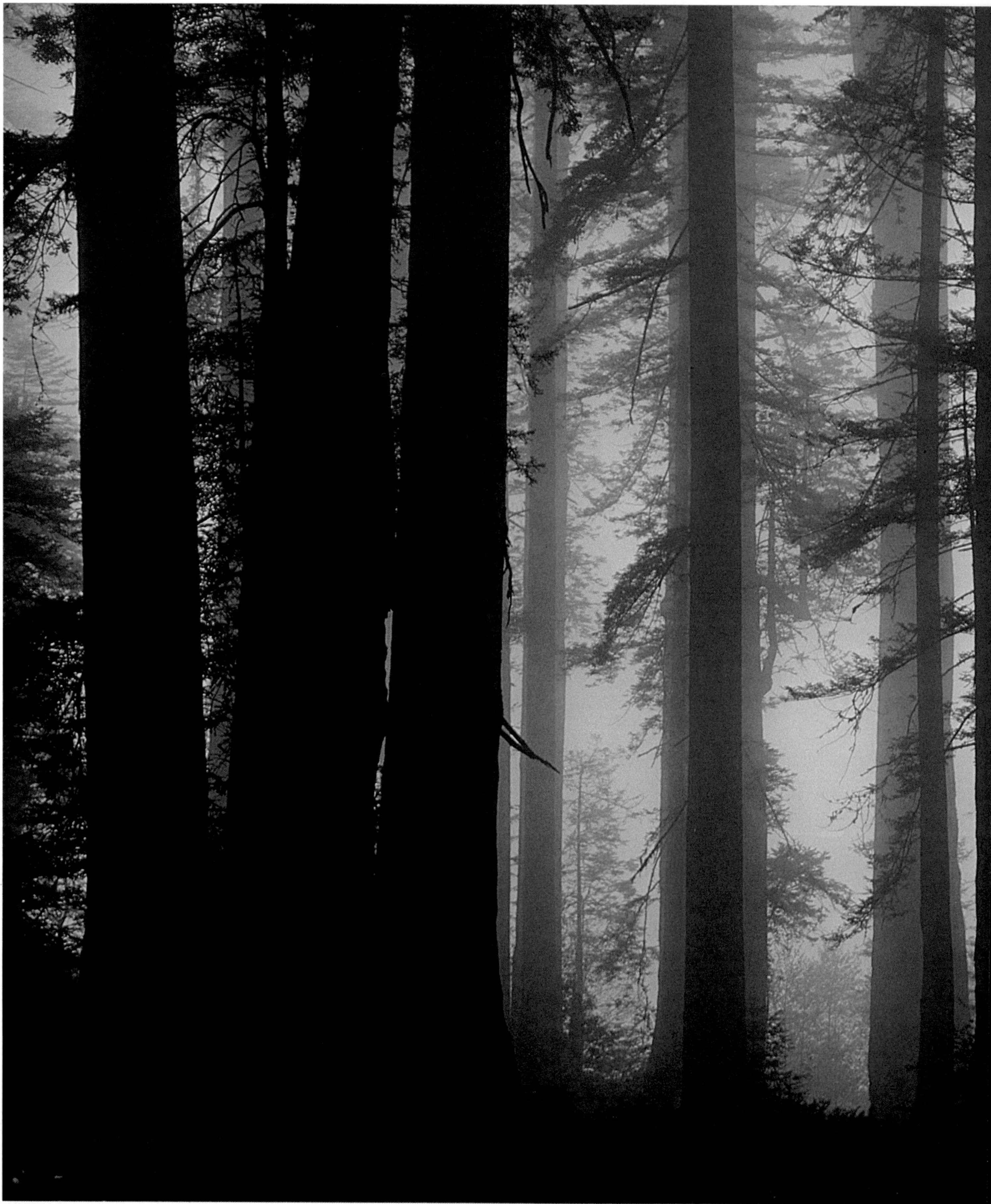

ncient redwoods 1,500 years old tower more than 250 feet in Lady Bird Johnson Grove, part of California's Redwood National Park. Morning fog regularly envelops the trees, providing them with life-sustaining moisture, especially during dry summer months. Congress established the park in 1968, after a study funded by the National Geographic Society revealed that logging had destroyed all but 15 percent of the original two-million-acre forest. Without federal protection, redwoods such as these looming above a visitor probably would not exist today.

N.G.S. PHOTOGRAPHER DAVID ALAN HARVEY

A mong spring's earliest arrivals, trilliums adorn the forest floor in Redwood National Park. The wild flowers—members of the lily family—display three translucent petals that appear white when they first open (below, right), then turn a dusky pink. A thousand plant and animal species find sanctuary in the park, which preserves the world's tallest trees.

*I*llegal plantation, round clumps of marijuana stand in rows on a mountainside in the King Range National Conservation Area, a BLM holding in northern California. Grown in remote areas, marijuana has become a problem on federal lands nationwide. Fertilizers and rodenticides spread around plots destroy wildlife and pollute streams. Sometimes resorting to violence, cultivators scare campers and employees off public lands. In 1983 local, state, and federal agencies joined forces in a program known as CAMP—Campaign Against Marijuana Planting. California officials eradicated this plot, one of 18 spotted from the air in the King Range.

*W*aging war on marijuana, BLM special agent-in-charge David Howard, left, and a local law-enforcement officer collect cannabis plants from public lands near Whitethorn, California, for removal to burn sites. Growers prefer the female cannabis (opposite, upper) for its high market value; one pound of buds—swollen areas at the top of the stem—may bring $2,000. In another raid on nearby BLM lands, agents use a helicopter (opposite, lower) to confiscate some 500 plants. Such crackdowns have helped deter would-be offenders in the state.

*L*andmark in San Francisco's Golden Gate National Recreation Area, Muir Woods (opposite) draws more than a million visitors a year. Set aside in 1908 as the first federally protected redwoods and dedicated to naturalist John Muir, the grove preserves the only virgin stand of the giant trees near a city. Ferns, red alder, California laurel, and western azaleas also flourish here. Golden Gate's scattered and diverse holdings encompass 73,000 acres in and around San Francisco. The Park Service recorded nearly 20 million visitors to the recreation area in 1983. Behind sun worshipers at Ocean Beach, graffiti on a seawall (below) underscore a common problem in heavily used parks: vandalism. An annual operating budget of 7.7 million dollars limits maintenance in Golden Gate to more serious problems affecting health and safety. The high cost of land hinders the development of urban parks, despite the recreational opportunities and breathing room they afford.

*R*ecreation takes many forms at Golden Gate, where land and ocean meet.
*Opposite, riders cross a coastal strip of private land bordering the park. Trails blazed by people
on foot or horseback and rutted by off-road vehicles worsen erosion of the unstable terrain. The
Park Service works with the owners to close the area to dune buggies, which use it to reach park
beaches. In Kelly's Cove (above), near the north end of Ocean Beach, strong tides challenge
surfers. Hang gliders (top) ride 20-mile-an-hour winds in the Fort Funston area.*

Western gulls wheel above Arch Rock at the eastern end of Anacapa, one of five islands in California's Channel Islands National Park. Nesting haven for several kinds of seabirds, the park also shelters more pinniped—fin-footed—species of aquatic mammals than any other place in the world. Opposite, California sea lions and northern elephant seals venture into sunset-gilded waters off San Miguel. Overgrazing and hunting threatened the wildlife of these rugged islands in the 1800s. Now oil from accidents—such as the 1969 Santa Barbara Channel spill—and seepage and spills from new drilling sites imperil the park. Ensuring some protection, regulations for the marine sanctuary here prohibit new leasing within six miles of the islands.

Kilauea—one of earth's most active volcanoes—erupts in January 1983 on the island of Hawaii. Below, molten lava courses through private lands of the Campbell Estate adjacent to 229,000-acre Hawaii Volcanoes National Park; a tree stump burns blue in the foreground. Opposite, lava's red glow illumines scorched ohia-lehua trees. Since its first eruption centuries ago, Kilauea has spread desolation. Lava from 12 outbursts in 1983 alone covered 6,400 acres, heightening public concern about a proposed geothermal plant on the estate.

PRECEDING PAGES: Fountains of lava explode as a new volcanic rift slices through virgin forest on the Campbell Estate. Though lava has already engulfed 14 potential drilling sites, planning for geothermal development proceeds.

olten lava shoots 200 feet into the air above Vent 1123—named for its eruption time of 11:23 a.m. A river of lava surges down the side of the newly formed cone. Nearby, a tributary moving more than a mile an hour covers a forest with aa, one type of lava (bottom). A kind called pahoehoe (below), closer to the vent, is more fluid and hotter at more than 2000°F. At left, pahoehoe drips over a lichen-strewn ledge and hardens into a stalagmite. By tapping the underground heat in this part of the island, developers believe they can supply a less costly energy source to the state, which depends almost entirely on oil. Adverse effects on neighboring Hawaii Volcanoes National Park could range from increased noise levels and pollution to destruction of wildlife habitats—such as those of the endangered Hawaiian hawk and honeycreeper.

WILLIAM L. ALLEN, N.G.S. STAFF (ABOVE AND RIGHT)

PAUL CHESLEY (ABOVE AND OPPOSITE)

336

*L*ures for albatrosses, paired decoys dot a grassy slope in the Kilauea Point refuge on Kauai. Albatrosses such as the two above normally breed on islands northwest of Hawaii. In the late 1970s their numbers increased dramatically on Midway, and they began appearing on Kauai. Working with the Fish and Wildlife Service, volunteers from a group called Earthwatch used decoys and sound recordings in an attempt to attract the birds onto the refuge, where fences would protect them from feral dogs. With nearly seven-foot wingspans, albatrosses need open slopes for takeoffs and landings. Officials plan to adopt chicks hatched elsewhere, hoping they will accept the refuge as home and return there to breed.

*One of the Far West's most
treasured showcases, Haleakala
National Park on Maui reaches
into the Pacific at Oheo Gulch
(opposite). The nene (below),*

*an endangered species of goose,
enjoys protection in Haleakala
Crater farther inland. Wildlife
officials reintroduced the nene—
the state bird—in the 1960s, after
hunting, farming, mongooses, and
wild dogs had eliminated it on
Maui. While the current Maui
population numbers no more than
150, the mere fact of the nene's
survival holds special significance
for Hawaii—a state credited with
the record for bird extinctions. For
Haleakala's 80 kinds of rare
plants, competition with exotic
species remains intense. Bamboo,
probably brought from India or
Southeast Asia by early
Polynesians, encroaches at lower
elevations and chokes out native
trees such as the one at left.*

Late afternoon shadows steal over cinder cones pocking the floor of Haleakala Crater, some 2,000 feet below the rim. Few plants can survive on the dry slopes of the cones, which formed around vents centuries ago. The spiny silversword (below) will soon flower after a maturation of 3 to 20 years, then quickly fade. Now protected by the park, silverswords have increased from fewer than a thousand in the 1920s to more than 46,000 today.

FOLLOWING PAGES: Sunrise bursts over Haleakala, Hawaii's legendary "House of the Sun." Eons of erosion shaped the 2.5-by-7.5-mile basin. Eruptions have strewed its floor with volcanic debris.

RON NAGATA

WILLIAM L. ALLEN, N.G.S. STAFF

Snowy ramparts of Mount McKinley—at 20,320 feet North
America's highest peak—tower beyond Wonder Lake in
Alaska's Denali National Park and Preserve.

Epilogue

$\mathcal{A}$ few years ago, on a balmy day in late summer, I joined some companions on the banks of the Noatak River in northern Alaska. There, with gravel crunching underfoot and mosquitoes buzzing around us, we launched three canoes into the river's headwaters.

The Noatak rises at the base of Mount Igikpak in the Brooks Range, runs westward across the state, then lunges southward to Kotzebue Sound on the Chukchi Sea. It lies entirely above the Arctic Circle and almost entirely above treeline. For the first 375 miles of its 435-mile length, there is no sign of man or his works. Then you reach the Eskimo settlement of Noatak, then nothing again until the sound and the little town of Kotzebue. We spent a month on the river.

I remember it as a peaceful and happy time, a leisurely glide through endless tundra beneath an endless sky. We had good weather and, in summer, 24 hours of daylight. We picked blueberries for lunch and caught grayling and salmon for dinner. A photograph above my desk shows me, my fishing pole in one hand, a nine-pound salmon held aloft in the other. Behind me is the river, and beyond that a country that looks to have no end to it. As we drifted and paddled, arctic terns hovered on the warm wind, and grizzlies, resembling golden boulders, browsed on lush hillsides. In the headwaters, the shallow water beneath the canoes was so clear it was invisible; the rocky bottom sped past my paddle tip. It was like looking down through a glass-bottomed boat.

At Noatak Village, a cluster of dwellings atop a crumbling bluff, we dined on caribou steak and attended a Quaker meeting. A young Eskimo boy showed me around. As we walked together, he told me about some large bones he had found on the beach. "Rib bones," he said, "from a big fish." "Maybe a whale," I suggested. He looked at me with scorn. "A whale is not a fish," he said. "A whale is a mammal."

By the time we reached Kotzebue, summer was over, and the nights were aglow with the aurora borealis, pale green curtains of fire that rippled across the heavens. We were so far north they were directly above us. I leaned my head back and gawked like a bumpkin.

Now, when I think of Alaska, I think of water as clear as glass, of rocks, of salmon, of space empty of humankind, of soggy tundra, of mellow days and daylit nights. And of Eskimo children who know more about whales than I do.

The Noatak drainage is the largest mountain-ringed river basin in North America still essentially untouched by man. Virtually every type of arctic habitat known to exist can be found within it, and its array of flora may be the most diverse in all the Far North. When my friends and I floated the Noatak, it was simply a long, unspoiled river winding through a huge basin in the vastness of wild Alaska. Today a 330-mile stretch of it is the Noatak Wild River, and the basin is part of the 6.5-million-acre Noatak National Preserve. The story of how that came to be is the story of federal lands in Alaska.

It begins in 1959, when Alaska became the 49th state. From its 365 million acres, Alaska was authorized to select 104.5 million for itself. But Native groups—Eskimos, Aleuts, and Indians—protested that the state was taking their traditional lands, so in 1966 Secretary of the Interior Stewart Udall halted the process. Nothing much happened until 1968, when oil was discovered on the North Slope. The oil companies wanted to build a pipeline to an ice-free port, and they needed to know who was going to own the land so they could begin negotiations. The state had to get its lands question settled.

The passage in 1971 of the Alaska Native Claims Settlement Act gave Natives 44 million acres of land and nearly a billion dollars. The same act, in its often cited Section 17 (d)(2), directed the Secretary of the Interior to choose up to 80 million acres "suitable for addition to or creation as units of the National Park, Forest, Wildlife Refuge, and Wild and Scenic Rivers Systems." Another section allowed the secretary to make additional withdrawals. All of these became known as the "d-2 lands," over which Alaskans, conservationists, developers, and Congress wrestled and fought, tussled and argued, debated and compromised for almost a decade.

Just before leaving office, on December 2, 1980, President Jimmy Carter signed into law the Alaska National Interest Lands Conservation Act (ANILCA), usually referred to simply as the Alaska Lands Act. It is an awesome piece of legislation, running to 180 pages of dense legalese. Awesome, too, are its provisions: The act put more than 103 million acres of Alaska into new or expanded parks, refuges, and other conservation units. It more than doubled the size of both the National Park and the National Wildlife Refuge Systems and added 25 free-flowing streams—among them the Noatak—to the National Wild and Scenic Rivers System. Fifty-six million acres were classified as wilderness, thereby tripling the size of the National Wilderness Preservation System. Ten new park units were created, including 19 million acres set aside in national preserves, which are managed like parks but open to sport hunting.

Laws do not enforce themselves. Much of any statute's effectiveness depends on the administration currently in office.

"Regarding ANILCA, the Reagan Administration has two primary goals," said William Horn, the Interior Department's deputy under secretary for Alaska. "To protect Alaska's natural resources and to fulfill the promises specified to Alaskans in the law. We think that the positive reaction of the Alaskans means we are succeeding. On balance, Congress has not expressed any substantive objection to our implementation of the act."

But many environmentalists were alarmed by the way the Reagan Administration began implementing the Alaska Lands Act. In June 1982, Senator Paul Tsongas of Massachusetts accused Secretary of the Interior James Watt of distorting the intent of the act: "Under the guise of implementing the law, the secretary is, in fact, undoing the law." The senator made some strong charges: "Through calculated use of the budget, selective enforcement of some provisions of the act but no enforcement of others, and by suspect interpretation of statutory provisions—the Alaska National Interest Lands Conservation Act is being transformed into the Alaska National Interest Lands Development Act."

Is it? Conservationists point to several Interior Department policies that seem to support Senator Tsongas's views. For example: One provision of the act exempts BLM lands in Alaska from being studied for inclusion in the wilderness system, but it does not prohibit such studies; it says, in fact, that the secretary "may" identify areas suitable for wilderness and may "from time to time" recommend them to Congress. But Secretary Watt used his discretion to *forbid* any further BLM wilderness studies in Alaska. In a policy directive he said, ". . . no further wilderness inventory, review, study, or consideration by the Bureau of Land Management is needed or is to be undertaken in Alaska. . . ." The BLM followed this directive with a memo to its staff: ". . . all work related to designation of public lands as wilderness in Alaska is to stop immediately."

Funding, critics claimed, was another means Secretary Watt used to circumvent the intent of Congress. "We'll use the budget system to be the excuse to make major policy decisions," he said. In Alaska, this meant withholding personnel and funds from conservation programs and lavishing them on

"Not in our generation, nor ever again, will we have a land and wildlife opportunity approaching the scope and importance of this one . . . given one great last chance, let us strive to do it right." As he urged his colleagues in 1979 to protect wild lands in Alaska, Congressman Morris Udall of Arizona expressed the convictions of conservationists nationwide. The Statehood Act of 1958 had initiated the complex process of allocating Alaska's 365 million acres to competing interests. The state itself was allotted lands totaling 104.5 million acres. No sooner had it begun selecting them than Native groups protested that their lands were being stolen. The federal government halted land transfers pending resolution of the dispute. The 1968 oil strike at Prudhoe Bay and the oil companies' determination to build a pipeline to an ice-free port increased pressure to end the freeze and distribute the land. The resulting Alaska Native Claims Settlement Act of 1971 awarded 44 million acres and nearly one billion dollars to Native corporations. One clause provided for the withdrawal of up to 80 million acres for national parks, forests, and wildlife refuges. Nearly a decade of debates, hearings, and compromises between developers and conservationists ensued before President Jimmy Carter signed the Alaska National Interest Lands Conservation Act on December 2, 1980. It expanded the three existing national parks—Denali (then called McKinley), Katmai, and Glacier Bay—and created ten new parks and monuments. The law also designated 32

National Parks
Wilderness within Parks and Preserves
National Preserves
National Forests
Wilderness within Forests
National Wildlife Refuges
Wilderness within Refuges
Bureau of Land Management lands
National Petroleum Reserve
Trans-Alaska Pipeline
Alaska Maritime N.W.R.

Alaska Maritime National Wildlife Refuge

ALEUTIAN ISLANDS

BERING SEA

Izembek N.W.R.

million acres of park wilderness, and accommodated sportsmen by setting aside 19 million acres of national preserves—managed like parks, but open to sport hunting. These additions increased the acreage of the National Park System by 150 percent. Rural Alaskans may continue traditional subsistence hunting, trapping, and fishing on most new federal reserves. Another compromise allows miners to develop valid claims that antedate new conservation units. Parts of Tongass National Forest received wilderness protection, but carefully drawn boundaries excluded mineral deposits and granted generous concessions to timber interests. The act also enlarged existing wildlife refuges and established nine new ones—more than doubling the size of the National Wildlife Refuge System. Today 27 million acres of BLM and Forest Service lands remain to be conveyed to the state.

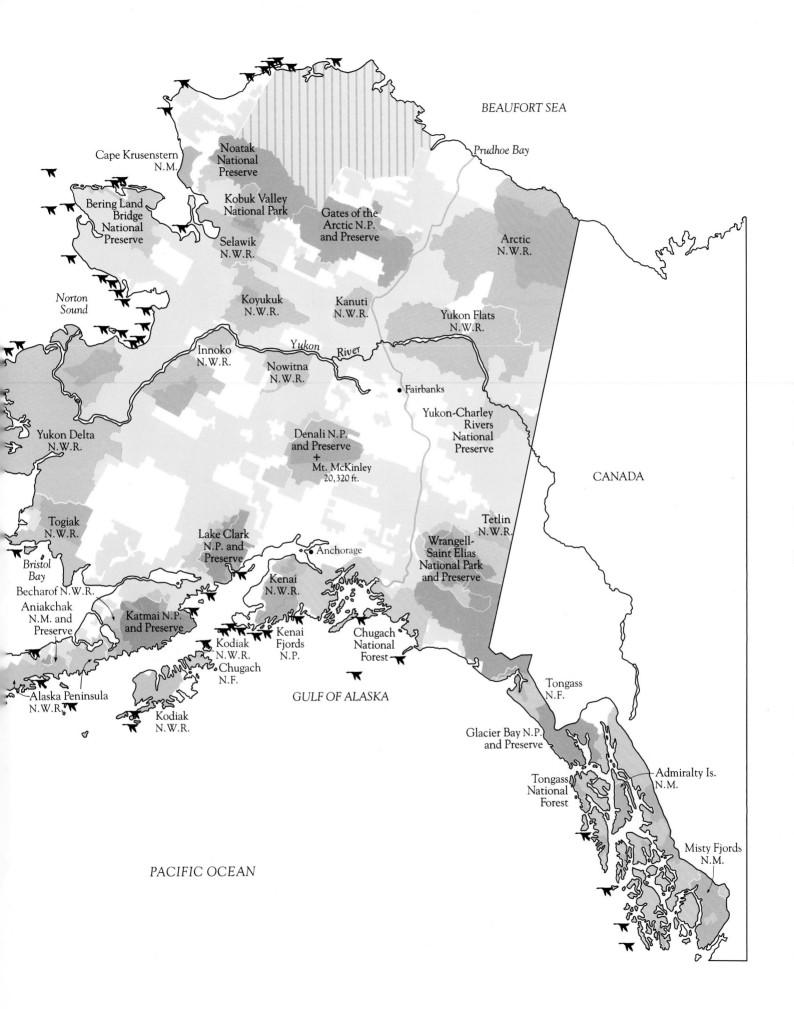

BEAUFORT SEA

Prudhoe Bay

Cape Krusenstern
N.M.

Noatak
National
Preserve

Kobuk Valley
National Park

Gates of the
Arctic N.P.
and Preserve

Arctic
N.W.R.

Bering Land
Bridge
National
Preserve

Selawik
N.W.R.

*Norton
Sound*

Koyukuk
N.W.R.

Kanuti
N.W.R.

Yukon Flats
N.W.R.

Innoko
N.W.R.

Yukon   River

Nowitna
N.W.R.

• Fairbanks

Yukon Delta
N.W.R.

Denali N.P.
and Preserve
+
Mt. McKinley
20,320 ft.

Yukon-Charley
Rivers
National
Preserve

CANADA

Togiak
N.W.R.

Lake Clark
N.P. and
Preserve

Tetlin
N.W.R.

*Bristol
Bay*

Becharof N.W.R.

• Anchorage

Kenai
N.W.R.

Wrangell-
Saint Elias
National Park
and Preserve

Aniakchak
N.M. and
Preserve

Katmai N.P.
and Preserve

Kodiak
N.W.R.
Chugach
N.F.

Kenai
Fjords
N.P.

Chugach
National
Forest

Alaska Peninsula
N.W.R.

Kodiak
N.W.R.

GULF OF ALASKA

Tongass
N.F.

Glacier Bay N.P.
and Preserve

Admiralty Is.
N.M.

Tongass
National
Forest

PACIFIC OCEAN

Misty Fjords
N.M.

development. For instance: Under the Alaska Lands Act, more than 43 million acres had been added to the state's national parks, but by mid-1983 only about 30 permanent employees had been added to manage them—one person for every 1.5 million acres. Today, Denali National Park and Preserve has 143 permanent and seasonal employees and an annual budget of 4.5 million dollars, while Tongass National Forest, with its heavily subsidized logging operations, has 700 employees and a budget of 59 million dollars.

Conservationists in Alaska worry about the politicization of resource management there. Several other issues also cause them concern: accelerated petroleum development, mining, and logging, accompanied by population growth and transportation corridors; land exchanges aimed at expediting resource development; threats to fish and wildlife populations; and amendments to ANILCA, such as a proposal to reopen parts of national parks to sport hunting. Some of these issues arise from compromises accepted by conservationists so that the Alaska Lands Act could be signed into law before President Reagan took office. A survey of some of Alaska's federal lands illustrates the problems.

The state's most famous park—Denali—surrounds the continent's highest peak, 20,320-foot Mount McKinley, north of Anchorage. It was established in 1917 and today receives about 350,000 visitors a year, a lot for an Alaskan park. Most come to see the wildlife and the scenery. Glaciers, spires of granite, and deep, rock-ribbed gorges ring tundra plateaus and broad valleys threaded by glacier-fed streams. Visitors riding a shuttle bus along an 85-mile primitive road may spot caribou, moose, Dall sheep, grizzlies, foxes, lynx, wolverines, marmots, porcupines, ground squirrels, and 155 kinds of birds.

Though sport hunting is now permitted in all but 8.7 percent of Alaska—including 75.4 million acres of wildlife refuges, 104.3 million acres of BLM lands, 19 million acres of Park Service preserves, and 23.2 million acres of national forests—hunters and commercial guides are not content. In 1983, Senator Ted Stevens of Alaska introduced legislation to open up 12 million acres inside the national parks to sport hunting by reclassifying them as preserves. The bill failed to pass, but everyone expects it to be reintroduced. It would permit sport hunting in 1.5 million acres of Denali's northern extension, which was specifically set aside as a wildlife sanctuary for animals that spend part of the year within the park. Conservationists say the hunting issue was settled when 19 million acres were designated preserves instead of parks to accommodate sportsmen. Further, allowing hunting inside national parks might set a precedent for other interests—mining, say, or oil and gas exploration—to invade them.

St. Matthew Island, 250 miles off the west coast of Alaska in the Bering Sea, was first given protection in 1909 and is now part of the Alaska Maritime Refuge; in 1970 it was included in the National Wilderness Preservation System. It's one of the world's richest seabird nesting areas, supporting about three million birds. The oil industry has long coveted the island as a base for exploration and production in the Bering Sea, and in August 1983 Secretary Watt engineered a land exchange that pleased the industry and angered environmentalists: Four thousand acres on St. Matthew were traded to three Native corporations in exchange for lands and easements in two other refuges. Unless the exchange is halted by the courts, construction will soon begin on an airport and roads on the island. Natives plan to lease the land—with storage tanks, oil transfer facilities, and worker housing—to an oil company.

On the mainland east of St. Matthew, the Yukon and Kuskokwim Rivers, Alaska's two longest, enter the Bering Sea and define, between them, the Yukon Delta, site of a 20-million-acre wildlife refuge, the largest in the system. About 18,000 Natives in 44 villages share the refuge with 170 species of birds. During their migrations, some birds from the Yukon Delta probably reach most provinces of Canada, every state in the United States and Mexico, all countries of Central and South America, Antarctica, virtually all Pacific islands, all Asian countries bordering the Pacific, Australia, and New Zealand. Recently, the populations of four species of geese have declined dramatically. For instance, in 15 years the number of cackling Canada geese has dropped from 376,000 to 26,000; that of greater white-fronted geese, from 495,000 to 80,000. Much of the decline can be attributed to hunting pressures and habitat loss along the birds' migratory routes outside Alaska, but the state's Natives have aggravated the situation. Largely dependent on the land for survival, Natives have for many years hunted the birds and their eggs in violation of a migratory bird treaty with Canada. A coalition of sportsmen has sued Interior in an attempt to make the department enforce the treaty. A more peaceable solution was reached in 1984, when Natives, California sportsmen, and wildlife agencies signed an agreement sharply reducing the number of birds Natives and sport hunters can take each year.

Far to the north, on the Beaufort Sea, the Arctic National Wildlife Refuge protects 19 million acres of mountains, arctic plain, and interior spruce forests. The most northerly unit in the refuge system, it is a fragile, slow-paced world, where a spruce can take three hundred years to attain a diameter of four inches. The 140,000-head Porcupine caribou herd covers more than a thousand miles on its yearly migration from Canada to calving grounds on the coastal plain within the refuge—and back again. A few polar bears den on the refuge's coast in winter, and ringed seals thrive in the frigid waters offshore. North America's largest discovery of oil and gas reserves was just 60 miles west of the refuge at Prudhoe Bay, and congressionally mandated exploration is now occurring on more than a million acres of coastal plain inside the refuge. Conservationists worry that tractor trains operating on inadequate snow cover are damaging the tundra.

Lake Clark National Park and Preserve comprises 2.6 million acres a hundred miles southwest of Anchorage. Its Chigmit Mountains rise from the western shore of Cook Inlet at the juncture of the Aleutian and Alaska Ranges, creating a realm of glaciers, waterfalls, forested slopes, and wild, white rivers. Inholdings owned by Native corporations or individuals are the problem here. The Nondalton Village Corporation has selected about 84,000 acres along the southern shore of Lake Clark, in the middle of the park, and has plans for development on a peninsula jutting into the lake. Lots costing $40,000 and up are being sold for luxurious second homes. The subdivision advertises underground electricity, telephones, cable television, an electronic security system, a 5,000-foot runway, and two hotels. The Park Service is concerned about the development, but it is reluctant to purchase the Native holdings because of their high cost and their relatively low resource value. And ANILCA prohibits the Interior Department from condemning Native lands.

Tongass National Forest, in southeastern Alaska, is the country's largest—16.9 million acres. It was established in 1907 by Teddy Roosevelt to halt destructive logging practices, and today, ironically, the American taxpayer is paying dearly to assure the continuation of extensive clear-cutting there.

In the early 1950s the federal government encouraged settlement of Alaska by creating jobs there. As one way of doing so, the Forest Service negotiated 50-year contracts with local timber operators, promising them enormous quotas at subsidized prices. The arrangement continues today. The Alaska Lands Act authorizes "at least $40,000,000 annually or as much as the Secretary of Agriculture finds necessary" to assure a harvest from the Tongass of 4.5 billion board feet a decade. Though the rates companies pay for the trees they cut are being reduced, the Forest Service's costs for managing the timber and building roads are soaring. They far exceed the timber-sale revenues; between 1970 and 1984 the difference, according to a Library of Congress analyst, was 312.5 million dollars. The Tongass is currently spending about 77 million dollars a year more than it takes in. The Forest Service points out that only two million acres are scheduled for logging, while five million have been set aside as wilderness; but three-quarters of the wilderness acreage is either unforested or unharvestable. Dense old growth along watercourses—critical fish and wildlife habitat—is disappearing faster every year. The agency warns that "the Tongass National Forest cannot accommodate all that is being asked of it." But the laws protecting the land and its wildlife are not as strong as those supporting the cutting.

*D*uring the debate in Congress on the Alaska Lands Act, Congressman Morris Udall of Arizona implored his colleagues: "Not in our generation, nor ever again, will we have a land and wildlife opportunity approaching the scope and importance of this one. . . . This time, given one great last chance, let us strive to do it right."

And are we, finally, doing it right? I put this question to a number of people who have been involved with land-use issues in Alaska, and their responses, as you might expect, varied.

William Miller, a second-generation Alaskan, spoke with me from a lodge north of Fairbanks where his family was holding a reunion. "The Alaska Lands Act was a good thing," he said. "It settled some very complex claims that were holding up development because the lands were so tied up in legal actions. But the federal government has been slow in releasing the state's selections. Maybe it's not been a *major* delay, but it's been an irritating one for people who want to get on with their businesses. Many Alaskans feel very strongly that the federal government kept too much land for itself. They'll tell you that the Feds have everybody by the throat up here. When I was a kid, you could do anything you wanted—go anywhere, build a cabin, file a claim, anything at all. Now there are strong restrictions on those sorts of things. Nevertheless, there's still an awful lot of space, and if you have a reason to develop some part of the country, you can generally find a way to do it."

David Morris, superintendent of Katmai National Park and Preserve, has been in Alaska five years. "I think the Park Service is doing a pretty darn good job," he told me. "The controversies that resulted from the passage of the Lands Act have quieted down even faster than we anticipated. Park Service staff and field operations have moved into the bush areas and are making some headway. And we've had some reasonable operating budgets lately. Our permanent staff here has doubled in the last four years, from three to seven. That sounds awfully small for four million acres, but you can't solve all problems by just throwing people at them. Happily, we're a society in which people can disagree. Some environmentalists argue that Alaska's resources are being developed too fast. But the pro-development people aren't getting everything they want, either. And we in the Park Service often find ourselves walking a thin line."

Lou Jurs worked in Alaska for six years, five of them with the BLM. He spent two years helping to prepare the BLM's environmental impact statement on oil and gas drilling on the North Slope. Lou said, "We're making the same political land-management mistakes in Alaska that we made in the lower 48, but on a much bigger scale and with better technology. If you read back through the history of the decisions that were made when the West was being settled, you'll find we're doing similar things in Alaska today. Even the attitudes of many Alaskans are similar to the Westerners' of a hundred years ago. For instance, a few years back a little ghost town near Denali was being considered for the National Register of Historic Places. A couple of prospectors had moved in there and reopened a few of the old mines. When they found out the town was being studied and might get some official protection, they bulldozed it down. They just didn't want anybody from outside coming in and looking over their shoulders at what they were doing. That seems to be a common attitude in rural Alaska."

Celia Hunter was a WASP—Women's Air Service Pilot—during World War II, ferrying pursuit planes from factories to bases and embarkation ports. Planes destined for the Soviet Union were flown by WASPs as far as Great Falls, Montana. From there they were flown by male pilots to Fairbanks, where they were turned over to the Russians. "The Air Force wouldn't let women fly to Fairbanks; they said they didn't have facilities for us along the route," said Celia. "That was baloney. They didn't have facilities for women *anywhere*." After the war, Celia and another WASP made it to Alaska on their own and, except for a year or two elsewhere, have been there ever since. They built and for 25 years operated Camp Denali, just north of what was then Mount McKinley National Park. Celia was president and later executive director of the Wilderness Society during the ANILCA negotiations.

I asked her, "Are we doing it right?" and she laughed. "ANILCA was passed during a Democratic administration, but now a Republican administration is implementing it. That's causing enormous problems. In every instance, when a provision of ANILCA is up for implementation, they interpret it in a way that runs counter to the intent of Congress. I'll give you an example. McKinley, Katmai, and Glacier Bay existed as protected parkland before the passage of ANILCA. The act added to their territory and stipulated that the original areas be designated wilderness. ANILCA also permits use of snowmobiles in the new parks and additions, and the administration is arguing that snowmobiles should therefore be permitted in the original areas, the wilderness areas. They're turning the whole thing topsy-turvy."

Ted Swem, now retired to the cool mountains west of Denver, was chairman of the Interior Department's interagency task force that identified potential parklands, refuges, and wild rivers in Alaska before passage of ANILCA. To my question he replied, "I find it very upsetting. There's been a lot of politics involved, something that hasn't normally affected the Park Service. For instance, in 1983 there was what many perceived as a purge of several top Park Service people in Alaska, including the regional director, the deputy regional director, and the superintendent of Glacier Bay National Park. They evidently ran afoul of the pro-development philosophy in Alaska and Interior and also the federal cochairman of the Alaska Land Use Council, a political appointee. They were all reassigned to the lower 48. In all my years with the Park Service, I never saw anything like it. The regional director and his deputy had about 60 years of experience between them, and their knowledge of Alaska was thrown out the window. The superintendent was responsible for protecting an endangered species—the humpback whale—and he did it so well he's now in Denver."

Bill Horn, Interior's deputy under secretary for Alaska, insists that the transfers were not politically motivated, and notes that the new regional director and his deputy are also career professionals with more years of experience in Alaska than their predecessors.

The angriest response to my question came from John Kauffmann, who worked twenty years for the Park Service, the last six in Alaska as a park planner, before retiring in 1978. "The answer to your question is *no*. There's a lot of fine print in the Alaska Lands Act that undermines much of the big print. By interpretation, rule making, and the withholding of funds, the administration can unravel the whole thing. It represents a sort of contempt for conservation, a 'now-we'll-get-back-at-'em' attitude. Some of the parks up there, like Gates of the Arctic, the one I worked on, were meant to survive as pristine wilderness for centuries, but parts of Gates are showing signs of wear after just four or five years. This is not a matter of nonpersonal threats like acid rain or strip-mining or clearcutting. This is deliberate misfeasance, as far as I can tell."

Appearing before the House Subcommittee on Public Lands and National Parks in June 1984, Secretary of the Interior William Clark rebutted some of these charges. He called the Alaska Lands Act "the greatest land legislation enacted in this century" and the capstone to two other major Alaska measures, the 1958 Statehood Act and the 1971 Alaska Native Claims Act. "These measures have essentially determined the land patterns in Alaska and the way is now clear to redeem the promises made to the state, the Natives, and the American people." He focused on those areas where, according to him, Interior was fulfilling congressional directives: He noted that acquisition of inholdings and land exchanges were proceeding; that the mammoth planning requirements were on schedule; that the state and the Native corporations were continuing to make their selections; that the wilderness review process had been incorporated into the management plans for parks and refuges, although the ban on BLM wilderness studies still stands. He also said that the combined land management budget for the BLM, the Park Service, and the Fish and Wildlife Service in Alaska had grown by 43 percent since 1982. And funds for operating the regional offices of the Park Service and Fish and Wildlife were up 30 percent in the same period. Staffing of Alaskan offices had increased 20 percent in the last three years.

*A*nd so the story in Alaska turns out to be the story we've heard throughout the rest of the country: complex issues, passionate disagreements, hard choices. Is new legislation needed to help resolve some of the controversies? In California, a sociologist told me, "I'd start with Aldo Leopold's axiom that a thing is right if it maintains the integrity and beauty of the environment and wrong if it doesn't. Massive alterations of the landscape should be forbidden until there is overwhelming evidence that they won't permanently harm the integrity of the land." Former Interior Secretary Stewart Udall warns that what one Congress does, another Congress can undo. "The overriding threat that looms over all BLM lands," he says, "is the prospect that some future Congress might do an about-face, reinstate the disposal concept of the 19th century, and transfer these lands out of the public domain."

As for me, after ten months of touring our federal lands, I felt I'd learned three crucial things. First, the greatest threats to these lands are greed and indifference. The one takes more than it needs; the other turns its back. And this, too: It is not always easy to find villains in these stories, and sometimes it turns out there are none. And, finally, our national estate—those patches and parcels of land scattered throughout the country—is indeed an inheritance, a bequest from our forebears more precious than gold and even harder to protect.

From those ten months I have a collection of mental snapshots, random memories of a gallery of speakers addressing the question of how the federal lands should be used and managed. Some thought federal management itself was the problem. One environmentalist said, "The issue is, in what ways is federal stewardship of the land impairing the land? I see that as the great threat: the momentum within agencies to manage more intensely, to make the lands produce more income. The managers are often as dangerous as no management." A BLM employee told me, "The BLM is 95 percent of the problem and 5 percent of the solution." Others oppose all federal ownership. A southwestern businessman, speaking of the public lands, said, "If 225 million Americans own and should continue to own 60 percent of the land in my state, why shouldn't we *all* own *all* of the land in *all* of the states? I don't believe that 90 percent of Alaska should be owned by the federal government and virtually none of New York and Iowa."

Is technology part of the problem? A forester said, "We've gone from a point in the past where every tree that was cut was physically touched and marked by a human being. Now computer print-outs have all the data, and we in the office are cut off from the forest."

"In the Park Service," said a ranger, "we're always being thrown into crisis management, reacting to problems." Said his partner, "The Park Service doesn't fight these threats nearly as well as people outside who love the parks. If we didn't have groups like the Sierra Club and the National Parks & Conservation Association, the parks would be in far worse shape than they are."

Are politics the problem? A BLM manager said, "Those of us involved with the resources here on the ground like to think we base our decisions on what the resources require. The resources speak at this level. But all the groundwork we do is turned over to politicians."

All of us use these resources in unexpected ways. A Fish and Wildlife man said, "If I'm sitting in my backyard and a skein of geese flies over, I'm using that wildlife resource." And is there room here for all God's creatures? A wildlife biologist told me, "Biologically, we can have grizzly bears. The habitat is still there, the bears are adaptable enough, and we know enough about their needs to protect them. But it will be decided by society, by you and me. If we want grizzly bears and are willing to make some sacrifices, then they'll survive." "I'm over-cautious," a refuge manager told me. "I'll admit it. But I figure if you're going to make a mistake, make it in favor of the animals, not man."

A militant environmentalist said, "When developers ask, 'How many wildernesses do we *need*?' I say, 'How many Brahms symphonies do we need?' Obviously, we don't *need* any, but the world would be a poorer place without them." Often those areas that are least known are least threatened. A newspaperman told me, "I think one of the best things you can do for a nice piece of wilderness is keep your mouth shut." I asked an authority on Indian rock art in Utah why he was revealing the locations of some new finds. "We've decided to sacrifice these sites in hopes of stopping the nuclear waste repository."

"These federal lands are our heritage," said a Utah conservationist. "They're what makes our country different from Europe. Europe has the great cathedrals—Chartres and Canterbury—but we have the redwoods and the Grand Canyon." A student told me, "I think of our federal lands as a huge village common, like in England—an area owned by everyone, used by everyone, and maintained by everyone." Water, too, is a common resource. "Mono Lake shows what happens when people don't stop to think about where their water comes from," David Gaines said.

And more random memories, of sights and sounds, keep flickering in my mind, like stills from a long movie. I remember Gerlach, Nevada, and its sign, "Where the pavement ends and the West begins," and the lady there who said, "The desert. That's what gets ahold of you." In the Smokies I heard Dolly Parton on my car radio, singing "Appalachian memories keep me strong." I remember standing in a sawmill south of Eureka, California; the huge building shook to its foundations as massive redwoods rolled onto the grapples that carried them through high-pressure hose baths and screaming saws; they emerged at the other end as neat piles of planks and shingles, ready to become paneling, ice cream buckets, and picnic tables.

I remember being stooped in Idaho by a prairie falcon coming at me out of the sun like a fighter plane. I remember waking during the night in the Nevada desert to a pack of coyotes yapping nearby like excited children. In the Monongahela, muscular loggers in grimy T-shirts did nimble little dances as they moved away from falling trees. I remember an anhinga in the Everglades juggling a fish like a circus performer before gulping it down. The Everglades twilights were filled with thousands of small white butterflies, drifting like confetti, and an osprey perched on a television antenna at the park motel.

I remember the look of astonishment on the face of a duck that was grabbed from below by an otter in a California harbor. The otter dragged the duck ashore, and I moseyed closer to watch. Too close. The otter went one way and the duck, streaming feathers and heaven-rending squawks, the other. I remember a fire in a Nebraska wheat field, its mushroom of smoke visible for 20 miles. I hit a skunk with my car near there and drove for an hour in twin clouds of stench and shame. I remember a CCC museum in Wisconsin, with bunks, uniforms, photos, heavy plates and cups. I remember little orange ribbons on the tips of thin stakes, fluttering like lilies in soft breezes.

Encircled by dawn's golden mist, a female moose searches a pond for aquatic plants, supplements to her diet of willow leaves and twigs. Denali's spruce forests—interspersed with meadows and small lakes—shelter some of the densest moose populations on the continent. Appearing ungainly, even comical, at a distance, the thousand-pound creatures become formidable at close range. Surprisingly swift both on land and in water, they fear only bears, wolves, and man.

But especially I remember a woman in West Virginia. She was behind the counter at a motel in Elkins when I stopped by in the morning to check out. The green hills of the Monongahela National Forest rose nearby. The woman was gaunt, bony, and very old. She looked cranky and out-of-sorts, so I was prepared to be on my best behavior. But as we did our business, she revealed herself to be warm and funny. We chatted, comparing notes on the weather—our disappointment with yesterday's, our hopes for tomorrow's. She nicked her thumb with her stapler and swore: "*Golly-ding!*" She confided to me an ambition of her husband's. "He wants to sell this place, buy a motor home, and drive it to Nome, Alaska. Alaska! *Nome!*" She fluttered her hands. "*I've* got no sense of direction. I've been lost in Macy's. I told him, 'Darlin', if that's what you want, we'll do it. But if the Lord shuts my book up there, bring me back here to my sweet West Virginia mountains.' " She looked me in the eye and lifted her arms in a helpless sort of gesture, part shrug, part benediction. "Sir," she said, "there's a strength in these hills. . . ."

She couldn't finish her sentence, but I knew what she was trying to say, having heard it from one end of the country to the other. Woody Guthrie used to sing it: "This land is your land, this land is my land, this land was made for you and me." To the old West Virginian, the forested Monongahela hills were hers.

We soon finished our business and I went on my way, but I've thought about her often since. I hope she made it to Nome. I hope she's up there now, agog beneath a flickering aurora. But I also hope she makes it home again, to her sweet West Virginia mountains.

RALPH HUNT WILLIAMS/WEST STOCK INC. (ABOVE); CLIFF HOLLENBECK (OPPOSITE, BOTH)

*S*hallow Toklat River meanders north past Divide Mountain in Denali National Park. Though these braided channels yield no gold, many other Alaskan rivers do. The state estimates that at least 600 placer mines disrupt as many streams. In the Kantishna Hills (below), a mobile processing plant separates gold from rock and dirt. The machine dumps rocks into a pile on the right. Finer sediments and gold flow down the sluice box at left. The heavy gold sinks and remains trapped in the trough, while churning water washes lighter material away. At bottom, the manager displays nuggets worth perhaps $50,000. Such operations alter streambeds, destroy food and spawning areas of fish, and can cloud the water as far as 50 miles downstream.

*I*ndependence and snow come early in wild Alaska: Scott Van Valin, at age seven, rows home on Lake Clark after school, and Jack Ross hurries to complete the Van Valins' new log lodge before winter sets in. Only an hour's flight from Anchorage, Lake Clark National Park and Preserve attracts more residents and tourists each year.

*I*n Katmai's spectacular Lake District, both waters and wildlife meet. Draining rain-fed Brooks Lake, the mile-and-a-quarter-long Brooks River empties into Naknek Lake and stains its turquoise waters inky blue. Glacial runoff and silt from the Valley of Ten Thousand Smokes give the lower lake its vivid color. When thousands of sockeye salmon fight their way up to the Brooks River in July, hungry bears arrive. Tourists emerge warily from Brooks Camp on Naknek's shore to watch the bears gorge themselves on salmon trying to clear Brooks Falls. Later the bears find the fish even more vulnerable in spawning grounds such as the tiny tributary below.

*G*iant Alaskan brown bear, renowned for his underwater fishing tactics, carries his catch to shore. Working his way downstream from Brooks Falls, he usually snags a salmon within 150 feet. He may devour as many as eight fish before returning to the woods for a rest. "Brownies" surpass their cousins the grizzlies in size and weight. Large Katmai males may grow to 7 feet and exceed 900 pounds. Downstream, a two-legged angler, seemingly oblivious of his competitor, casts for rainbow trout. As the fame of Brooks River spreads, contact between humans and the huge carnivores will increase. Park Service personnel strive for a balanced policy that enables visitors to watch the bears while protecting the animals and one of their prime feeding areas.

merald green sedges and darker shrubs thrive along sloughs in the immense floodplain of the mighty Yukon River. Here the Yukon Delta Refuge plays host to multitudes of waterfowl and shorebirds in summer. At right, an emperor goose herds fuzzy goslings toward food. These small, stocky geese summer along Alaska's west coast and winter in the Aleutian Islands. Below, a red-throated loon defends its nest of mud and wet vegetation at the water's edge. When disturbed, the loon dives into the water, surfaces a short distance away, and tries to distract its predator.

As days shorten in early fall, the loons fly south to spend the winter on the Pacific coast from Alaska to Baja California.

*S*porting ivory tusks more than two feet long, male walruses float in fog-shrouded waters of Bristol Bay off Togiak National Wildlife Refuge. Both boon and bane, their overgrown canine teeth help walruses clamber onto ice floes, frighten enemies, and settle quarrels among themselves. But the ivory also attracts Native Alaskan hunters who covet it for scrimshaw. Separate herds of male and female walruses migrate up and down Alaska's western coast. Plans to auction oil leases in Bristol Bay worry both environmentalists and fishermen; a spill there would imperil the food chain on which walruses, fish, birds, and people depend.

FOLLOWING PAGES: Alarmed by a fishing boat, seabirds take to the sky at Togiak. Between May and September, one and a half million black-legged kittiwakes and common murres nest here on the coastal cliffs of Cape Newenham.

*C*oastal mountains climb into the clouds at Misty Fjords National Monument in southeast Alaska. Wilderness designation protects 94 percent of the monument, but the Pacific Coast Molybdenum Company controls mineral-development rights within 152,610 acres at its center. Core sampling indicates that Quartz Hill (opposite, upper) may hold one of the world's largest known molybdenum deposits. A helicopter (opposite, lower) carries out samples for testing, and a research vessel on Boca de Quadra (below) conducts studies to determine the possible impact of tailings dumped in the bay. Controversy still exists over the location of necessary roads, towns, docks, and dump sites and the protection of the area's fish and wildlife.

*P*erpetual fog obscures the brooding mountains and interlacing waterways of Tongass, the nation's largest national forest, encompassing nearly 17 million acres in Alaska's panhandle. The mild maritime climate, with up to 200 inches of rain a year, nurtures 400-year-old forests of spruce, cedar, and hemlock. Ancient broken-topped trees support huge nests and serve as perches for bald eagles (above). Eagles require nesting sites with unobstructed views of the surroundings and clear flight paths to coastal waters where the birds feast on fish and carrion. Acting on the mistaken belief that eagles competed with the new canning industry, the Territory of Alaska encouraged their slaughter in 1917. Bounty hunters shot 100,000 eagles before policy changed in 1952. Today, 4,000 pairs still nest in southeast Alaska, but logging of their old-growth habitat continues to reduce their range. All the lower 48 states already list our national bird as threatened or endangered.

*H*eavy equipment rumbles, clanks, and roars through the Tongass. One logger (below, right) measures tree sections to gauge their weight for helicopter removal. Another operates a seven-foot chain saw to rip in half a giant spruce log too heavy to be lifted in one piece. Helicopters carry the 10,000-pound sections to a transfer point for loading onto trucks.

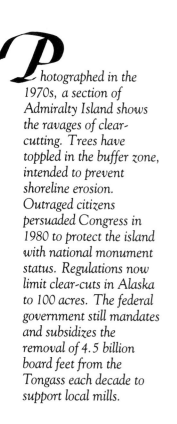

*P*hotographed in the 1970s, a section of Admiralty Island shows the ravages of clear-cutting. Trees have toppled in the buffer zone, intended to prevent shoreline erosion. Outraged citizens persuaded Congress in 1980 to protect the island with national monument status. Regulations now limit clear-cuts in Alaska to 100 acres. The federal government still mandates and subsidizes the removal of 4.5 billion board feet from the Tongass each decade to support local mills.

JAMES H. KATZ (ABOVE)

Riggs Glacier still surrenders part of its length to the sea each year. Salt water melts and undermines the glacier's face, sending icebergs crashing into the bay. Fanciful shapes such as the 150-foot-long cat (top) delight visitors. But nature's sculptures do not last; they capsize, break apart, or melt within weeks. More stable terrain confronts three seasonal rangers (above) on a two-day trek across Geikie Glacier.

*C*olossal face of Riggs Glacier looms above the 65-foot tour boat M. V. Thunder Bay. A mile wide and rearing 140 feet out of the water, the glacier is but a remnant of the 4,000-foot-thick ice sheet that scoured Muir Inlet 200 years ago. The park's 16 tidewater glaciers draw increasing numbers of tourists, who marvel at the rugged scenery, the abundant birdlife, and the whales cavorting just offshore. As their ship nears a glacier, passengers can hear the ice rumble, pop, and crack as the stresses shift. Lucky observers will catch the glacier calving, dropping huge blocks into the bay. Farther from the glacier than it seems, this boat keeps a respectful distance from the ice face. Falling bergs cause dangerous waves that can swamp kayaks or slam slabs of floating ice into larger vessels.

Spanning 14 feet, flukes of a humpback whale break the surface of Glacier Bay near the photographer's kayak. Gentle mammals, humpbacks gained renown for their haunting songs and playful antics. When a tour boat comes too close or moves too fast, a whale may breach (opposite, right), flinging its 45-foot, 40-ton body out of the water and descending with an explosive splash. In 1978 most of the two dozen humpbacks that spent the summers gorging on krill and small fish in Glacier Bay left early; only a few have returned. Researchers suspect boat traffic, and the Park Service has issued regulations to control it, hoping the whales will reappear.

TOM BEAN (ABOVE AND TOP)

DAVE MILLS

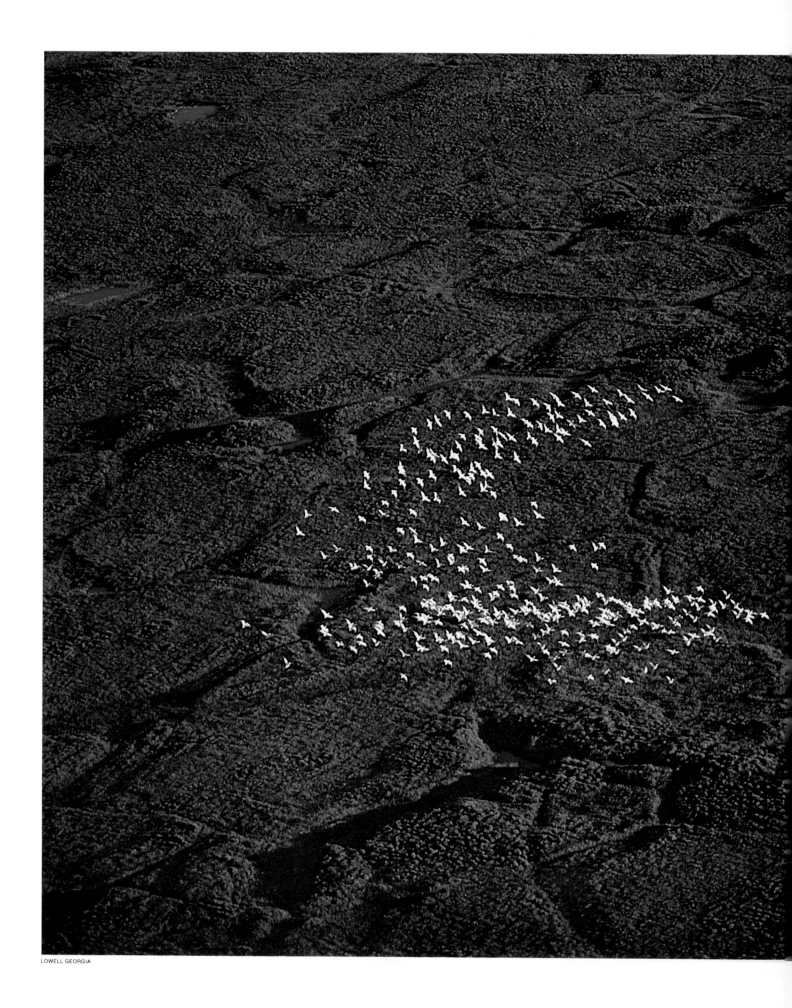

*F*lurry of snow geese sweeps over the tundra of Arctic National Wildlife Refuge. The birds arrive from Canada in late August to feed and to form flocks for the fall migration to Oregon and California. Fierce freeze and thaw cycles have made patterns in the tundra. The spongy cover of lichens, sedges, and mosses hides a layer of permafrost up to 2,000 feet thick. The 19-million-acre refuge extends from the ice-caked Beaufort Sea, across coastal tundra plains, over the Brooks Range, and down into the boreal forests of interior valleys. It protects an unusual diversity of northern habitats and gives the arctic animals that frequent them the room they need to survive.

FOLLOWING PAGES: A polar bear, weighing more than a thousand pounds and measuring nine feet from nose to tail, searches for choice bits on a whale carcass off Barter Island.

WILL TROYER/ALASKAPHOTO (ABOVE); STEVEN C. KAUFMAN (OPPOSITE, BOTH)

Fringed by sedge meadows, Lake Schrader appears inviting during the brief arctic summer, but the stark Franklin Mountains beyond attest the harshness of Alaska's Arctic Slope. Willow catkins (below) bloom as soon as snow starts melting in mid-May. Tougher than it looks, arctic bell heather (bottom) graces north-facing slopes in the Brooks Range, where late-melting snowdrifts last far into summer.

FOLLOWING PAGES: *Female caribou and month-old calves rush east across the tundra to join males for the journey to Canadian wintering grounds. Named for a river it must cross, the 140,000-head Porcupine Herd travels more than 1,000 miles each year. In this endless cycle of migration, each move has a reason and each place a season, demonstrating the animals' remarkable adaptation to these barren lands. Oil may lie beneath the caribou's calving grounds. Is it more important than this herd, symbol of the wildness and freedom of our last frontier?*

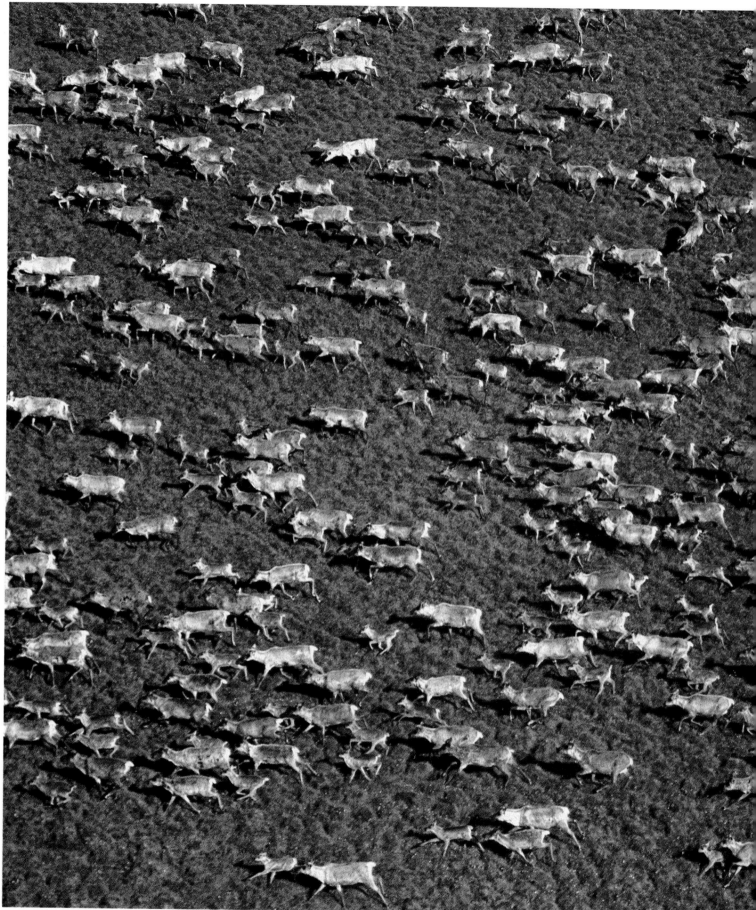

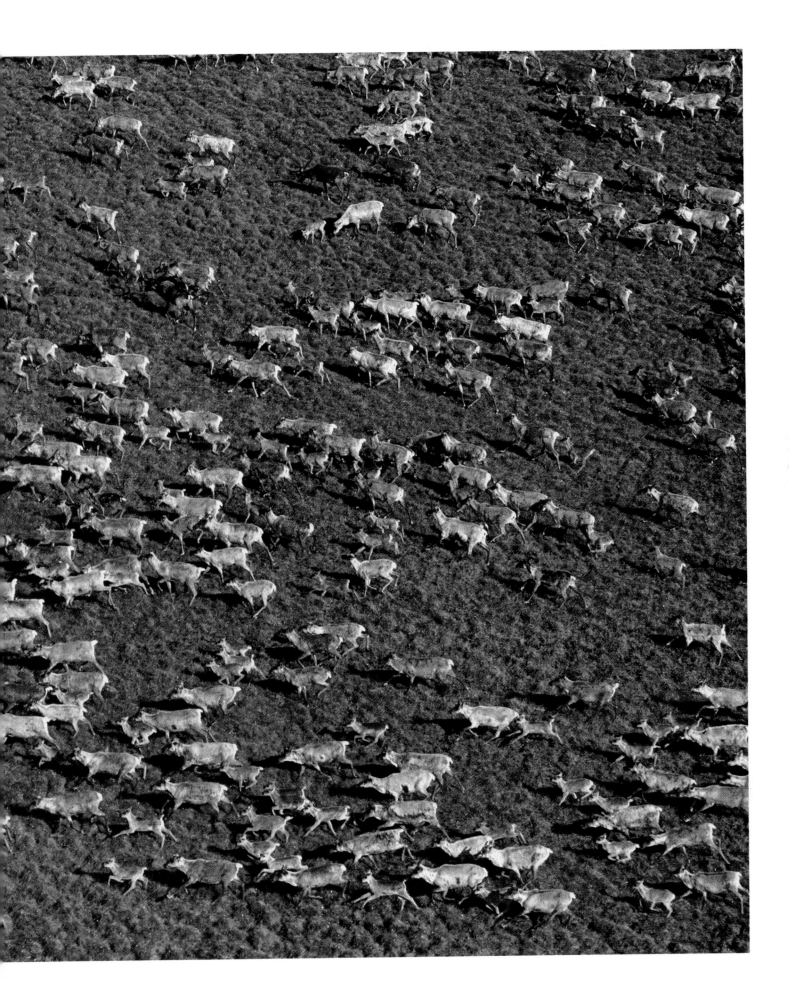

Acknowledgments

The Special Publications Division wishes to express its gratitude to the men and women of the Bureau of Land Management, the National Park Service, the U. S. Fish and Wildlife Service, and the U. S. Forest Service for their cooperation and assistance during the preparation of this book, which we dedicate to them.

We are particularly indebted to Jan Bedrosian of the BLM and Diane O'Connor of the Forest Service. From the planning of *Our Threatened Inheritance* to its completion we also received valuable guidance from William C. Reffalt and Terry Sopher of The Wilderness Society, Charles S. Watson, Jr., of the Nevada Outdoor Recreation Association, Terri Martin of the National Parks & Conservation Association, and David Cline of the National Audubon Society.

We thank the individuals and organizations named or quoted in the book, and those cited here, for so generously sharing their experience and expertise with us: Susan Alexander, David Ames, Sam Baker, William Berg, Ann Bishop, William Booker, Gary Brown, Harry Crandell, Douglas Cuillard, Leslie Dawson, John G. Dennis, Roger Di Rosa, K. L. Drews, Glenn Elison, Robert M. Ellis, Jon W. Erickson, Clyde Fiske, Ralph Fries, Wayne Gagne, Roy Geiger, Dave Glowka, Paul F. Haertel, Tom Henry, Jack Hession, Mark Hilliard, Steve Hinderer, Dennis Holland, Lloyd Hulbert, Destry Jarvis, Frank Johnson, Richard Knight, George Kyle, George A. Lawrence, Henry Little, Lloyd Loope, Bruce Louthan, Matt Millenbach, Roger R. Miller, John J. Moscatelli, Bruce Moorhead, Shaaron Netherton, John C. O'Brien, Stephen Osgood, Kenneth P. Owen, James D. Rasmussen, Craig Rieben, Gordon Roberts, Edward Ruth, Vernon L. Saline, Tom Sayre, Charles E. Scott, Patrick Smith, Shirwin Smith, Tom Stehn, Jim Stratton, David Tremayne, Brock Tunnicliff, Sharon Urban, Stephen Veirs, John W. Voigt, Jesse Warner, T. H. Watkins, Dave Webster, Jane Whalen, Nicholas Whelan, and Edward E. Wood, Jr.

Additional Reading

The reader may wish to consult the *National Geographic Index* for related articles and books. The Society's publications covering federal lands include *Alaska's Magnificent Parklands; America's Wonderlands: Our National Parks; Wild Lands for Wildlife: America's National Refuges;* and *Wilderness U.S.A.*

The reader may also find the following books helpful: GENERAL: Craig W. Allin, *The Politics of Wilderness Preservation;* Paul Brooks, *Speaking for Nature;* Marion Clawson, *The Federal Lands Revisited;* Paul W. Gates, *History of Public Land Law Development;* Aldo Leopold, *A Sand County Almanac;* Maxine E. McCloskey and James P. Gilligan, editors, *Wilderness and the Quality of Life;* E. Louise Peffer, *The Closing of the Public Domain;* James B. Trefethen, *An American Crusade for Wildlife;* Stewart L. Udall, *The Quiet Crisis;* T. H. Watkins and Charles S. Watson, Jr., *The Lands No One Knows;* William K. Wyant, *Westward In Eden.* BUREAU OF LAND MANAGEMENT: Marion Clawson, *The Bureau of Land Management;* William Voigt, Jr., *Public Grazing Lands.* NATIONAL FORESTS: Richard C. Davis, editor, *Encyclopedia of American Forest and Conservation History* (2 vols.); Michael Frome, *The Forest Service* and *Whose Woods These Are: The Story of the National Forests;* Gifford Pinchot, *Breaking New Ground;* William Shands and Robert G. Healy, *The Lands Nobody Wanted;* Jack Shepherd, *The Forest Killers.* NATIONAL PARKS: Eugenia Connally, *National Parks in Crisis;* William C. Everhart, *The National Park Service;* Alfred Runte, *National Parks: The American Experience;* Joseph L. Sax, *Mountains Without Handrails.*

NATIONAL WILDLIFE REFUGES: George Laycock, *The Sign of the Flying Goose;* Robert W. Murphy, *Wild Sanctuaries;* Laura and William Riley, *Guide to the National Wildlife Refuges.*

Books on specific subjects covered in individual chapters include: LAND OF THE EASTERN SEA: Marjory Stoneman Douglas, *The Everglades: River of Grass;* Reginald V. Truitt, *Assateague—The "Place Across."* LAND OF PASTURES AND FORESTS: Robert H. Boyle, *Acid Rain;* Wilma Dykeman and James Stokely, *Highland Homeland: The People of the Great Smokies;* Gregory S. Wetstone and Armin Rosencranz, *Acid Rain in Europe and North America: National Responses to an International Problem.* LAND OF THE PASTORAL PLAINS: Alexander B. Adams, *Sunlight and Storm;* Durward L. Allen, *The Life of Prairies and Plains;* Robert P. Allen, *The Whooping Crane;* David F. Costello, *The Prairie World;* David Hawke, *Those Tremendous Mountains;* Tom McHugh, *The Time of the Buffalo;* Russel McKee, *The Last West;* John Madson, *Where the Sky Began.* LAND OF SIERRAS AND PEAKS: Stephen Fox, *John Muir and His Legacy;* Aubrey Hains, *The Yellowstone Story: A History of Our First National Park;* Dean Krakel II, *Season of the Elk;* Paul Kruger and Carol Otte, *Geothermal Energy;* John Muir, *Steep Trails.* LAND OF SWEET-AIR'D PLATEAUS: Donald L. Baars, *The Colorado Plateau;* Ada and Frank Graham, *The Changing Desert;* John C. McGregor, *Southwestern Archaeology;* Polly Schaafsma, *Indian Rock Art Of The Southwest;* T. H. Watkins and others, *The Grand Colorado.* LAND OF THE WESTERN SEA: Andrew J. Berger, *Hawaiian Birdlife;* Joseph E. Brown, *Monarchs of the Mist;* Sherwin Carlquist, *Hawaii: A National History;* Peter C. Howorth, *Channel Islands;* Glen Kaye, *Hawaii Volcanoes;* Janet Kear and A. J. Berger, *The Hawaiian Goose;* Karen Liberatore, *The Complete Guide to the Golden Gate National Recreation Area;* Gordon A. Macdonald and Agatin T. Abbott, *Volcanoes in the Sea;* Jim Mack, *Haleakala;* Henry C. Warren, *Olympic.* EPILOGUE: Dale Brown, *Wild Alaska;* William E. Brown, *Alaska National Parklands: This Last Treasure;* George Calef, *Caribou and the Barren-lands.*

Periodicals that regularly feature articles on the federal lands include *Alaska Geographic, Audubon, Defenders, National Parks, Sierra,* and *Wilderness.*

The many publications of the Bureau of Land Management, the National Park Service, the U. S. Fish and Wildlife Service, and the U. S. Forest Service provide a wealth of information about these agencies and the federal lands in their care.

EDITOR'S NOTE: The number, size, and status of federal holdings change from one year—or one month—to the next. New parks and refuges are established; more wilderness areas are designated; national forest and Bureau of Land Management acreages are in constant flux. The official government designations and acreages given in this book were the latest available at press time.

Library of Congress CIP Data

Fisher, Ronald M.
  Our threatened inheritance.

  Bibliography: p.
  Includes index.
  1. Nature conservation—United States. 2. National parks and reserves—United States. 3. Natural areas—United States. 4. United States—Public lands.
I. Blair, James P. II. National Geographic Society (U. S.) Special Publications Division. III. Title.
QH76.F57 1984   333.95'16'0973   84-13976
ISBN 0-87044-512-X (regular edition)   ISBN 0-87044-536-7 (deluxe edition)

Index

Composition for OUR THREATENED INHERITANCE: NATURAL TREASURES OF THE UNITED STATES by National Geographic's Photographic Services, Carl M. Shrader, Director, Lawrence F. Ludwig, Assistant Director. Printed and bound by Kingsport Press, Kingsport, Tenn. Film preparation by Catharine Cooke Studio, Inc., New York, N.Y. Color separations by the Lanman Progressive Company, Washington, D. C.; Lincoln Graphics, Inc., Cherry Hill, N.J.; and NEC, Inc., Nashville, Tenn.